connectedness

About Thinkers50

Thinkers50 is the world's most reliable resource for identifying, ranking, and sharing the leading management and business ideas of our age.

Founded in 2001, the Thinkers50 definitive ranking of management thinkers is published every two years. The Thinkers50 Distinguished Achievement Awards, which recognize the very best in management thinking and practice, have been described by the *Financial Times* as the "Oscars of management thinking."

Since 2016, the Thinkers50 Radar has been identifying emerging thinkers with the potential to make a significant contribution to management theory and practice. The Thinkers50 Booklists of Management Classics and Best New Management Books, introduced in 2022, highlight the most influential management books past and present, as selected by the Thinkers50 Community.

DES
DEARLOVE
Co-founder, Thinkers50

LISA
HUMPHRIES

connected*ness*

HOW THE **BEST LEADERS** CREATE
AUTHENTIC HUMAN CONNECTION
IN A
DISCONNECTED WORLD

WILEY

Copyright © 2025 by John Wiley & Sons, Inc. All rights reserved, including rights for text and data mining and training of artificial technologies or similar technologies.

Published by John Wiley & Sons, Inc., Hoboken, New Jersey.
Published simultaneously in Canada.

For general information on our other products and services or for technical support, please contact our Customer Care Department within the United States at (800) 762-2974, outside the United States at (317) 572-3993 or fax (317) 572-4002.

Wiley also publishes its books in a variety of electronic formats. Some content that appears in print may not be available in electronic formats. For more information about Wiley products, visit our web site at www.wiley.com.

Library of Congress Cataloging-in-Publication Data is Available:

ISBN 9781394285778 (cloth)
ISBN 9781394285785 (ePub)
ISBN 9781394285792 (ePDF)

Cover Design: Paul McCarthy
Cover Image: © Getty Images | Osakawayne Studios

SKY10085541_091924

Contents

Foreword

Learning from one another sets human beings apart from every other species on the planet. It isn't our big brains (though that doesn't hurt). It isn't that we have both spoken and written language (though that doesn't hurt either). And it certainly isn't because we are the largest, fastest, or most threatening of creatures. No, what makes humans unique is our unparalleled ability to learn from each other, both at once and across time.

It is learning that has given us the ability to reach a total population size that is vastly larger than would be the case for animals of an equivalent size. It is learning that has allowed us to survive, even thrive, in astonishingly diverse environments. Indeed, humans can be found in virtually all habitats on Earth, a quality unique to our species. And it isn't that humans simply adapt to the environments they find themselves in—they actively alter the environment through their command of energy and matter. Humans can innovate and build upon insights and discoveries made far from where they happen to be, in both space and time. With the press of a button, humans can access and build upon centuries of accumulated knowledge, generate more of it, and in turn share it with other humans who can do the same.

In this timely book, authors explore the implications of human connection and communication in an age of exponentially developing technologies. Both are essential to the extraordinary accomplishments of our species.

Let's explore three situations in which acknowledging participants' humanity has fundamentally shifted business outcomes.

Human Unpredictability and the Challenge of Scaled Systems

The very concept of scaled systems—systems that are designed to create outputs in a systematic and predictable way—is unique to humanity. Wonders such as the assembly line, globally precise supply chains, and the entire worldwide shipping industry are marvels of productivity. And yet, the very precision and repeatability that makes scaled systems so powerful is also often an enemy to the human beings enmeshed in them. As Paul LeBlanc, former president of Southern New Hampshire University, observes, scaled systems are built to ensure predictability and reliability (McGrath, 2024). Humans are capable of designing such systems, but when it comes to those that are intended to deliver care, they often fall short. Providing education, health care, recovery from the criminal justice system, and addiction treatment are all situations in which scaling struggles.

Humans are unpredictable. Their very ability to learn means they can do things like game the system, avoid sanctions, do things in ways that are more convenient for themselves, or learn bad habits that they in turn can pass along to others (Bloom, 2024). Similarly, rigidly built scaled systems with a one-size-fits-all approach often leave out solutions for those who do not fit their prescribed patterns. Evidence suggests that the more complex a scaled system becomes, the more resources need to be dedicated just to maintaining it (Ehrenreich, 2020). That said, we may well be on the brink of discovering a new solution to the perennial dilemma of the fragility of scaled systems.

With the advent of artificial intelligence and machine learning, historical processes of human learning can accelerate. This in turn means that people with less expensive expert training can take actions and make decisions that previously required highly skilled experts. Further, instead of having systems that rely on predesigned solutions to succeed, humans can be at the touchpoints in which variability arises in the system. A fascinating example of a system that has achieved this is Nashville's CareBridge Health, which uses technology to surround its Medicare and Medicaid patients with the equivalent of 24/7 care and monitoring, bringing in expensive experts only when warranted. The rest of the time, the healthcare teams of physicians, pharmacists, nurses, social workers, and others providing care address issues such as preventing falls and limiting the appearance of wounds. The result is a system that profitably serves its patients at scale.

Human Learning Through Connections and the Debate Over Where Work Takes Place

It is a taken for granted assumption in much of the literature on workplaces that being together in a common place fosters learning, trust, companionship, and innovation. And yet, we also know that relying on working at the same place in person is not systematic. Further, the richness of communication between people is limited. As Thomas J. Allen famously discovered, once people are located more than about 60 feet apart, the richness of the information they exchange with one another drops off dramatically—from a high of 80% of shared, rich information to lows of something like 20%. And our wondrous channels of communication—telephone, email, short messages, and so on—don't make any difference to this reality (McGrath, 2023). As Allen himself noted, we don't substitute such communication vehicles for one another. When it comes to complex learning and problem-solving, there is no substitute for people being physically together (Allen and Henn, 2006).

This is perhaps the reason so many companies are hungry for their people to return to their offices—to the point at which some are punishing those who don't "badge in" (Cutter, and Chen 2023) enough with poor performance rating and financial consequences. Work by Keith Ferrazzi (2024) and others, however, suggests that companies have misunderstood the implications of the Allen rule. This is that the Allen effect takes place in situations of "serendipitous" bonding—bumping into one another accidentally, for instance. The level of team bonding reported by teams in Ferrazzi's study, on a 5-point scale, hovers on average around 2.8. That is hardly world-changing levels of team effectiveness! While the level of team bonding did drop a bit during the pandemic, the level achieved through serendipitous bonding leaves a lot to be desired. Instead, Ferrazzi suggests putting in place practices that foster the creation of bonding, trust, and common commitment proactively. The practices of team formation and execution that we have inherited from the past are not fast enough or reliable enough for the level of performance teams need to achieve today.

In other words, evidence suggests that intentionally designing teams for mutual success, bonding, and trust is what matters to human groups, not where they randomly happen to be working.

Humans as Costs—Leaving Value on the Table

Sadly, both in the United States and across the globe, systems have emerged that treat people, particularly frontline people, as cost centers. Efficiency-oriented systems therefore seek to minimize those costs as much as possible. As Zeynep Ton has argued in her marvelous books, *The Good Jobs Strategy* (2014) and *The Case for Good Jobs* (2023a), we have created a virtual epidemic of bad jobs. Low pay, unpredictable hours, little opportunities for advancement, and few opportunities to learn a variety of skills have cemented many employers' activities as essentially treating valuable humans like poorly performing robots. The business effects are not great either—high turnover, decreased customer satisfaction, poor productivity, and high levels of active disengagement are all outcomes.

Instead, Ton's work suggests that thinking of employees as units of revenue, rather than of cost, can yield tremendous benefits, even in low-margin sectors of the economy. As she puts it, ". . .what happens if your turnover level is one fifth of the industry average? That means that now for every new worker you can spend five times as much on hiring, on training, on performance management without increasing your hiring, training, or performance management budget. Can you imagine the competitive advantage that these companies have when they operate with such low turnover? There are so many other things that they can do. For example, they can ensure that their customers don't wait. They can ensure that their customers get service from people who are empowered, who know exactly what they're doing. They can ensure that their employees can constantly improve performance. These are all the things that are not available to companies that operate with high turnover" (Ton, 2023b).

Given that human learning is cumulative, it isn't surprising that firms that have figured out how to keep people, help them learn together, and adopt practices that are good for the enterprise outperform those that don't. One fascinating example of this is in the transaction led by Peter Stavros of KKR, in which CHI Overhead Doors was acquired by the private equity firm. In a departure from the standard playbook, however, every employee received an ownership grant of shares in the company through an Employee Stock Ownership Plan (ESOP), and when the company was eventually sold to Nucor Steel, employees made life-changing returns on their equity. What made this possible was attention to day-to-day improvements at the company. KKR had acquired the company in 2015 for US$700 million and sold it to Nucor Corp for US$3 billion in early 2022.

It became one of KKR's best investments historically, on the basis of treating humans as the ingenious, cooperative creatures they can be.

Connections—No Permission Required

Some companies, such as CHI Overhead Doors, have found that humans can put their ingenuity and learning to marvelous use, given the right organizational design and structure. Ricardo Semler, chief executive officer of the Brazilian company Semco, explains the success of a similar approach in his 1993 book, *Maverick* (1993). Semler observes, "We hire adults and then we treat them as adults. Think about that. Outside the factory, workers are men and women who elect governments, serve in the army, lead community projects, raise and educate families, and make decisions every day about the future. Friends solicit their advice. Salespeople court them. Children and grandchildren look up to them for their wisdom and experience. But the moment they walk into the factory, the company transforms them into adolescents. They have to wear badges and name tags, arrive at a certain time, stand in line to punch the clock or eat their lunch, get permission to go to the bathroom, give lengthy explanations every time they're five minutes late, and follow instructions without asking a lot of questions."

Other organizations offer early examples of facilitating more human connection and agency in their workplaces. Buurtzorg is a self-managing network of nurses in the Netherlands. Morning Star in the United States has grown extraordinarily in its tomato-processing sector. Haier in China makes appliances using the principles of micro-enterprises. The Ner Group in Spain espouses a flat hierarchy as part of its secret sauce. South Africa's Bidvest prides itself on decentralization, particularly in its services area.

As William Gibson once reportedly said, "The future is already here; it just isn't evenly distributed yet." So too with the human side of our changing technological universe. Let the gems in this collection show you the promise of a more connected future.

—Rita McGrath
Columbia Business School, New York, June 2024

References

Allen, T. J., and Henn, G. (2006). *The organization and architecture of innovation.* Routledge. Chapter 3, P58. https://books.google.co.uk/books?id=J5-ls6fV_3YC&lpg=PP1&pg=PA58&redir_esc=y#v=onepage&q&f=false

Bloom, N. (2024). *A very 2023 start-up—a badge-swiping app for folks with RTO mandates* [online]. Available at: https://www.linkedin.com/posts/nick-bloom-86b79510b_a-very-2023-start-up-a-badge-swiping-app-activity-7145790445481046016-j_gs

Cutter, C. and Chen, T-P. (2023, Sept. 25). Bosses aren't just tracking when you show up to the office but how long you stay. *Wall Street Journal.* https://www.wsj.com/lifestyle/careers/attention-office-resisters-the-boss-is-counting-badge-swipes-5fa37ff7?st=n8v01syax9vt950&reflink=d esktopwebshare_permalink

Ehrenreich, B. (2020). How do you know when society is about to fall apart? *New York Times.* https://www.nytimes.com/2020/11/04/magazine/societal-collapse.html

Ferrazzi, K. (2024). How the world's best teams engineer trust. *Forbes.* https://www.forbes.com/sites/keithferrazzi/2024/05/17/how-the-worlds-best-teams-engineer-trust/

McGrath, R. (2024). *What the world needs now . . . is love and AI?* [online]. Rita McGrath Group. Available at: https://www.ritamcgrath.com/sparks/2024/05/what-the-world-needs-now-ai/

McGrath, R. (2023). *WFH? RTO? Remembering the Allen Curve and why it matters now* [online]. Medium. Available at: https://rgmcgrath.medium .com/wfh-rto-remembering-the-allen-curve-and-why-it-matters-now-6698d744070b

Semler, R. (1993). *Maverick: The success story behind the world's most unusual workplace.* Warner Books.

Ton, Z. (2014). *The good jobs strategy.* New Harvest.

Ton, Z. (2023a). *The case for good jobs.* Harvard Business Review Press.

Ton, Z. (2023b). *Why good jobs are good for business (with Zeynep Ton)* [online]. Pitchfork Economics. Available at: https://pitchforkeconomics.com/episode/why-good-jobs-are-good-for-business-with-zeynep-ton/

Introduction

On a recent trip to Tibet, the Harvard professor and happiness guru, Arthur Brookes, met the Dalai Lama. His Holiness imparted six lessons on how to transcend our narrow focus on ourselves and shift our attention to other people instead. Brookes asked him why we find it so hard to focus on other people rather than ourselves—to which the Dalai Lama replied that we are under an illusion of ignorance about our individuality. The hidden truth is that we are all interconnected. We are all interdependent.

So how can we learn to live interdependently? Lesson no. 1 from His Holiness is that the way to remember the truth of interdependence throughout the day is to put love at the center of your work. No matter what your job, find a way to remind yourself that someone needs you, and the work is making their life better. In some jobs (raising kids), says Brookes, this is more obvious than in others, but it's true of all productive activity.

It may seem a bit of a stretch from the mountaintop monastery in Tibet to the busy and boisterous world of modern business, but it's not such a huge leap. In November 2023, when we invited the world's thought leaders to join us in London for the 2023 Thinkers50 Awards Gala, it was the first time the Thinkers50 Community had been able to meet in person since the COVID-19 pandemic. One of the three themes of the Gala was Reconnecting (the other two were Rethinking and Resetting).

Reconnecting

The Reconnecting theme was important because we had not gathered face-to-face as a community since 2019. The 2021 Awards Gala was a virtual event, and although it was inspiring to get together online, for 2023 we sensed a pent-up hunger for in-person human connection. We weren't disappointed. The sense of connection in the room and throughout the two-day 2023 Gala was extraordinary and has been remarked upon many times by those who experienced it. It reminded us of what it is to be human. It reconnected us with old friends and introduced us to new ones in a way that simply is not possible online.

A video call is not the same as being present in the same room; connecting digitally is not the same as connecting physically. The pandemic may have hastened the advance of technology in a time of crisis, but it also brought the realization that we may have been losing the human touch with colleagues, peers, customers, managers, leaders, family, and friends over the last two decades, as the digital world unfolded before us. It's easy to pin the blame for the disconnection that many of us feel on COVID-19, but in truth, it was already there: a creeping sense of separation and isolation that has become widespread in our modern society. Many more people now live alone and at a distance from family and friends. Technology, while at one level offering new ways to connect, has also contributed to our isolation.

There is an epidemic of loneliness.

In his turn of the century book *Bowling Alone*, Robert Putnam explored the decline of social capital in the United States, including the decrease in civic engagement and social connectedness since the 1960s. Putnam used the metaphor of bowling alone to illustrate the trend, explaining that while the number of people who go bowling had increased, the number who bowled in leagues had declined. Putnam put this down to a combination of factors, including the rise of television, two-income families, migration patterns, and changing generational attitudes. He argued that this had led to a decline in the quality and frequency of social interactions, resulting in a reduced sense of community and social trust.

Today, we can add a few more factors to Putnam's list: the amount of screen time we spend across multiple devices—including gaming, smart phones, and virtual work—as well as the lingering impact of the pandemic and the impending impact of artificial intelligence (AI). Some of the trends Putnam's book outlined have since reversed—most notably participation in US elections, which has risen. (Roughly two-thirds—66%—of the eligible population turned out for the 2020 presidential election—the highest for any national election since 1900.) But sadly, this can also be equated with a growing polarization in politics—and the disconnection and anger that many voters feel, a phenomenon that has been amplified and exacerbated by social media.

At the Thinkers50 Awards Gala, when we announced the topic of this book and invited contributions, we did not realize how acutely the theme would resonate. The response was almost overwhelming. It struck a nerve with people at the event and beyond. The fact that it coincided with the rapid advancement of generative AI certainly played a part too. What it is to be human and to connect with other humans was and continues to be on the minds of those who research, write, and speak about the future of business and management.

Game Changer or Whole New Game?

Right now, AI is still in its infancy, but it is already having a profound influence on how we work and live.

Few doubt that AI has the power to transform business, but how do we ensure that it does so in a way that benefits human beings and society? AI promises groundbreaking productivity and efficiency gains, but it also raises concerns about job losses, algorithmic biases, ethical dilemmas, and a host of other issues. It is also the question on the minds of business leaders: Is AI simply the next in a series of "disruptive innovations," or is it a new paradigm altogether? Do our existing strategy and innovation frameworks, tools, and theories still hold in this brave new world? Or do we need new thought-leadership to make sense of and navigate humanely through the AI inflection point?

Many of these questions remain unanswered and will only become clear in the coming years. But one thing does seem certain: AI threatens to remove many of our opportunities for connection. Meetings can be missed and summarized in seconds. Interactions with chatbots have already replaced human-to-human customer service (to the point where we often no longer know if we are talking to a person or a machine). Many tasks previously performed by human beings will be taken over and executed by more efficient algorithmically tuned AI tools. So where does that leave us?

The truth is that we don't yet know. What is certain, however, is that the fundamental human desire —need—to connect will not go away. We are hardwired for human connection. The question, then, becomes how will we connect with the new technology—will we fight it or embrace it? Will human beings and AI duel or dance? And how can we create stronger and more nuanced connections through technology?

"In the intricate dance of life and work, genuine connections are the rhythm that keeps us moving forward," observed Martin Lindstrom, branding and business culture expert, at the 2023 Thinkers50 Awards Gala. Lindstrom is right. There is something very special about human beings connecting. Something almost magical. That magic was present in the room in London's Guildhall when the Thinkers50 Community came together. Its potential is present wherever human beings come together and connect.

Collective Effervescence

"Things happen here that don't happen in real life," Norman Cook, AKA Fatboy Slim, declared when he came on stage at the Glastonbury music festival—a gathering of 200,000 people in a field in Somerset, England. Sociologist Émile Durkheim called this "collective effervescence," which, Wharton organizational psychologist Adam Grant explains, is "the energy of being in a group with a shared purpose. It's the joie de vivre of being in synchrony with strangers on a dance floor, colleagues in a brainstorm, friends on a soccer field, or family at a holiday dinner" (Grant 2021). It refers to the unifying excitement generated when people experience the same heightened emotion, an emotional contagion that can stimulate human connections from a music festival or sports event to a wave of creativity or innovation.

Grant reminds us that joy is a group phenomenon, a team game. "Joy shared is joy sustained," he says. In a nod to the Dalai Lama and Buddhist doctrine, he advocates "a Declaration of Interdependence."

Things happen when people get together, at an event, in a meeting, in the workplace, or even in a queue at the sandwich shop. Community matters. Relationships matter. "Every relationship that you form and nurture has a significant impact on you and can be the difference between success and loneliness. I've learned to never underestimate the power of investing in community," says Ruchika Tulshyan, author of *Inclusion on Purpose* (2023).

It's worth repeating. Relationships matter. Community matters. Harnessing the power of connections is the way to build trust and boost productivity. Connections (building relationships) are also intrinsic to good leadership.

Connections are essential to the sharing of ideas to make the world a better place, which is the mission of Thinkers50.

So how can leaders foster better connections between their people, customers, and other collaborative organizations, in this brave new world? How can we create our own pockets of collective effervescence? And what do the leaders of tomorrow need to know about human connection?

That's the question we put to the thinkers who make up the Thinkers50 Community. This book is their response. It is the second of our curated collections of short essays addressed to the leaders of the present and future, to help them not only to survive but also to thrive (Dearlove 2023). As ever, we hope that the advice and fresh thinking they contain will help you—the leaders of tomorrow—nurture and sustain the human touch on your journey.

Readers' Guide

The topics covered in the following pages center around the theme of human connection. The book is structured to help readers dip in and dip out or read as a complete guide.

How can we cultivate positive working relationships? Michael Bungay Stanier provides a framework. Andrew Barnes argues the benefits of implementing a 4-day week (something we have adopted at Thinkers50 and heartily recommend). How can we reconnect when we have lost touch? Pia Lauritzen reveals the power of questions. Making every word count: Matt Abrahams illuminates on building effective communication skills. Taking the lead in the dance with AI, Kate O'Neill outlines a human-centric approach to AI, and Hamilton Mann addresses the thorny scourge of biases in AI models.

There are lessons for leaders too, from Kirstin Ferguson on intellectual humility; developing a human touch from Susie Kennedy; perfecting meeting intelligence (MQ) from Thomas Roulet and Soulaima Gourani; and tackling the loneliness epidemic from Constance Noonan Hadley.

How do we create a connecting culture within our organizations? Poornima Luthra presents seven steps to active allyship; Malissa Clark unpacks the issues of remote work versus return-to-office; and Neri Karra Sillaman shows us that resilience is stronger in a community than within an individual. We also need to connect with true inclusivity, and Ludmila Praslova offers the canary code to embracing neurodiversity.

Focusing on people development and nurturing talent, Kandi Wiens addresses burnout; Jenny Fernandez explains how to unleash the powers of Gen Z; and David Lancefield shows how to cultivate strategic people through empowerment, reframing, and teamwork.

Connecting the Dots

Connection is our most important human superpower. Lack of connection is our biggest threat as individuals and as a species. Connections matter. They are what make us human. We are interdependent and our work is interdependent. On our own, we are just individual dots. Together we are so much more. The future of management and business is all about how we connect those dots.

—Des Dearlove & Lisa Humphries, London, June 2024

References

Dearlove, D. (2023). *Certain uncertainty: Leading with agility and resilience in an unpredictable world*. Wiley.

Grant, A. (2021, July 10). There's a specific kind of joy we've been missing. *New York Times*. https://www.nytimes.com/2021/07/10/opinion/sunday/covid-group-emotions-happiness.html

Ruchika, T. (2023). 7 leadership lessons in 7 years. *Inclusion in Leadership*. LinkedIn. https://www.linkedin.com/pulse/7-leadership-lessons-years-ruchika-tulshyan

We, Human

1

Every Working Relationship Can Be Better

Here's How

Michael Bungay Stanier
Author of The Coaching Habit

Okay, perhaps not every working relationship. But *almost* every one.

I know that's a bold statement. It's also an urgent one.

Our happiness and our success at work are deeply dependent on the quality of our key working relationships, not just our bosses, our team, and our collaborators, but also our peers, our customers and clients, and our vendors.

Think of what it's been like to work with those key people. When things are good between you, there's a strong likelihood that the work is good too and you feel at your best. When things between you are off, the work is a struggle, and you feel stressed.

Hope Is Not a Strategy

You know this to be true from our lived experience. And yet, mostly, you do nothing about it. It's in the lap of the gods, you've got your fingers crossed, you're rolling the dice, you're hoping it will be good this time, and then you wait and see.

You start each working relationship with mixed feelings, some balance of hope and anxiety. Your past experiences and to some extent your inherent wiring will determine your own particular blend of optimism and pessimism.

Sometimes you've got lucky and found yourself working with someone who's fabulous. You clicked. You were greater than the sum of your parts. You brought out each other's best, and you managed to step lightly through the tricky moments.

Sometimes you've got unlucky. They wound you up, set you off, and brought out the worst in you (just as you did for them). You were diminished by the experience, "less" not just in the quality of the work you did and the impact it had, but in the way you felt about yourself.

And mostly, the working relationships have been somewhere in the middle. They're mostly okay. There are ups and downs. You can live with it, but it's been defining.

But what if you stopped just *hoping* that you'd get lucky and actually did something about it?

What if you were active in shaping the working relationships you had so that they were closer to what you hoped for? What if each of your key working relationships was the best version that it could be?

What if it could be the best possible relationship (BPR)?

The Best Possible Relationship

Spoiler alert: not every working relationship can be wonderful. Would that it could be true . . . but, no. However, every one of them could be better. The good, the bad, the ugly: imagine each of them 10% better than they currently are. Can you see the difference that would make on your impact, your stress, your happiness, your sense of self?

The goal is to build the BPR with your key people. A BPR has three defining qualities. It is safe, it is vital, and it is repairable.

Amy Edmondson, Thinker50's 2023 #1 management thinker, has been championing psychological safety for 25 years now. It's become part of our corporate vocabulary, and there's a general understanding that individuals and teams perform better if they feel safe: safe to talk about what's not working, safe to show up as who they are. Psychological safety is table stakes for a BPR. And while it's necessary, it's not sufficient.

I've been in working relationships that were "safe," but they also felt stifling. They were nice, they were pleasant, and they were boring. That's why the second quality of a BPR is vital. This is psychological bravery. It's a willingness to challenge, to provoke, to say the hard truth, to have healthy conflict, to step out to the edge of what's known, to feel your way forward in the half-light.

The final quality of a BPR is repairable. Reading across the work of the doyens of romantic relationships—Esther Perel, Terry Real, John Gottman, Dan Siegel, and others—two things become clear. First, the relationships that thrive and have longevity are ones that get repaired. Second, most of us are not great at repairing relationships. We tend to "fight or flight" it: either we lash out and try and hurt the other person back, or we retreat and suffer the pain in silence.

Each BPR finds its own ideal mix of safe and vital, as the two individuals find the balance in their relationship. Equally, each BPR understands that, even with the best of intentions, there's always a moment where something goes wrong. A misunderstood word, a failed commitment, a lack of blood sugar. So each BPR knows that repair will at some stage be necessary and is willing to do that work.

If a BPR—safe, vital, and repairable—is the goal, how do you get there? What's the practice that makes the difference?

A Keystone Conversation

The answer is simple but not easy. It's to have a conversation about how you'll work together before you start the work. Or if you've already begun working with them, a pause, and a conversation about how you might tweak and fine-tune your working relationship to make it better.

The keystone metaphor is obvious enough. It's the joining piece between two columns, and it's the stone that allows the arch to settle, to bear stress, and to grow stronger over time.

It's not easy, and for two reasons. First, because work shouts loudly. It's there, it's the main thing, and it's important—or urgent or enticing. You've spent your whole career cracking on with it and getting the work done. You're measured on your work. Your role is defined by the work you're meant to be doing. You have deep muscle memory to just get on and get going with the work.

The second reason is that a conversation about how you do the work is an unusual and (somewhat) vulnerable conversation. It's uncommon, so it's daunting. It requires you to share something of yourself. It requires you to be willing to see other people for who they are. It requires you to know something of yourself. It can feel risky, and truth is that it can be risky. Anytime you chose to "lower your shield," to use Brené Brown's phrase, there's both danger and opportunity.

What Do You Talk About?

If you simply asked (and answered) the question, "How can we best work together?" that would be fantastic. That would already put you in a minority of people more actively shaping their working relationships.

But you can go deeper, be more curious, and get more specific. Broadly speaking, you're seeking to exchange information on two areas: what we should amplify and what we should avoid.

The idea of amplification draws upon such established approaches to change as Appreciative Inquiry and Positive Deviance. Both these strategies come from the idea that we should figure out what works and then do more of it. One powerful question, which I first learned from the author and management philosopher Peter Block, is, "What can we learn from successful past relationships like this one?" What was said and done by you and by the other person? What was not said and not done by the two of you? And now, what does that tell you about what's useful for this current relationship?

The flipside can be equally useful, this time in seeking out what to avoid. "What can we learn from past frustrating relationships like this one?" Mistakes were made. Triggers were set off. Irritations were flared. What happened? What was their role? What was yours? And now, how does looking at this past dysfunction help you navigate this current relationship?

You're both figuring out that if we had more of X and less of Y, we're more likely to enjoy working together and more likely to have success while doing it. Beforehand, you would just be guessing at what the X and the Y was, as would that other person. Now you both get to find out for real.

But What About [Name of Terrible Person]?

You've probably got at least one person in your working life who you're thinking, "This would never work with them. They are terrible, horrible, and no good." And yes, you're probably right. Not that person.

But that leaves everyone else.

Every one of those other working relationships could be better. You could make them better. The thing to do is to be the person who moves first. Someone said, "No one likes to be the first person to say hello, but everyone likes to be greeted." You can be the first person. You can make every working relationship better.

Biography

Michael Bungay Stanier is the author of *The Coaching Habit: Say Less, Ask More & Change the Way You Lead Forever* (Page Two Books, 2016), the best-selling book on coaching this century. He is also the founder of training and development company, Box of Crayons. Michael's latest book is *How to Work with (Almost) Anyone* (Page Two Books, 2023). He was the recipient of the Thinkers50 2023 Coaching and Mentoring Award.

2

The Four-day Week

Here's Why

Andrew Barnes
*Founder of Perpetual Guardian and cofounder
of 4 Day Week Global*

In 2018, I initiated a trial of a four-day workweek (reduced hours, but on full pay) for the 320 employees in my own business, Perpetual Guardian, New Zealand's largest Trustee company. The announcement and the results of the trial led to global media headlines numbering in the tens of thousands, and prompted me to write a book, *The 4 Day Week* and to establish a not-for-profit organization, 4 Day Week Global, which assists companies, organizations, and governments all over the world to introduce a four-day/reduced hours working week with the objective to create a million years of free time.

To date, we have run six-month pilots in the United States, Canada, Ireland, the United Kingdom, Australia, New Zealand, and South Africa, with current work underway in a further 10 countries. Alongside the pilots we coordinate a comprehensive university-led research program to assess the impact on both employers and employees, and I propose to draw on the research results to illustrate the effect reduced-hours working has on human connectivity.

I often describe myself as feeling a bit of a fraud when it comes to talking about the four-day week in the context of its social impact, as my objective for the original experiment at Perpetual Guardian was to determine if the incentive of gifting more time off without a reduction of pay could incentivize higher levels of productivity. We now refer to this as the 100:80:100 rule: 100% five-day pay, 80% time, 100% five-day productivity and customer service. While this objective was exceeded, more surprising was the effect the initiative had on the well-being of our employees.

Alongside the four-day-week trial, we commissioned qualitative and quantitative research to ensure that we had objective and verifiable data on the impact of the change to the working week. The results painted a clear picture of the ways in which increased non-work time improved the quality of employees' lives.

A consistent theme was that employees had more time to accomplish tasks in their personal lives which were often squeezed in or put off in the course of a five-day work schedule. Some employees reported more time to learn and contribute via formal and informal study and professional development, while others dedicated additional time to travel, leisure and consumption activities, or volunteering.

However, the dominant outcome was having more time to participate in family life. This included working parents (and grandparents) having the opportunity to be more actively involved in children's lives, by sharing meals, attending day-care or school activities, and talking and connecting with their children, partners, and wider family and friend networks.

Whilst these results were encouraging and were certainly the impetus behind the creation of the global 4 Day Week campaign, the data set was small, and the results could potentially have been influenced by the placebo effect of the trial and the attendant publicity on the employees. Subsequently we have run trials involving more than 200,000 employees across a wide variety of businesses, industries, and countries, and we are now able to draw more robust conclusions upon the impact on individuals of reduced-hours working.

But first, a general observation. While on one level we have never been more connected, with billions of us using Facebook, Instagram, TikTok, and a plethora of emails, apps, and social media groups to communicate and engage with our communities and other individuals all over the world, on another level, true connectivity appears to be plumbing new depths. Recent studies show that loneliness is rising at an exponential rate with one in four young people in a recent Gallup poll describing themselves as lonely. An analysis by Meta of 125,000 respondents found that each succeeding generation reported increasing levels of loneliness, despite these technological connections. At another level, while 3 in 10 US adults (rising to 6 in 10 for Americans under 50 who have never been married) are using dating apps, the percentage of dating app users across all demographics who feel dissatisfaction with the apps has risen, with just under 50% of all users reporting they feel somewhat negative about online dating as opposed to the traditional methods of meeting a potential partner via social, work, or family connections.

An inescapable conclusion is this illustrates the limitations of social media as a facilitator of true relationships between individuals and individuals and society. As we have turned to technology to facilitate communication, increasingly those messages or Instagram moments are sometimes curated to project an image of ourselves that doesn't necessarily reflect either our true selves (especially in dating apps!) or our vulnerabilities and true feelings. We have lost the human aspect of connection which, I believe, only occurs when individuals feel they are valued and when they are able to spend time with the people they love and value in both their families and the wider community.

So far, so good, but how does this relate to the impact and imperative for a four-day week? Our original experiment had hinted at the possible social benefits of a reduction in working hours, and we were determined that the associated research would focus on this, while still ensuring we monitored the productivity outcomes which had been central to the initial experiment at Perpetual Guardian.

Our thesis remains that if a reduction in the working week is to be achievable, and, more importantly, sustainable, it has to demonstrate a four-day week doesn't come at the expense of business. I therefore make no apology in a book focused on human connection, to firstly present the business perspective of our July 2023 "The 4 Day Week: 12 Months On" research report by Professor Juliet B. Schor, Professor Wen Fan, and Guilin Gu of Boston College. This report updates the results from the 4 Day Week Global US and Canadian pilot in 2022 and provides an insight into the longer-term impact of the four-day week beyond the trial's conclusion.

The business reaction was encouraging. On a scale of 1–10, from very negative to very positive, companies rated the overall impact of the trial as 8.7/10. As a tool to attract new employees, the four-day week was rated as 8.7/10, with both productivity and performance scoring 7.7/10. Respondents recorded revenue as having increased by 15%. The number of employees who were seriously considering leaving their jobs fell significantly, with 32% saying they were now less likely to leave. As for their plans post-trial, 100% of the respondents are definitely planning, or leaning toward, continuing the four-day week policy. So from a business perspective, a four-day-week is a viable solution that appears to have sustainability beyond the trial environment. This is also borne out by our other research reports into our other national trials and the results from the Perpetual Guardian experiment, now entering its sixth year!

We also asked participating employees for their reaction at the end of the six-month trial and, not surprisingly, a staggering

96.9% of employees said they wanted to continue a four-day week, while only two respondents leaned toward not continuing. Not a single person said they didn't want to continue working on a four-day-week schedule.

We also asked employees to report how much it would cost to entice them back to a five-day-week role; 13% said no amount of money would induce them to take a five-day schedule. Another 13% said they would require a more than 50% pay rise, while 42% would require a 26% to 50% increase.

I think we can draw two conclusions from this research. Firstly, and most obviously, a four-day week is extremely popular with both employers and employees, the latter notwithstanding that it comes with work performance obligations. Secondly, employees put a higher value on the time they have off than their employer appears ready to pay for it, probably because it is impossible to put a price on the benefits afforded by additional free time, which is then deployed in ways that appear to fulfill human physiological and psychological needs as well as fostering real connections.

As humans, we have physiological needs, among them the requirement to eat, to sleep, and to find shelter. Work, or rather the income received from it, enables individuals to meet these needs, albeit there is some evidence to suggest that modern working practices are adversely impacting the second of these, with many employees reporting a higher incidence of insomnia or sleep deprivation.

Almost 7 in 10 employees in the US and Canadian pilot experienced reductions in burnout, while 40% reported feeling less stressed, and 59% reported a decline in negative emotions. Significant increases were observed in participants' physical and mental health, and 40% experienced fewer sleep problems following the implementation of a four-day week.

Our UK trial demonstrated that when employees were gifted more time off, they often used the opportunity to volunteer and engage more with their local communities. This is backed up by two separate studies, conducted in 2019 and 2021 by Henley Business School, of 2,000 UK-based employees and 500 business leaders, including businesses that had already implemented a four-day week.

Sixty-six percent of employees indicated they would likely spend the time meeting up with friends and 67% meeting up with their families. Volunteering, at 36%, was another popular option, as was theater or cinema going (45%) and eating out (48%). Of importance to improving personal health, taking part in sports (45%) and having more time to cook at home (59%), possibly leading to less fast and takeaway food, also scored highly.

Equally, humans have psychological needs: to feel they are doing a good job (competency), that they have control over their time (autonomy), and the need to feel related or connected to other people (connection). A consistent theme from the various research reports linked to our four-day-week pilot programs is that these three psychological needs appear to be fulfilled as a consequence of a reduced-hours, outcome-focused workweek.

With the introduction of a four-day week (based on the 100:80:100 principle) employees are given more control over their work and are empowered by management to find solutions so as to deliver on clearly articulated outcomes. In the "One Year On" report, 51% of employees reported better control of their schedules linked to a big improvement in self-reported productivity, with a 57% increase in workers' current work ability compared to their lifetime best.

In all successful implementations of a four-day (reduced-hours) workweek, there appears to be an exponential focus on teamwork as an enabler of performance, with participants reporting a mutual willingness to help each other out, with greater sharing of information and delegation of tasks linked to an increase in appreciation and trust for the ability and reliability of their team members.

The post-trial results for teamwork and team cohesion conducted by Professor Haar, a leading New Zealand researcher in human resource management and organizational behavior, on the Perpetual Guardian trial indicated outcomes 25% higher than national country averages and still significantly higher (11%) than the pre-trial data.

In the same research, Professor Haar saw significant increases in job satisfaction and work engagement, to levels that he described as easily the highest he had ever seen in his New Zealand data, supporting the hypothesis that employees felt themselves to be more fulfilled in the workplace via more collaboration.

Outside the workplace, the evidence also suggests as people have more time they take up hobbies and reconnect to family and community. This appears to be confirmed by the "One Year On" data, which indicated work-to-family and work-to-life conflict declined for 6 out of 10 participants. Similar results were seen in our UK pilot data, with parenting time by men doubling throughout the trial (to 35%). Increased engagement not only contributes to reducing stress, but it also creates the opportunity for an active recovery from the pressures and impositions of work as well as fulfilling an individual's psychological need for connection.

In a world where we are increasingly disconnected, either via the intrusion of work time into our lives, or by the disintermediation of technology into our community and connections, it is increasingly clear that the way we work today is fit neither for human health and well-being nor for the productivity and profitability of business. If we take seriously the transformative change of the four-day, reduced-hours week, as well as other productivity-driven models of flexibility in work, we can start to address the significant challenges we currently face as a species.

But don't take my word for it. Take the plunge and initiate a trial in your own workplaces. After all, what's the worst that could happen?

Biography

Founder of Perpetual Guardian, New Zealand's largest corporate trustee company, Andrew Barnes is author of *The 4 Day Week: How the Flexible Work Revolution Can Increase Productivity, Profitability and Well-Being, and Create a Sustainable Future* (with Stephanie Jones, Hachette, 2020). He is also cofounder (with his partner, Charlotte Lockhart) of the 4 Day Week Global movement, which has spearheaded four-day-week trials across the world. Andrew has served as an advisor to governments and sits on the advisory boards of both the US and Ireland 4 Day Week campaigns and on the board of the newly created Wellbeing Research Centre at Oxford University. A founding member of the World Wellbeing Movement, Andrew was named to the Thinkers50 Radar Class of 2024.

3

Why We Lost Touch with Each Other and How We Reconnect

Pia Lauritzen
Inventor of Qvest and Question Jam

Will the use of technology take over human connection in the future?

This was one of the questions asked in a study I recently conducted in a global community of young leaders. As in all the studies I have run in the past 20 years, I did not ask any questions myself. Instead, I used Qvest.io, the flipped survey platform I developed to allow groups of people to ask each other questions about a topic they have a shared interest in. In this case, I invited 92 members of UNLEASH, a nonprofit organization with a mission to accelerate positive change toward the Sustainable Development Goals, to exchange questions and answers about the future.

Across countries, fields of study, and professions, people in the study expressed fear that we are losing our "human touch."

Some were concerned about the consequences of emerging technologies. Others asked:

"What will happen if we lose generations of wisdom to a capitalist society?"

"How can we stay hopeful when everything everywhere seems to be falling apart?"

"What are some effective ways to fight disinformation with science?"

"How can we use culture and art to strengthen democracy and decrease polarization?"

"How do we teach students to learn from our collective history, the good, the bad, and the ugly?"

It only seems fair that the leaders of tomorrow are concerned. Despite incredible scientific and technological advances, we humans still fight each other. One might even argue that human strife is worse now than it was a few decades ago. There is war again in Europe. The situation in the Middle East is worse than it has been for a long time. Social media is accused of increasing polarization. And the climate crisis has us blaming each other for not doing enough—or doing the wrong things—instead of bringing us together to make a joint effort. At the same time, companies still struggle with silos and lack of strategic alignment. And the great focus on inclusion and diversity indicates that many people do not feel seen, heard, and respected. It seems like we have lost touch with each other. But why? And how do we reconnect?

The Missing Link

After spending 20 years researching the nature and impact of questions, I have arrived at an answer that only indirectly has to do with technology and capitalism.

The answer is that there is a missing link in our collective understanding of human connection: something essential to our ability to connect with each other that we consistently, yet unknowingly prevent each other from doing.

The answer can be traced back to 375 BCE Greece where Plato wrote his world-renowned dialogs, featuring the even more renowned Greek philosopher, Socrates.

Socrates was Plato's mentor, but unlike other mentors, he didn't tell his students what to think and how to do it. Instead, he asked them a lot of questions. Like today's coaches, Plato believed, "When people are asked questions, they can produce the right answers to anything by themselves." But then he added, ". . .provided that the questioning is done properly" (*Phaedo*). Much has been said and written about the impact of Plato's ideas on Western thought and civilization. But neither philosophers nor social scientists have examined how this idea that questioning is something that must be done "properly" affects the way people act and, even more importantly, *interact* with each other.

Combining philosophical research with more than 30,000 questions asked by people from around the world (collected and analyzed through the flipped survey platform I mentioned earlier), I have found that two things happen:

1. We have become obsessed with asking the right questions in the right way.

2. We consider some people better suited than others to ask questions.

The Power of Questions

My research shows that when we humans ask questions, we automatically connect with each other and commit to a shared purpose. This means that the best way to reach important goals together is to ask each other questions.

However, to unleash the power of questions, no one must withhold important questions or prevent others from asking questions. And that is precisely what the idea that questioning must be done "properly" makes us do.

While the obsession with asking the right questions in the right way makes many refrain from asking questions out of fear of asking wrong questions in the wrong way, the idea that some people are better suited to ask questions than others has given certain professions a monopoly on asking questions.

Throughout 2,400 years of Western history, philosophers, mentors, coaches, teachers, scientists, journalists, lawyers, leaders, and human resource consultants have considered it their job to ask the right questions that lead to the right answers. Meanwhile, everyone else has been reduced to respondents, i.e., someone who *responds* to questions rather than asking them themselves.

When (thought) leaders from philosophers and scientists to business leaders and consultants consider it their job to ask *the right questions* in questionnaires, opinion polls, and interviews, they not only monopolize the power of questions, they also systematically prevent large groups of people from asking their own questions. When people are prevented from asking their own questions, they are also largely prevented from connecting with each other and the world they share.

The Monopoly

If the reason we lost touch with each other is that the human behavior that links us all together has been monopolized and institutionalized, we need to take a closer look at the people and professions that hold this monopoly.

I have identified three categories of (thought) leaders whose understanding of themselves and their profession makes it harder for others to connect and commit to a shared purpose: *philosophers, scientists and technologists,* and *business leaders and consultants.* Although it may sound strange, teachers, journalists, lawyers, and others concerned with seeking and sharing the truth fall under the category of philosophers.

Let's look at the three categories one at a time:

1. **Philosophers:** As we already learned from Plato, philosophers are concerned with asking the *right questions* that lead to the *right answers.* They know that *what* and *how* they ask is decisive for whether or not they succeed in their work. And they spend time thinking, reading, hearing, and maybe even teaching, writing, and talking about the art of asking good questions. The trillions of search results for "how to ask" on Google testify to the fact that many share this understanding of questions. It also testifies to the idea that it takes time and expert knowledge to ask good questions.

2. **Scientists and technologists:** While scientists ask questions to get *correct* answers, technologists design and develop technology to make it easy to get *quick answers.* However, the focus on answers rather than questions is the same. Questions are seen as merely a means to an end, and it is the exception rather than the rule that scientists and technologists pay attention to the role questions play in their work. (Stuart Firestein's book, *Ignorance: How It Drives Science*, is a brilliant example of such an exception.)

   Advances in science and technology are the main reason why questions have remained a blind spot in our collective understanding of human connection. By not paying attention to their own understanding of questions as a simple means of getting quick, correct answers, scientists and engineers have built the same understanding of questions into all the systems that make up the infrastructure of our societies.

This means that we unknowingly subject ourselves to this understanding when we implement scientific theories, methods, technologies, and tools in our daily work and lives. Like the scientists and engineers who developed the theories and technologies, we don't think about it. But every time we type a question into a search engine or rely on AI to solve our problems, we reinforce the view of questions as a means of quick answers rather than something we do to connect and collaborate with each other.

3. **Business leaders and consultants:** The third category of leaders whose understanding of themselves and their profession makes it harder for others to connect and commit to a shared purpose is, paradoxically, those whose job it is to create connection and commitment across large groups of people. Business leaders and consultants, but also political leaders and their advisors, are less concerned about whether their questions and answers are *right* and more about whether they have the information and insight they need to make *good decisions*.

Their focus on making good decisions makes it vital for leaders to continuously receive important information. And their focus on receiving important information not only makes them dependent on their relationships with the people they work with, it also makes them dependent on people they are not in direct contact with, e.g., shop floor employees and customers. And this is where the monopoly of questions comes into play.

To collect data from people they do not personally interact with, leaders and consultants rely on the methods and technologies developed by scientists and tech designers. Interview techniques, questionnaires, surveys, opinion polls. They all reflect and reinforce (1) that some questions are better than others and (2) that some people are more entitled to ask questions than others (e.g., HR consultants and coaches).

In addition to reinforcing the monopoly held by philosophers, scientists, and technologists, business leaders and consultants risk focusing so much on getting important information themselves that they forget that others also depend on information and meaningful interaction to make good decisions. They may have tools that help them ask and collect answers to their own questions, but if they don't have tools that help others do the same, they make it harder, rather than easier, for their employees and other stakeholders to connect and commit to a shared purpose.

The Democratization

"Will the use of technology take over human connection in the future?" The person asking the question in my UNLEASH study received the following answer from one of the other participants: "The use of technology will reduce human connection, but it will not take over human connection."

I tend to agree with the person writing this. But I also agree with another participant in the study who stated: "We are living through an incredibly fascinating time in human history." And I think the key to our future is to take our history seriously. After 2,400 years of monopolization, I am curious and optimistic about what can happen if we set out to democratize the power of questions.

Democratization requires a fundamental shift in how we think and talk about all three categories of monopoly: instead of obsessing about asking the right questions in the right way, we must trust ourselves and each other to ask the questions that help us connect and collaborate on solving important problems.

When designing and developing technology, we must ask ourselves and each other whether quick and easy is always the answer. What if complex technology inhibits rather than enhances our own ability to navigate complexity? What does it take to develop technology that supports human curiosity, critical thinking, and creativity? Can technology be designed to make us less reliant on technology?

And instead of focusing solely on their own decisions and their own sources of information, leaders must focus on creating a culture where everyone seeks out the information and interaction they need to solve important problems together.

Who knows. By democratizing the power of questions, we may not only prevent the use of technology from taking over human connection, we may end up strengthening it.

Biography

Pia Lauritzen is a Danish philosopher and the inventor of the digital Qvest and Question Jam platforms. She holds a PhD in philosophy and has published five books, including *Questions* (Johns Hopkins University Press, 2024). Pia is a regular contributor to *Forbes*, and her 2019 TEDx Talk is titled, "What You Don't Know About Questions." In 2023, she was selected for the Thinkers50 Radar List for "providing powerful proof that questions, rather than generic answers, will shape our futures."

4

One Simple Change to Improve Your Connections

Amanda Nimon-Peters
Professor of Leadership, Hult International Business School, Dubai Campus

Are You a Rational or Emotional Thinker?

Maybe you think of yourself as rational. When faced with a problem or decision, you might see yourself as a logical, factual, reasoning-based thinker. Or perhaps you are driven by intuition or instinct. You might believe it is best to "go with your gut" or "listen to your heart." You might even feel you swap between the two, sometimes basing a decision on facts, sometimes basing it on feelings. Right now, you might be picturing a spectrum, with rational thinking at the opposite end from emotion-led thinking.

Whichever description you believe fits you best, neurobiology has demonstrated that almost all human thinking, almost all the time, is both. Further, the emotional aspect comes first; indeed, it determines what data we pay attention to. Thus, although some of our thinking is more methodical and logical, and some of our thinking is more reactive and instinctive, most of our thinking, most of the time, is shaped by emotional reactions (Kahneman 2003). Neuroscientists have coined the term **emotional thought** to represent their findings that cognitive processes are actually embedded within the processes of emotion (Immordino-Yang and Damasio 2011).

Put in simple terms: in any given situation, situated within a sea of millions of potential stimuli or bytes of information, your brain's automatic, subconscious, emotional reactions will determine the data you consciously consider. This process includes whether or not you are paying attention, what you are paying attention to, how you evaluate that data, how you code it into memory, and whether or not you are motivated to do anything about it (Immordino-Yang 2011; Li et al. 2020).

What This Means for Our Attempts to Influence Others

These observations about the brain are highly relevant to the way we go about influencing others. Commonly used strategies are less effective than you might expect, mostly because our brain processes information in a way we don't expect.

For example, one of the most commonly used strategies when people at work attempt to influence their colleagues is rational persuasion (Higgins et al. 2003; Manning 2012; Lee et al. 2017). This means deploying a series of logical or factual reasons to convince another to act. Yet, unless the recipients report to you directly, this is a pretty ineffective strategy. One meta-analysis of 49 studies, covering the workplace behavior of almost 9,000 people, found that the correlation between using rational persuasion and getting to the desired outcome was around 0.35, indicating rational persuasion influencers are successful about 12% of the time (Lee et al. 2017). Further, we often behave as if the more logical reasons we add to our arguments, the more convincing we will be. Instead, the opposite seems to be true. The average effectiveness of rational persuasion drops when would-be influencers combine their reasons (Falbe and Yukl 1992; Schwartz et al. 2015; Bélanger et al. 2018).

Why are logic and facts less persuasive than we expect? Because we are less rational and logical than we believe ourselves to be. Essentially, we are driven by emotional thought rather than pure and undiluted logic.

Think back to the last time you wrote an email, prepared a presentation, or introduced yourself. Chances are that your primary consideration was to determine which facts, data, or information you needed to convey. You might also have considered how to structure that information in a logical, rational sequence. This seems like perfectly sensible behavior, but as we have seen, it is a less effective communication paradigm than it may appear. When we structure a message according to data and information, we leave ourselves open to the audience's attention being hijacked by an emotional response to the topic or the specific words used or how they feel about the sender of the message (i.e., you), as well as whether the message itself is perceived as of benefit, threat, or simply neutral to the receiver.

In essence, our deep, unconscious reaction to how a person makes us feel has a significant effect on how we interpret what that person says.

One Simple Change to Dramatically Improve Your Influence and Your Connections

The key to applying this understanding in your own life is accepting the need to flip the script. Instead of starting every communication by considering "What do I need to say to this audience?" ask instead, **"How do I want them to feel?"**

Your success in effectively generating a beneficial emotional response in others—and hence a greater likelihood of a positive outcome—will be affected by both your ability to say the right things as well as your skill in avoiding the wrong things.

What to Do: Generate a Feeling of Affiliation

You are more likely to influence others to listen to you, help you, remember you, or do the things you ask when you target their emotional reactions through the behavioral science principle of **affiliation** (Nimon-Peters 2022). The principle of affiliation is based on the brain's fundamental and ongoing classification of others as either "like me" or "not like me." Visualize it as a process by which your brain is continually seeking information to determine whether another should be included inside a Venn diagram with you or excluded as an outsider. Those boundaries can change from one situation to the next, such as when a supporter of the opposing team ("not like me") is the only other person at the soft drink stand who speaks your language ("like me").

Among the first to describe this phenomenon, social psychologist Henri Tajfel found stark differences in people's behavior toward others based on whether or not they perceived them as members of the same group (Tajfel 1974). The distinction can be conscious or unconscious and is probably a survival-driven mechanism, given we are more likely to be safe and cared for with people who are in our tribe or part of our team than with outsiders. Indeed, humans can make in-group versus out-group distinctions from as early as 17 months of age (Jin and Baillargeon 2017).

Once we perceive another person as "like me," our behavior toward them becomes measurably biased. This behavior includes a tendency to disproportionately favor them when sharing resources as well as a more positive interpretation of their actions, words, facial expressions, and motives [(Tajfel 1970; Tajfel et al. 1971; Saarinen et al. 2021). Neuroscientists have measured that our brains experience less effort and less anxiety in conversations between people with higher similarity compared to conversations between people with lower similarity, even when discussing the same topics (Descorbeth et al. 2020).

In today's workplaces, our colleagues are often very different in gender, background, age, nationality, function, expertise, and even fashion sense! People will classify you as either like them or not like them whether or not either party is aware of the process, so this diversity runs the risk of an automatic "not like me" classification. Even if the other person looks a lot like you, and irrespective of what *you* may feel about *them*—you should always aim to proactively trigger a sense of affiliation.

There are three ethical, research-backed methods for generating a feeling of affiliation between yourself and others. One or all of these should factor highly into your plan to address the question, "How do I want them to feel?"

1. **They feel that you have important similarities in common with them.** The number-one technique for creating a sense of affiliation is to highlight a real similarity between you. You are looking for a positive feature, something that the person would be proud of or happy to acknowledge. This will have the dual effect of inducing positive emotion, at the same time as highlighting your similarity. The more important the feature for social identity, the stronger the effect will be.

2. **If you have genuine praise to share, share it!** Receiving praise activates the brain's reward center in a manner similar to that when someone is given money (Izuma et al. 2008). Compliments benefit the emotional well-being of both givers and receivers, and yet the average person refrains from

giving compliments because we consistently underestimate how positive the effect will be (Zhao and Epley 2021a). The positive effect of a genuine compliment is stronger than a generic one (Boothby and Bohns 2021), occurs even when the person is someone you just met, and does not reduce as multiple compliments are received over time (Zhao and Epley 2021b). In the workplace, praise for a peer or direct report has a stronger effect than praise for a supervisor (Gordon 1996).

3. **Demonstrate that you care about the things that matter to them.** Research has shown that even people lower in trust feel more cared for when they are asked about their day or their other experiences by someone who listens to their answers (Cortes and Wood 2019). If you are a manager, take the time to know your people's goals and acknowledge these when you interact with them. In a face-to-face conversation, paraphrase something the other person said. A paraphrased reflection is more effective in generating positive feelings than a simple acknowledgment of what was spoken (Weger et al. 2010).

It's Not Just Being Likable!

All of these actions help you send a message to the other person's brain that you are part of their tribe and that you have their back. When understood accurately, the principle of affiliation is substantively different from simply being friendly or likable. With an inaccurate understanding of the concept, you might think the most important action is to bring donuts to work, spill your innermost secrets, or generally behave in an agreeable manner. With an accurate understanding, you can engage in simple action steps that are appropriate in any professional environment, whatever your level of seniority.

When generating a sense of affiliation, it's key to remember you are targeting how the person **feels**. Don't bombard the other with lots of information: that is behaving as if your goal is to communicate lots of facts and figures. In fact, thanks to a phenomenon called the "dilution effect," providing additional content in your message can divert people's attention away from the important element (Zukier 1982). It's also key to trigger the sense of affiliation at the moment of interaction rather than assume it already exists. As noted, the boundaries between "like me" and "not like me" can change with the context.

What else is in it for you? Just as research demonstrates that giving compliments has a positive effect on the giver as well as the receiver, a sense of affiliation not only influences the positive behavior of others toward you, it will influence your positive behavior toward others also.

What to Avoid: Triggering a Distraction or Negative Emotion

When considering the actions you will take to affect how a person feels, there are easy mistakes you might make that will have the opposite effect. This is a particular risk in communications in which you include lots of information because the chance of an unintended consequence increases.

1. **Take care with the words and topics.** Our intended communications are frequently hijacked by a receiver's reflexive reactions. One of the earliest researchers in the field of listening described how attention wandered in a classroom of university students because audience members were distracted by their emotional reactions to specific words or topics (Nichols 1960). Once distracted, the receiver will remain that way for some time. Despite popular beliefs, our brains

have evolved to single task, and multitasking is almost always a misnomer (Madore and Wagner 2019). This means that once an aspect of your communication triggers a tangential thought process in the audience, that thought process has been substituted for paying attention to your message. For example, if you want receivers to attend to one point (a deadline), avoid mentioning any topic that might produce a stronger emotional reaction (possible layoffs).

2. **Be careful with the negative things you say about people.** It's not just about saying positive things; it's also avoiding a pattern of criticizing or being negative. A phenomenon known as "spontaneous trait transference" describes the documented effect that when people describe others, the traits they mention become associated with them, even when they are not describing themselves (Mae et al. 1999). Hence, saying positive things about other people not only makes that other person feel good, but the compliments also rub off on you in the minds of people listening in.

If you can stay mindful of the phenomenon of emotional thought and act upon the principle of affiliation, you can forge stronger connections. Encode these positive action steps in your daily behavior and you will see an improvement in your level of influence, as well as the meaningful connections in both your personal and professional lives.

Biography

Amanda Nimon-Peters is an Australian behavioral scientist and professor of leadership at Hult International Business School. She is the author of *Working with Influence: Nine Principles of Persuasion to Accelerate Your Career* (Bloomsbury, 2022) and holds a PhD and MPhil from the University of Cambridge. Amanda's objective is to develop data-aware, principle-driven leaders to be influencers for positive change. She is a member of the Thinkers50 Radar Class of 2024.

References

Bélanger, J., Haines, V.Y., III, and Bernard, M. (2018). Human resources professionals and the cost/benefit argument: rational persuasion in action in municipal organizations. *The International Journal of Human Resource Management*, 29(16), pp. 2431–2454.

Boothby, E.J. and Bohns, V.K. (2021). Why a simple act of kindness is not as simple as it seems: Underestimating the positive impact of our compliments on others. *Personality and Social Psychology Bulletin*, 47(5), pp. 826–840.

Cortes, K. and Wood, J.V. (2019). How was your day? Conveying care, but under the radar, for people lower in trust. *Journal of Experimental Social Psychology*, 83, pp. 11–22.

Descorbeth, O., Zhang, X., Noah, J.., and Hirsch, J. (2020). Neural processes for live pro-social dialogue between dyads with socioeconomic disparity. *Social Cognitive and Affective Neuroscience*, 15(8), pp. 875–887.

Falbe, C.M. and Yukl, G. (1992). Consequences for managers of using single influence tactics and combinations of tactics. *Academy of Management Journal*, 35(3), pp. 638–652.

Gordon, R.A. (1996). Impact of ingratiation on judgments and evaluations: A meta-analytic investigation. *Journal of Personality and Social Psychology*, 71(1), pp. 54–70.

Higgins, C.A., Judge, T.A., and Ferris, G.R. (2003). Influence tactics and work outcomes: A meta-analysis. *Journal of Organizational Behavior: The International Journal of Industrial, Occupational and Organizational Psychology and Behavior*, 24(1), pp. 89–106.

Immordino-Yang, M.H. (2011). Implications of affective and social neuroscience for educational theory. *Educational Philosophy and Theory*, 43(1), pp. 98–103.

Immordino-Yang, M.H. and Damasio, A. (2011). We feel, therefore we learn: The relevance of affective and social neuroscience to education. *LEARNing Landscapes*, 5(1), pp. 115–131.

Izuma, K., Saito, D.N., and Sadato, N. (2008). Processing of social and monetary rewards in the human striatum. *Neuron*, 58(2), pp. 284–294. 10.1016/j.neuron.2008.03.020.

Jin, K. and Baillargeon, R. (2017). Infants possess an abstract expectation of ingroup support. *Proceedings of the National Academy of Sciences*, 114(31), pp. 8199–8204.

Kahneman, D. (2003). Maps of bounded rationality: Psychology for behavioral economics. *American Economic Review*, 93(5), pp. 1449–1475.

Lee, S., Han, S., Cheong, M., Kim, S.L., and Yun, S. (2017). How do I get my way? A meta-analytic review of research on influence tactics. *The Leadership Quarterly*, 28(1), pp. 210–228.

Li, L., Gow, A.D.I., and Zhou, J. (2020). The role of positive emotions in education: A neuroscience perspective. *Mind, Brain, and Education*, 14(3), pp. 220–234.

Madore, K.P. and Wagner, A.D. (2019). Multicosts of multitasking. In *Cerebrum: The Dana Forum on Brain Science* (vol. 2019). Dana Foundation.

Mae, L., Carlston, D.E., and Skowronski J.J. (1999). Spontaneous trait transference to familiar communicators: Is a little knowledge a dangerous thing? *Journal of Personality and Social Psychology*, 77(2), pp. 233–246.

Manning, T. (2012). The art of successful influence: Matching influence strategies and styles to the context. *Industrial and Commercial Training*, 44(1), pp. 26–34.

Nichols, R.G. (1960). *The supervisor's notebook* (vol. 22, no. 1). Scott, Foresman & Co.

Nimon-Peters, A. (2022). *Working with influence: Nine principles of persuasion to accelerate your career*. Bloomsbury Publishing.

Saarinen, A., Jääskeläinen, I.P., Harjunen, V., Keltikangas-Järvinen, L., Jasinskaja-Lahti, I., and Ravaja, N. (2021). Neural basis of in-group bias and prejudices: A systematic meta-analysis. *Neuroscience & Biobehavioral Reviews*, 131, pp. 1214–1227

Schwartz, D., de Bruin, W.B., Fischhoff, B., and Lave, L. (2015). Advertising energy saving programs: The potential environmental cost of emphasizing monetary savings. *Journal of Experimental Psychology: Applied*, 21(2), pp. 158.

Tajfel, H. (1970). Experiments in intergroup discrimination. *Scientific American*, 223(5), pp. 96–103.

Tajfel H. (1974). Social identity and intergroup behaviour. *Social Science Information*, 13(2), pp. 65–93.

Tajfel, H., Billig, M.G., Bundy, R.P., and Flament, C. (1971). Social categorization and intergroup behaviour. *European Journal of Social Psychology*, 1(2), pp. 149–178.

Weger, H., Jr., Castle, G.R., and Emmett, M.C. (2010). Active listening in peer interviews: The influence of message paraphrasing on perceptions of listening skill. *International Journal of Listening*, 24(1), pp. 34–49.

Zhao, X. and Epley, N. (2021a). Insufficiently complimentary? Underestimating the positive impact of compliments creates a barrier to expressing them. *Journal of Personality and Social Psychology*, 121(2), pp. 239–256.

Zhao, X. and Epley, N. (2021b). Kind words do not become tired words: Undervaluing the positive impact of frequent compliments. *Self and Identity*, 20(1), pp. 25–46.

Zukier, H. (1982). The dilution effect: The role of the correlation and the dispersion of predictor variables in the use of nondiagnostic information. *Journal of Personality and Social Psychology*, 43(6), pp. 1163–1174.

5

Connection Through Communication

Matt Abrahams
Lecturer in organizational behavior at Stanford University's Graduate School of Business

Communication is our primary method of building connections with those around us. It's through our words and the way we convey them that we establish rapport, develop trust, and foster a sense of shared understanding. By honing our communicative abilities, we not only improve our interpersonal relationships but also contribute positively to the well-being of others. The process of articulating our thoughts and actively receiving messages from others is at the heart of collaboration and teamwork. Through mindful communication, we create an environment where ideas thrive, perspectives are valued, and collective goals are achieved.

Communication is a powerful tool for meaningful and productive human connection and collaboration. To help bolster and catalyze human connection, we need to

- manage communication anxiety to put ourselves and others at ease;

- address our curse of knowledge and passion by crafting our messages in an audience-centric way; and
- craft engaging, concise messages to enable attention, stickiness, and remembering of our messages.

Manage Anxiety

Communication anxiety is a widespread concern, with an estimated 70% of individuals experiencing some level of nervousness when speaking in public. This anxiety can significantly hinder our ability to effectively convey messages and build deep, meaningful connections with our audience. However, by adopting a comprehensive approach that addresses both the physical symptoms of anxiety and its psychological sources, individuals can significantly enhance their communication skills, thereby facilitating better, deeper interpersonal connections.

Symptoms

Physical symptoms of communication anxiety, such as increased heart rate, sweating, or shakiness, can be overwhelming. But by deploying specific management techniques, we can get our symptoms under control. Deep-breathing exercises are pivotal in managing these symptoms because they help slow down the autonomic nervous system, reducing heart rate and cortisol levels, thereby instilling a sense of calm. Purposeful movement and gestures can help dissipate the energy released by adrenaline, combating shakiness and promoting a more composed presence. Hydration, particularly with warm water, and the use of lozenges can address dry mouth, a common symptom that can disrupt speech fluidity. Furthermore, holding something cold can counteract the body's heat response during anxiety, reducing blushing or sweating and helping maintain a cooler, more stable body temperature.

Sources

The psychological sources of communication anxiety often stem from a fear of negative judgment or failure, rooted in an evolutionary fear of jeopardizing our status within a group. To combat these sources, reframing our perspective on public speaking from a threatening activity to an opportunity for building a shared, collaborative experience can significantly alleviate anxiety. This reframing involves shifting focus from achieving perfection to fostering a genuine connection with the audience. It acknowledges that effective communication is more about engagement than flawless delivery.

Present-oriented activities can help maintain focus on the current moment rather than worrying about future outcomes or dwelling on past experiences. These activities, ranging from doing something physical (e.g., walking around the block) to engaging in mindfulness exercises, can ground speakers in the present, reducing the mental burden of anxiety.

Expanding comfort zones by gradually seeking more challenging speaking engagements and finding supportive allies or groups can further mitigate the sources of anxiety. Such environments encourage positive risk-taking and provide a safety net for experimentation and growth, allowing individuals to build confidence in their speaking abilities over time.

Practical steps for addressing communication anxiety also include engaging in repetitive practice and seeking feedback. This process allows for the refinement of speaking skills and the development of resilience against the fear of public speaking. Feedback, particularly from trusted peers or mentors, can provide constructive insights and encouragement, further reducing the apprehension associated with speaking engagements.

Ultimately, managing communication anxiety and fostering deep interpersonal connections require a holistic approach that combines managing symptoms with addressing the root causes of anxiety. Through consistent practice, mindfulness, and a focus on connection over perfection, communication can transform from a source of apprehension into a powerful tool for personal and professional growth. Embracing these strategies can lead to more confident, impactful communication, enabling individuals to establish deeper connections and navigate the complexities of interpersonal interactions with ease and assurance.

Be Audience-Centric

Understanding and overcoming the "curse of knowledge" and "curse of passion" are critical steps in enhancing our communication. These "curses" represent the challenges we face when our familiarity with a topic or our excitement about it creates a gap between us and the audience. It's essential to bridge this gap through audience-centric communication, a method that prioritizes the listener's interests, preferences, and level of understanding, and invites a connection rather than simply commanding attention.

To communicate effectively, we must first appreciate why our knowledge and passion could be barriers. With the curse of knowledge, we might inadvertently use language that's too specialized, or we might skip over explanations that are vital for the audience's understanding because we assume the audience already knows. Our passion, while typically a positive force, can sometimes overwhelm listeners if not channeled properly. It can lead us to dominate conversations or to miss cues from our audience that signal confusion or disinterest.

Recognizing these challenges is only the first step; addressing them requires careful strategy and thoughtful implementation. We begin by tailoring our message to ensure it's relevant to our audience. This doesn't mean diluting our content. Rather, we must present it in a way that is engaging and resonates with the listener's interests. It's about molding our delivery, tone, and examples to fit within the context of their experiences and expectations.

Crafting this tailored message also involves enhancing comprehension. We do this not through oversimplification but by aligning our delivery with the audience's level of understanding. This might mean breaking down complex concepts into fundamental truths or relatable insights, or it might involve using storytelling to illustrate points in a way that's memorable and impactful.

Building a connection is where the true power of audience-centric communication shines. By showing that we understand and value our audience's perspectives, we establish trust. Trust is the foundation upon which persuasive and meaningful communication is built, turning the act of speaking into an opportunity for dialogue and mutual understanding.

The strategies for audience analysis are as varied as the audiences themselves. It begins with reconnaissance—gathering direct and indirect information about our audience before the communication takes place. For planned communication, we might conduct surveys or analyze attendee lists to gauge interest and background. In more spontaneous settings, careful observation and brief interactions can offer clues about the audience's level of knowledge, engagement, and interest.

Reflection is also a critical part of audience analysis. We can draw upon our own experiences and use empathy to anticipate audience reactions. In planned settings, we can reflect on similar past experiences or discussions to inform our approach. In more spontaneous situations, our intuition and recent interactions can guide our responses.

Research is equally important. We must be diligent in learning about our audience's likely interests, knowledge base, and attitudes. For planned communication, this might involve a deep dive into industry reports or social media analysis. In impromptu scenarios, we might rely on quick searches or insightful questions to gather information on the fly.

By employing these audience-centric strategies, you ensure that your communication resonates deeply with your audience, fostering understanding, engagement, and meaningful connections. It transforms your communication from a one-way transmission of information into a dynamic exchange, where both you and your audience are active participants in the creation of shared understanding. This not only makes your communication more effective but also lays the groundwork for trusting relationships and collaborations that are enriched by mutual respect and understanding.

Focus Messages

Effective communication is the cornerstone of connection, the bridge between individuals in personal and professional realms. To not only reach but truly connect with others and forge lasting relationships, our communication must be clear, focused, and resonant, much like a well-composed piece of music that lingers long after the last note has been played.

In our fast-paced world, where attention is a precious commodity, concision is paramount. It's about making every word count and ensuring your message cuts through the noise. This concision isn't about curtailing the richness of your message but about distilling it to its purest essence. Much like the advice, "Tell the time, don't build the clock," the art lies in providing enough information to be clear and comprehensible without overwhelming the listener with unnecessary details. The "billboard test" is a litmus test for clarity; if your message can be grasped at a glance, much like a billboard by the roadside, you have achieved concision. Beginning your communication with the bottom line up front (BLUF) is not just about brevity; it's about respect for the listener's time and attention.

To cultivate relevance is to align your message with the interests and needs of your audience. As mentioned in the previous section, it is all about understanding their perspectives—their knowledge, attitudes, and motivations. By doing so, you craft messages that resonate, that are salient, and that are remembered. It's about being empathetic to the listener's experience and using language that includes rather than excludes. Engaging with questions, employing analogies, and sharing relatable stories are the tools that make your content stick.

Striving for accessibility means translating complex information to make it digestible for your audience. We often overcomplicate our messages, making them inaccessible and thereby erecting barriers to connection. By tailoring your communication to the audience's level of understanding, you show that you value their comprehension and engagement. Visual aids, like diagrams and infographics, serve as bridges, helping to convey complex data in a form that is easily navigated and understood.

Precision in communication is about setting a clear objective. What do you want your audience to take away? It is framing your content with a clear beginning, middle, and end, much like a tour guide who outlines the journey ahead and sets the right expectations from the outset. This structure acts as a roadmap for your audience, helping them to follow along with ease and contributing to the lasting impact of your message.

Implementing these strategies involves both planned and spontaneous communication. For planned communication, challenge yourself to pare down your messages, seeking feedback from others to help refine and focus your content. In spontaneous communication, ask yourself the essential point of your message before you begin, and let this guide your delivery.

But beyond the mechanics of message delivery, these principles hold a deeper significance in the realm of human connection. When we communicate with concision, relevance, accessibility, and precision, we do more than share information—we invite others into our world. We ensure our messages not only reach our audience but also resonate with them on a deeper level. This resonance is what transforms information into connection, enabling us to build relationships that endure beyond the immediate interaction. We demonstrate care for their experience, and we build trust.

In the end, we can do many things to make our communication more effective, connected, and useful to us in our social relationships. We can manage our anxiety, be audience centric, and focus our messages appropriately. Thus, in practicing the art of effective communication, we practice the art of relationship-building. We learn that to connect truly with others, we must speak not only to be understood but also to understand. In each exchange, we have the opportunity to bridge gaps, to unite ideas, and to join hearts and minds in a shared human experience. This is the true power of communication: not merely to transmit information but to transform relationships and, in doing so, to enrich our shared existence.

Biography

Matt Abrahams is an executive coach, consultant, and author of *Think Faster, Talk Smarter: How to Speak Successfully When You're Put on the Spot* (S&S/Simon Element, 2023). He is also host of the *Think Fast Talk Smart* podcast. As a lecturer in organizational behavior at Stanford University's Graduate School of Business, Matt teaches popular classes in strategic communication and effective virtual presenting. He received Stanford GSB's Alumni Teaching Award in recognition of his teaching students around the world.

6

The Power of Pausing

Jeanette Bronée
*Culture strategist, global keynote speaker,
author, and founder of Path for Life*

In our busy world, trying to keep up with the relentless pace and constant uncertainty around us can quickly consume our focus and attention. Feelings of fear and stress have permeated our workplaces, creating cultures that foster reactivity rather than mindful response. We often feel like we're stuck in survival mode. We barely have a moment to catch our breath, let alone connect with ourselves and others. We live on a hamster wheel where we make decisions based on FUD—fear, uncertainty, and doubt.

In our tech-driven environment, we're supposed to be more connected than ever. However, feelings of isolation and loneliness have skyrocketed. We can access information about anything, anytime, yet we're confused about what we need to thrive.

This disconnected way of going about our personal and professional lives has become our new normal.

Something has gone seriously wrong in our pursuit of progress, and we've lost sight of the essence of life—human connection.

We are craving the very thing that we are sabotaging.

Business Is About Relationships

Even though we are going further into the digital age, we still live in a relationship economy. Sales, customer service, leadership, culture, and work are all about relationships. But as our ability to connect has diminished, so has the quality of our conversations, which is the foundation of a healthy work environment.

Over the last 20 years, I've coached and consulted thousands of individuals and leaders to manage stress and burnout as well as unlock their full potential at work. No matter if I'm working with a new team member or a veteran leader, the challenge that consistently emerges is this lack of connection. My clients tell me they feel alone and unsupported, that their work isn't appreciated, and that the only thing that matters is the results they achieve. The rollover effect of these feelings of insignificance has led to a loss of motivation and meaning in their work.

As I've transitioned to also being a keynote speaker on workplace performance and culture, these same feelings and issues are voiced time and time again. We've stopped trusting ourselves and each other. We fight in meetings to get a word in. Instead of connecting, communicating, and collaborating with purpose and care, people often tell me that they've stopped trying and have opted to just "go with the flow."

Despite this bleak scenario, there's a silver lining. Even now, when it seems like we are too far down the rabbit hole, humans possess unique abilities that set us apart.

We can choose what we care about and consciously decide where to focus our attention.

We can reclaim agency and build relationships that are not just transactional but meaningful.

We can stop the fragmentation we are experiencing and embrace human connection as the foundation of our work culture.

Instead of thinking we are a problem to solve, it's time we unleash our human advantage—our ability to think, engage, and act with intention and purpose. We need to do this because adopting a mindset of collective care is the solution to the splintered human experience ruling our work and personal lives.

This begins by transforming the very nature of our conversations through a simple, yet profound answer: Power-Pausing.

What Is Power-Pausing?

Power-Pausing is not just a practice, it's a philosophy. It's that small moment, that gap in time, where we can pause, listen, and ask more questions. Rather than reacting, Power-Pausing allows us to respond and engage with discernment and care. It creates space in our minds to challenge our perceptions and change our behaviors.

Our intention fuels our attention—that's the power of the mind. When under stress, our mind is hijacked by perceived danger, and we become stuck in instinctive, automatic behaviors. We become critical and focus on what's not working instead of being curious about how to make it work. We focus on our own survival rather than engaging and collaborating, making us feel even more isolated and disconnected. We become "Why not-ers." Our mind floods with questions like, "Why can't I do this?" "Why can't I solve this?" This compulsory thinking only escalates the FUD that is permeating so many of our workplaces and lives.

However, the beauty of Power-Pausing is that it allows us to take back our power of choice. By embracing this transformative tool, we can realign our intention and redirect our attention to what matters most: connecting, communicating, and collaborating with care to create impact together.

Power-Pausing gives us the power of presence.

It gives us the power of change too.

The Three Stages of Power-Pausing

Power-Pausing consists of three stages: the physical pause, the emotional pause, and the mental pause. Each stage helps us reclaim agency over how we think, engage, and act with care.

POWER PAUSING
THINK, ENGAGE, & ACT WITH CARE

WHAT DO YOU NEED SO THAT YOU CAN...?

1. The physical pause
When we are stressed and feel stuck, our bodies tense up, and our breathing tightens as cortisol fills our brains. The first stage in Power-Pausing gives us space to become aware

we are in survival mode so that we can reconnect with ourselves and shift out of our reactive behaviors.

By pausing and taking a few deep breaths, we can calm down our nervous system. This allows us to reset our attention, think more clearly, and redirect our focus onto what we need so that we can move forward.

2. The emotional pause

We've been taught that our emotions aren't welcome in the workplace. This leads us to repress and ignore much of how we truly feel in stressful situations. However, our emotions are what give us our human advantage. They provide us with important insights into what we need to communicate with empathy to build trust and belonging.

To improve our ability to connect with ourselves and each other, we can pause, listen to, and acknowledge how we feel, and ask what we need so that we can reclaim emotional agency.

3. The mental pause

This third stage of pausing taps into the cognitive brain, which is how we access our growth mindset and become more agile and collaborative. By doing so, we can navigate challenges to make better, faster, and more inclusive decisions for ourselves and as a team.

To discover the keys to unlocking a growth mindset, we can pause, listen, and ask ourselves what we need to act with more curiosity, courage, and creativity to get unstuck and accomplish our goals.

Each pause is designed to be used in action. You can Power-Pause anywhere and anytime: while walking, before you respond to a question, when you start a new task, or when you pick up the phone. You can especially use it in meetings to reset, refocus, and re-engage with intention and care.

Once we pause and listen inside, the pivotal question that redirects our attention onto the outcome we want to achieve is, "What do we need so that we can . . . ?"

When we change the question, we change the outcome.

Neuroscientist Amishi P. Jha, PhD, says that 50% of the time, our mind wanders and doesn't stay engaged with what is happening right in front of us, meaning we are missing half of our lives.

This is why Power-Pausing is so crucial. Imagine how much time you'd save and the impact you could make by pausing to reclaim agency over how you think, engage, and act.

Let's dive into how you can use Power-Pausing to cultivate transformative conversations.

The Business Case for Pausing

Culture is an ecosystem of relationships, starting with the one we have with ourselves.

It isn't utopian to think that human connection can be at the core of our work cultures. In fact, it's not even something we need to create. It existed, but we lost the power of collective care when we decided to start working in silos, production lines, and work environments that celebrated the highest performer, thinking that would encourage everyone to work harder. But this has proven to be catastrophic for connection. To create the future we want to see, this is the moment when we must rethink high performance and unlock our human advantage.

I've seen firsthand the damaging effects that a lack of pausing to listen, reflect, and connect has caused in countless companies. Failing to do so ensures participants fail to engage with curiosity and creative input. For example, I was hired to coach a C-suite executive—let's call him Sam. Sam's team had complained that he never listened to them or included their ideas. They felt demotivated, and several considered leaving for jobs where they would feel valued and could make a greater impact. Likewise, it became clear that Sam was frustrated with his team; he felt they were disengaged and not doing their jobs properly. In our sessions together, we implemented Power-Pausing to help overcome the difficulties both he and his team were facing to create an environment that encouraged productive collaborations.

After Sam outlined the challenges he was encountering, I asked him to pause for a moment and notice how he was feeling. He noted agitation, irritability, and underlying anger. I asked him to pause for a little longer to get to the root cause of these feelings and the mindset behind them. He admitted he felt under immense pressure to deliver a new product in a short time frame and felt stuck because the team was not performing to his expectations.

Once Sam took the time to express these thoughts and emotions, he realized he was operating in survival mode. He blamed his team for the lack of progress and failed to see his role in this disconnect. He was focusing solely on his vision for the project without considering the team's well-being and input. I asked him to pause and focus on the process of working with the team and what he needed to redirect his attention back to how he could best support them so they could do their best work.

As a leader, asking someone why they have not done something will get the conversation stuck in defensive explanations. However, the pivotal question, "What do we need so that we can . . . ," redirects our attention so we can achieve our goals.

- If you feel critical, you can ask, "What do I need so that I can listen with curiosity?"
- If you feel overwhelmed, you can ask, "What do I need so that I can prioritize better and communicate that more clearly?"
- If you feel distracted, ask, "What do I need so that I can be more present and mindful?"

We decided that Sam would practice Power-Pausing in team meetings to notice if he was feeling impatient and if his mindset was critical or curious. Instead of jumping in to tell team members what they needed to do, Sam committed to listening and allowing his team members to express their concerns and share ideas. When he did speak, he would ask his team members questions about how they would solve the challenges and what they needed so they could move forward.

To build trust and help shift toward this new ethos, I attended a team meeting. However, before getting started, I explained that there was one new rule: at any time, anyone could raise their hand and say, "Let's pause on this. What do we need so that we can . . . ?" whatever challenge they needed to solve together.

Immediately, each team member felt more empowered to work with Sam, seeing him as a constructive and supportive thinking partner rather than an overseer obsessed with controlling every detail. In their meetings, Power-Pausing gave them the space to speak up, communicate, and collaborate with more curiosity and courage, allowing them to access their collective growth mindset.

Power-Pausing is not a one-and-done quick fix. It's an ongoing process that allows us to recognize our patterns of thinking and feeling and how they affect our actions and interactions. When under stress, many of us succumb to our reactive habit of grasping for answers in an attempt to resolve the issue as quickly as possible. However, a team that Power-Pauses together develops the crucial skill of asking more questions to explore all the possibilities available. When this is practiced over time, it cultivates the connective tissue of a high-performing team. This is how we co-create solutions and foster trust in our relationships, where people feel seen, heard, and supported in their growth.

Let's Pause on This

By embracing Power-Pausing, we can transform our human connections and conversations, making them more meaningful and productive. We are not just improving our individual lives but also contributing to a larger shift in our society.

To cultivate this shift and establish relationships as the bedrock of our organizations, we must engage with CARE: curiosity, awareness, respect, and empathy. Power-Pausing is how we achieve this. It allows us to shift from a "Me" perspective to a "We" perspective. It takes us away from frustration and confusion within our teams and gives us the tools to be conscious and clear about our objectives.

In today's world, with technology evolving at beyond imaginable speeds and change happening all around us, it is easy to feel defeated and that the only way to keep up is to overextend ourselves.

However, right now, we have the unique opportunity to pause, listen, and ask questions with the same curiosity that humanity has used for centuries to evolve and innovate.

The future is no longer about survival of the fittest. It's about connection. It's about collaboration. It's about harnessing our human advantage.

Can you imagine what could change if we embraced a culture of pausing?

We would have a culture built on collective care.

May the Pause be with You.

Biography

Jeanette Bronée is the author of *The Self Care Mindset: Rethinking How We Change and Grow, Harness Well-Being, and Reclaim Work-life Quality* (Wiley, 2022). She helps individuals, leaders, and organizations rethink the intersection between an evolutionary growth mindset, collective well-being, and workplace performance. She's a three-time TEDx speaker and has spoken at the United Nations about the power of care at work. Jeanette founded Path for Life® in 2004 to raise awareness about preventing burnout in the workplace and to provide tools for achieving better work/life quality. More recently, she launched the Pause on This podcast to encourage dialogue about building cultures of *we*, where people stick together. She works with major companies such as Microsoft, BlackRock, IBM, and Siemens and cares deeply about building a strong culture of healthy human relationships, starting with the one we have with ourselves.

AI and Us

7

AI and the Future of Human Connection

Kate O'Neill
Founder and chief tech humanist, KO Insights

As we ponder the opportunities for greater human connection, our minds may not exactly leap to the realm of robots and artificial intelligence (AI). In fact, AI is often seen as a threat to human connection. Deepfakes, clumsily generated content, synthetic intelligence standing in the way of genuine human relationships, these are all valid areas of concern. But what if these threats were offset by exponential opportunity? Could AI—can AI—serve as an invaluable tool to amplify human connection and deepen our understanding of one another and ourselves? What would it take to get it right?

After all, AI is increasingly integrated into our everyday lives. From automated intelligent systems in industries to personal assistants in our homes, AI has become an essential (if sometimes invisible) part of our reality. But as we continue to develop these systems, we must ask crucial questions: How can we ensure that we are nurturing meaningful human experiences and fostering fulfilling relationships amidst this technological evolution? How can our choices benefit human thriving rather than just benefiting business bottom lines? Isn't it possible that we can do both? To take on this dualistic objective, we have to start by understanding something of the complex nature of how we experience AI.

Funhouse Mirror: How Humans Experience AI

AI presents a conceptual challenge for us. On one hand, as a technology that exists within other technologies (like smartphones and cars), AI already belongs to a category of tools that we use to enhance our experiences and capabilities.

On the other hand, the more overt and direct our interactions with AI interfaces become, the more we talk about the technology as an existential threat: a nonhuman entity that could potentially outthink and outmaneuver us. Thousands of years of evolutionary instinct have trained us to confront our threats, to sniff them, to look for their weakness. Naturally we want to know where this so-called "AI" fits in the realm of existence relative to ourselves. We at least often perceive synthetic intelligences as an entity we must philosophically and existentially contend with.

We don't generally think this way about interactions with tech where AI fulfills more of a background, supporting role: again, within our smartphones or cars, say, or within complex tech-powered devices in our lives that increasingly have "smart" AI capabilities, like refrigerators, depending on how lavish your kitchen setup is.

And the conversational interface is our most confusing challenge yet. Even though AI has been an ever-present behind-the-scenes part of our tech-accelerated lives for decades in one form or another, conversational interfaces have changed the way we think about it. Bringing *interaction through language* into the mix heightened the sense that something is different here.

Let's have a look at why that is.

The Pivotal Role of Language and Meaning

Language is the fundamental human technology, and meaning, if you'll pardon the comparison, is its operating system. Language is the means by which we share knowledge and culture, the means by which we tell stories, make jokes, warn others of danger, and comfort those who are grieving.

Language is also the principal means by which we construct our very sense of self. We use language not just to communicate our thoughts and feelings to others, but to think and feel about ourselves.

Meaning, then, is what language *does*. Meaning is both enabler and essence.

Meaning Is at the Heart of Every Type of Human Connection

Human beings are equipped with the starter hardware for meaning-making through language: the capacity to produce and comprehend an infinite range of sounds (or, in the case of sign languages, gestures) and to combine these into an infinite variety of sentences. We share this capacity with other animals that communicate: bees, chimpanzees, parrots.

The advanced capacity for meaning-making, though, is an innate part of human nature, and as far as we know, ours alone. It is not a cultural artifact that we learn from others; it is something we are born with. Language is an instinct, like the ability to walk or talk. We don't have to be taught how to produce or comprehend language; we do it naturally, without effort. And since meaning is what we use language for, we attach great significance to our ability to signify.

Which is why it comes as no surprise that the latest human existential crisis is driven by language—as utilized by AI in large language models and through generative AI tools.

Here's the twist, though: machines have a very different interpretation of meaning. Their understanding is algorithmic, based on patterns and probabilities.

Humans are conditioned to encounter language as a vehicle for meaning. We are not as well equipped to think of language as merely a tool of probability or processing.

This distinction in the way humans and machines use language is important because it is the basis for what makes us unique as a species. It is also the basis for much of the research that I do—as a strategist and theorist, and perhaps not coincidentally, as a linguist by education. In my work, I explore how meaning relates to experiences, how technology augments those experiences, and how we can be more intentional in the design of our technology and experiences to create new meanings.

We humans explore meaning in many different ways, from semantics to patterns to existential and cosmic ponderings. But all these ruminations about meaning have two things in common: First, they are all fundamentally about **what matters**. Second, they are all connected to our **embodied sense of experience** in the world. We make meaning through our senses.

Machines create a different form of meaning, one that is algorithmic, based on patterns and probabilities. Even if a time comes when synthetic intelligences more frequently inhabit mobile bodies, this key difference in the process of meaning-making from the origins of our existence as humans and AI is a crucial point of consideration as we navigate the complexities of our AI-integrated future.

AI's Potential in Enhancing Human Connection

Of course there is a Tower-of-Babel-sized irony in language as the key to understanding the human experience and connectedness, since the multiplicity of human languages have created challenges in human connection since language began.

But here we already have demonstrated proof of the power of AI: machine translation apps have already aided communication between people who don't share a common language. As these functions become more seamless in emerging devices and experiences, we can start to see how they could enhance human connection by facilitating global connection, cultural exchange, and mutual understanding.

As those functions and capabilities find their way more seamlessly into emerging devices and experiences where translation is the default—along with technologies like augmented reality or other forms of spatial computing—AI has the potential to further break down barriers of distance and language. The meaning in the shared cultural layer that we use to interpret the world around us is what allows us to communicate in nuanced ways with each other and what allows us to understand the world around us. But it varies as much from culture to culture as from language to language.

In the very near term, AI+AR (augmented reality) tools could facilitate global connection, cultural exchange, and mutual understanding. By contextualizing differences in cultural norms, AI could help people better understand one another, fostering a greater sense of global community.

From AI to IA—Intelligence Amplification

The key to achieving these outcomes lies in shifting our perspective from AI to intelligence amplification (IA). The latter term is about as old as the former, but it shifts the focus more toward us, where we need it to be. Instead of focusing solely on how AI can replace human tasks, we should examine how it can amplify our human capabilities.

Whatever we call it, we need to examine its potential more closely.

It's easy, for example, to recognize the utility and the convenience AI brings to our lives. Spam filters, for example, have been making our lives a little tidier for years now.

But take it a step further, and you could even make a case that AI has helped to foster human connection by eliminating some of the noise that comes with capitalistic endeavors at absurdist scale. That's **AI as a tool of focus**, helping to elevate the priority of relevant human experience by suppressing what is not relevant.

Or look at recommendation algorithms on entertainment and ecommerce sites, which have long been helping us discover new books, movies, songs, and products we enjoy—and along the way find new communities to which we may belong, as fandoms arise and coalesce. We can think of this as **AI as a tool of affinity**, where the algorithmic optimization in this set of examples acts as part of identity development.

AI is far more than chatbots but far less than the all-seeing robot wizard many people imagine.

For one thing, machine intelligences, for now, are specialized. When they're good, they're good at a given task or task area, which is why we've seen mind-blowing results on protein folding, for example.

What's an unsolved area in your field that could truly benefit humanity to solve? How can you invest into the research and development of that solution?

Leaders, strategists, designers, those building and shaping technology have a role to play in rethinking the next steps in the evolution of our world. They must ensure that as we use AI in the experiences they create for humans to encounter, interact with, consume, and be served by, that we're not minimizing and detracting from our humanity but instead using every tool in our chest toward personal growth, understanding, and connection.

The Responsibility of AI Developers

AI's potential to enhance human connection will depend largely on the decisions we make today. We have a responsibility to guide the development of AI in a way that prioritizes human connection and fosters a sense of community. When guided by a human-centric approach, AI holds immense potential to enhance human connection.

As humans and consumers and users, we have little to fear from AI itself. We have everything to fear from misaligned business values.

After all, the most bullish of AI enthusiasts often talk about its potential in terms of productivity and focus on what we gain by automating the meaningless tasks in our lives. That's a valid point of focus, but it must be in balance. Imagine if we automated everything in the world and all we focused on was what was meaningless, rote, or routine. At scale that would mean a world filled with meaninglessness, where nothing had any personality, nothing resonated with anyone.

Instead, as we develop new systems and interactions increasingly fed by data, we can be sure to develop increasingly meaningful interactions and experiences. As behavioral economics demonstrated the power of the nudge, we have the opportunity to think about engineering relevance, sense, and nuance into more our automated experiences. That's right: we have the opportunity to become **nuance engineers**.

But some of this comes down to measurement and optimization. And how does AI figure out what we need? We tell it.

How do we do that? Sometimes explicitly, in the original modeling of data sets and design of algorithms. But in many if not most cases, the machine models we are using learn through reinforcement, which means that we are all training AI by how we use it.

Measuring Connection

All models are false, but some are useful.

—**George E. P. Box**

Whatever we measure is only part of the story, always. But our goal in integrating AI into our processes should be to make our measures more meaningful so that our optimizations can be more meaningful.

How should business measure what it means to foster connection?

How can we choose measures of business effectiveness that also align with when customers are most delighted?

How can we train algorithmic intelligences to optimize for happiness, for meaning, for thriving, when we don't know how to measure it?

We have to start measuring somewhere. I can propose a few possible measures. For example, memorability is a proxy for meaning when it comes to a brand experience. Net promoter score (NPS) is a measure of referral willingness. That is a proxy for satisfaction or, ideally, delight. It's not a guarantee, but it's directional.

To get a measure like NPS you do have to ask. Ideally, we will want to gather feedback without sacrificing too much of our privacy, liberty, and human agency to get there. That's a challenge at a time when many leaders would prefer a shortcut, rather than asking people directly, to set up sensors or use proxies that involve tracking and surveillance. I urge you to resist this unless there is no alternative.

Think about the conundrum of measuring the productivity of a software programmer: the temptation through the years has been to measure lines of code. But the most elegant solutions are often shorter. They just take longer to arrive at and refine.

We should still want to learn and encourage learning, still want to be creative and foster creativity. We will still need to struggle now and then to arrive at new learning and creative solutions. Our measures should include the grace to guide that.

As we develop measurement models, we can provoke ideas by asking our team questions like the following: What might we learn by asking? What might we learn by observation? What might we learn through experimentation? What do we need to measure? What do we need to optimize? What do we need to maximize?

The more we track the measurable attributes that directionally influence our thriving, the more we can use automated intelligence to help steer our way there.

Data, Privacy, and Trust

Of course data—in particular, lots and lots of *personal* data—play a key role in how connected these experiences feel. So this approach requires a healthy respect for privacy, for data minimization, for robust data management practices and cybersecurity, which means we need to think about data and trust.

In communication and human connection, one of the big—and growing—gaps is in trust. People distrust institutions, governments, and each other. They distrust corporations the least.

Therein lies an enormous opportunity for corporate leaders to take a leading role and look for solutions that move us forward—responsibly, ethically, and with meaningful connections in mind.

Can we connect the progress of our companies with the progress of society, and move ahead on what matters: the climate crisis, inequality, job insecurity, access to basic needs like housing, health care, education, and so on?

We cannot make this progress without trust. And we should not make this progress without reason to trust. That means we need all of us—you, me, and every other leader out there—making trustworthy decisions.

A Human-centric Approach to AI

At this point, the question is not "Can AI make us better connected?"—the answer to that is a resounding *yes*—but "Can we prioritize human connection to such a degree that we use the most powerful set of tools we've ever developed in service of that goal?"

We already have a roadmap: the United Nations Sustainable Development Goals. We have begun to see how AI can help us advance those goals. I have been tracking AI developments along these lines for years and have seen advancements such as AI-mediated efforts to optimize solar panel arrays, to more efficiently manage water in areas where it is scarce, and much more. Many of these initiatives are run by for-profit companies in public-private partnerships with government or through foundations, or simply as standard matters of business operations. Nonprofit initiatives are wonderful, but there is more good to be done than can be done by nonprofits alone. We need for-profit businesses bought into making a better world too.

As a leader, you can start your journey here: https://sdgs.un.org/goals. Review the list of Sustainable Development Goals, and identify which one best aligns with your company's existing purpose.

This approach means that we can collectively set a goal to create a world where AI can enhance our ability to connect, to understand, and to empathize with one another; one where we can use AI and other automative tools to build stronger bonds, deeper relationships, and more meaningful exchanges; one where we use every tool in our chest toward personal growth and understanding—in alignment with business goals rather than *solely in service* of business goals at the potential expense of our human thriving.

Shaping Our Technological Future

It is important to keep asking "How will AI change our lives?" so that we can monitor and manage the impacts of technology on a grand scale, but that question necessarily casts humanity in a passive role. We must also ask more proactive questions: "How can we use the strengths of AI to solve human problems at scale? How can we develop AI to create the opportunity for more meaningful experiences? How can we harness AI to foster greater human connection?"

By reframing our questions this way, we put humanity not only at the center, but at the *helm* of our technological future. Through this reframing, prioritizing human connection and leveraging AI as a tool to amplify our human capabilities, we can steer toward a future where AI uplifts humanity in developing a more connected, more relevant, and more meaningful world for us all.

Biography

Known as the "Tech Humanist," Kate O'Neill is founder and chief executive officer of KO Insights, a strategic advisory firm. Previously, she held the first content management role at Netflix, developed Toshiba America's first intranet, and founded [meta] marketer, one of the first digital strategy and analytics agencies. Kate has appeared as an expert tech commentator on the BBC and NPR and her latest book, *What Matters Next: A Leader's Guide to Making Human-Friendly Tech Decisions in a World That's Moving Too Fast* (Wiley, 2025), helps leaders have greater confidence in making decisions about rapidly evolving technology that stands to affect humanity's future. Emerging technology, Kate argues, offers the potential to solve human problems at scale. In 2023, she was shortlisted for the Thinkers50 Digital Thinking Award.

8

Tech Is Cool, but People Are Warm

Giuseppe Stigliano
Chief executive officer, marketing professor, global keynote speaker, and senior advisor

Imagine Sarah and Alex, a young couple brimming with excitement as they step into a well-known consumer electronics store. The occasion is special: they are about to select a TV screen for the living room of their first shared apartment, marking the start of a new chapter in their lives together. A sense of anticipation hangs in the air; they envision cozy evenings cuddled on the sofa, binge-watching their favorite series on a screen that fits just right into their new space.

However, their enthusiasm begins to wane as they start interacting with a sales representative. The rep, armed with a clipboard, launches into a barrage of questions: "Are you looking for plasma, LCD, or OLED screens? What size are you considering? What kind of audio system do you need?"

These questions, while technically relevant, feel cold and impersonal—akin to the filters one would apply on an e-commerce website. The couple look at each other, perplexed; this was not the experience they had anticipated. In a world increasingly dominated by digital transactions, the couple had sought something different from their visit to the store—a human connection. They were looking for a welcome that only a physical store could offer: a smile, a warm greeting, an interaction that felt personal and attentive. They didn't just want a TV; they were in pursuit of an experience that acknowledged their individuality and their journey.

Sensing their discomfort, a seasoned salesperson—let's call her Mia—notices the couple and approaches them with a different tactic. She begins with a smile and a genuine, "How can I help you make your living room perfect?" Mia's questions are different; they are designed to understand not just what Sarah and Alex want, but why they want it. "How often do you watch TV? What are your favorite programs? Do you enjoy movies, or is music more your thing? And gaming—does that interest you? How far is your couch from where the TV will be? Do you get a lot of sunlight in the room?" These questions, simple yet insightful, immediately put Sarah and Alex at ease. They feel understood, cared for, and guided. Mia's expertise allows her to translate their needs and preferences into technical specifications, ultimately recommending a selection of models that perfectly align with what the couple truly need and desire.

This anecdote exemplifies a fundamental truth: in the age of digital dominance, the unique value of brick-and-mortar stores lies in their ability to offer what online cannot—a personal, warm, and human shopping experience. The ritual of sales, celebrated within the temple of a physical store, hinges not on replicating the digital interface but on transcending it. By fostering genuine connections, understanding the subtle nuances of customer needs, and providing informed, personalized guidance, retailers can create memorable experiences that resonate with customers on a deeply human level.

However, there is no one-size-fits-all approach to balancing the need for human intervention with the pursuit of digitally enabled efficiency; it all boils down to the specific needs, wants, and desires of each customer persona.

For businesses worldwide, striking the perfect balance between the calculated precision of technology and the innate warmth of human interaction isn't just a strategic move—it's the essence of a unique selling proposition. The truth echoes through the corridors of innovation: technology will never replace humans entirely, but those who fail to leverage its power will be surpassed by those who do. This isn't a grim prediction; it's a pragmatic look ahead to a future where adaptability is the benchmark of survival and innovation the cornerstone of growth.

Historically, those at the forefront of utilizing state-of-the-art tools have consistently outpaced their competitors. Today, we stand at an unprecedented inflection point. General-purpose technologies—artificial intelligence, blockchain, Internet of Things, 5G, etc.—are transitioning from distant marvels to present-day realities. Their convergence is set to redefine our world. Each brings a transformative potential that, if harnessed, can expand boundaries and reshape industry contours. Yet, devoid of human creativity, empathy, and ingenuity, their cold precision might become sterile, their revolutionary promise unfulfilled.

Imagine a world where shopping is a silent transaction with a machine, customer service a loop of prerecorded voices, offices a labyrinth of blinking LEDs and whirring machines, devoid of the hum of human collaboration. Efficiency reigns, but at the cost of personal touch, stripping commerce of its soul. In contrast, a business model that employs technology as an invisible maestro, orchestrating the operational symphony from behind the scenes, allows the front stage to sparkle with the drama and dynamism of human interaction. Here, technology is an invisible partner, setting the stage for humanity to deliver the emotive performance of connection, creativity, and complexity that defines our species.

Consider a retail environment where clerks greet you with a knowing smile, not just from memory but informed by insights provided by technology. They accommodate your preferences not just leveraging data analytics but also through an understanding bolstered by experience, using this insight to enrich the customer experience with a warmth no machine could replicate, like in the story of Sarah and Alex. Visualize a customer service environment where representatives, equipped with comprehensive customer relationship management data, deliver a service that goes beyond mere efficiency and embodies genuine empathy. They listen, reassure, and celebrate, elevating the interaction above the transactional level. Thanks to advanced technology, efficiency is ensured upstream in the process, allowing the organization to focus downstream on adding "human" value—a game changer in customer relations.

This synthesis of technology and humanity is where my global interactions with executives across industries have yielded profound insights. The ability to drive concrete outcomes within an organization relies on our capacity to translate "theory" into "practice"—an alchemy refined through experience. Here, "practice" is a rich tapestry interwoven with variables such as organizational culture, management biases, unique contexts, digital literacy levels, competitive landscapes, and geopolitical climates.

Yet, it's important to acknowledge the potential flipsides of the aforementioned approach.

From my dialogues with more than 150 industry leaders and my own critical assessment, five pivotal elements emerge that warrant careful consideration:

1. Overemphasis on human touch

While prioritizing human interaction is crucial, it's important to identify scenarios where technology can offer more efficient solutions.

For instance, in handling simple inquiries or transactions, such as checking a bank balance or booking appointments, automated systems can provide quick and accurate responses, freeing human staff to address more complex issues that require empathy and nuanced understanding.

2. Technological determinism

Technology is not simply a tool; it shapes human experience and societal structures significantly.

For example, the widespread use of social media platforms has reshaped communication practices and fostered a culture of instant gratification, altering the way we form relationships and perceive privacy.

3. Data privacy concerns

The use of customer data to tailor personalized experiences must be balanced with ethical data management practices.

An example of this is the recommendation algorithms used by e-commerce platforms, which analyze user browsing and purchase history to suggest products. While these provide a customized shopping experience, they also raise concerns about the extent of data collection and the potential for misuse, underlining the need for strict adherence to privacy laws and ethical standards.

4. Scalability challenges

Implementing a high-touch, personalized approach can be challenging to scale, especially for businesses that serve a large and diverse customer base.

For example, a boutique hotel chain may excel in offering personalized guest experiences at a few locations, but replicating this level of personalization across dozens of properties worldwide can be resource-intensive and difficult to manage consistently, highlighting the need for scalable solutions that balance personalization with efficiency.

5. Cultural variability

Preferences for human interaction versus automated services can vary significantly across different cultures. In some regions, customers might prefer the efficiency and anonymity of automated systems, while in others, personal interaction and relationship-building may be valued above all.

For instance, in Japan, there is a high acceptance of automation and robotics in service delivery, reflected in the popularity of vending machine cafes and robot-staffed hotels. Conversely, in countries like Italy, personal interaction in settings such as retail and hospitality is often prioritized, reflecting a cultural emphasis on personal connection and warmth.

In the dance of the digital age, where robots and humans move to the same rhythm, it's the role of businesses to choreograph a ballet that harmonizes the efficiency of automation with the subtlety of the human touch. Each company must find its unique balance, leveraging this harmony as its competitive edge. The distinctive selling propositions of tomorrow will be defined by this equilibrium.

In conclusion, as I advocate for a balanced approach, it's imperative to address and mitigate the risks outlined. We must be vigilant of the broader societal impacts of our technological tools, maintaining the highest respect for data privacy, carefully considering the scalability of personalized approaches, and remaining attuned to the cultural differences in customer service expectations. Recognizing these potential pitfalls is not admitting defeat but adopting a strategic stance that reinforces the proposition I advocate—in a world increasingly steered by technology, it is our humanity that will distinguish the lasting successes of our ventures.

At this pivotal crossroads of human and technological evolution, the choices we make today will define our trajectory. As we stand on the brink of a future where machines and humans are inextricably linked, let us write a narrative where technology is celebrated for its cool efficiency, but people are revered for their warm connections. Let us pledge to harness the power of our innovations to cast our humanity in the best possible light, creating a world where technology enhances rather than eclipses our human touch.

Biography

Giuseppe Stigliano is an entrepreneur and manager with more than two decades of international marketing and communication experience. He has served as chief executive officer at three international agencies, partnering with more than 300 companies globally. He holds a PhD in marketing and economics and serves as an adjunct professor at several renowned universities and business schools. Giuseppe is a member of the Thinkers50 Radar Class of 2024.

9

Ask Not What AI Can Do for You—Ask What You Can Do for AI, to Serve Humanity

Hamilton Mann
Group vice president for digital marketing and digital transformation at Thales

Rapid advancements in artificial intelligence (AI) systems, especially large language models (LLMs) like OpenAI's GPT, have raised concerns about their potential threats to humanity, political systems, democracy, and the very concept of truth.

A critical worry is that if not meticulously designed and controlled, AI systems like ChatGPT may amplify existing biases and contribute to political polarization.

Indeed, AI models trained on vast datasets may inherit societal biases, and their outputs can reinforce these biases when generating content. This could exacerbate divisions in society and hinder productive political discourse.

The Impartial AI Holy Grail and Its Paradoxes

Some have embarked on a quest for an impartial AI, integrating ideals of neutrality, fairness, and justice. This pursuit acknowledges that while AI systems will inevitably retain biases, regulation should act as a safeguard, mitigating the impact of these imperfections and protecting society from potential harm.

Paradoxically, it is this very thesis—and not AI itself—that presents a substantial threat to humanity.

The assumption that AI can be made wholly responsible and trustworthy results in a dangerous dependency where humans may begin to rely solely on machine judgment, perceived as more objective than human decision-making, and culminates in a significant abdication of human responsibility.

A study titled "Human Cognitive Biases Present in Artificial Intelligence" by Martinez et al. (2022) points out that biases detected in AI mirror discriminative social biases present in society, emphasizing the necessity of understanding basic and general principles of cognition and cognitive biases that affect our relationship with AI.

In essence, the challenge lies not in making AI systems unbiased, but in recognizing and addressing the inherently human biases they reflect.

As highlighted by O. C. Ferrell (2024), biases in AI, influenced by biased data, algorithmic design choices, and the implicit biases of developers, are a reflection of societal inequalities.

Our inability to recognize biases in their true scale and manifestation in the real world leads to a misconception that AI systems are amplifying these biases. However, this reflection is more a revelation of existing societal biases than an amplification.

Even if well intentioned, the pursuit of creating a bias-free AI risks creating echo chambers that, in turn, can perpetuate illusions and misunderstandings, leading us to underestimate the true impact and prevalence of our own biases within society. This would inadvertently mask the deeper, more pervasive biases that are embedded within our social structures and cultural norms.

It is akin to asking, as in the famous Disney animated film, "Mirror, mirror on the wall, who is the fairest of them all?" while expecting AI to show only our best selves and ignoring all the imperfections that make us perfectly human.

In recognizing this, we must leverage AI not only as a technological advancement but as a means to uncover, understand, and better address the biases, often unnoticed or unacknowledged, that permeate our society and contribute significantly to various social issues.

The Dual Nature of Biases

Whether we consider their positive or negative effects, human biases are inherent to the imperfect but unique condition of being human.

The commitment bias, which refers to our tendency to stay committed to a chosen course of action, even when faced with challenges, has been instrumental in the accomplishment of numerous great human achievements.

Take, for instance, the Apollo 11 moon landing mission.

The commitment bias of NASA and the astronauts involved in achieving the monumental goal of landing on the moon was unwavering. Despite the immense technical challenges, risks, and uncertainties, they remained deeply committed to their mission.

It fueled years of relentless work, innovation, and problem-solving, ultimately leading to the historic success of Apollo 11 and beyond.

Pagnini et al. (2023) provide insights on the critical need for resilience and dedication in facing the unique challenges of space exploration, in a study exploring the psychological adaptation and countermeasures in space missions. The study highlights how the commitment to overcoming extraordinary obstacles is essential for the success of missions like the Apollo 11 moon landing.

As another example, the negativity bias, which causes humans to pay more attention to negative information or threats, has played a pivotal role in driving advancements in safety and security.

Consider the development of safety features in automobiles. The awareness of the potential dangers of road accidents and the negative consequences associated with them has been a driving force behind the continuous improvement of safety technologies in vehicles.

This bias has pushed engineers and innovators to invest in technologies like airbags, anti-lock brakes, and collision avoidance systems, all aimed at mitigating the negative outcomes of accidents.

Evidence provided in Catherine J. Norris' (2019) study underlines the evolutionary advantage of negativity bias as more critical for survival to avoid harmful stimuli than to pursue potentially helpful ones.

Without the negativity bias, the urgency to prioritize safety might not have been as strong, and we might not have witnessed the significant reduction in road fatalities and injuries that these innovations have achieved in making our daily lives safer.

As a matter of fact, when it comes to human biases, outcomes are not solely negative.

The Specific and Systemic Biases in Society

AI systems offer a window into both.

Specific biases are those that emerge in situations where our knowledge is incomplete or when we are confronted with unfamiliar contexts. In these scenarios, our cognitive process compensates for the lack of information by generating preconceived notions or precontextualized pieces of information or ideas to fill the gaps, completing the missing puzzle pieces, so the situation appears certain.

This often subconscious act allows us to form a coherent picture of an otherwise ambiguous situation, leading us to mistakenly accept these generated perceptions as factual truths while they ultimately stem from our own creative capacity.

Such biases highlight our innate tendency to seek clarity and certainty, even in the absence of complete information.

In contrast, systemic biases operate on a much broader scale, ingrained within the very structures and institutions that govern and regulate society.

These biases are the result of specific biases becoming normalized and integrated into societal systems, thereby influencing the rules, norms, and practices that dictate social interactions. They often manifest in the form of institutionalized preferences or disadvantages that affect entire groups based on characteristics such as origin, gender, or other social identifiers.

Both specific and systemic biases interplay with each other, and this makes the biases "system" even more complex.

While specific biases originate from individual experiences and perceptions, they can gradually permeate into the larger societal context, contributing to the formation of systemic biases. Conversely, systemic biases can reinforce and validate individual biases, creating a feedback loop that perpetuates these prejudices across both personal and societal levels.

The Specific and Systemic Biases in AI Models

Modifying specific and systemic biases is complex: they often function invisibly, silently dictating what is considered the norm, shaping culture, lifestyle, and societal etiquette.

In this context, AI systems act as a medium through which the continuous interaction between specific biases and broader systemic biases is played out. This self-perpetuating cycle of action and feedback, encompassing mental, social, and societal aspects, is computationally mirrored in AI.

Foundational AI models, such as OpenAI's GPT, are particularly illustrative of this phenomenon. These models are trained on extensive datasets sourced from a wide range of internet materials, which inherently contain the dynamics, inequalities, stereotypes, and dominant ideologies prevalent in the data and in the value systems from which these models have been trained.

Consequently, these foundational AI models become carriers of systemic biases, reflecting some of the existing societal disparities and prejudices.

As an example, such an occurrence has been illustrated in the research conducted by Buolamwini and Gebru (2018) highlighting that the facial recognition systems were highly inaccurate when it came to classifying the faces of women of color. In this groundbreaking paper, the authors further demonstrated that the model was most accurate for people who identified as male and of white skin tone.

On the other end of the spectrum, we have AI models that are derived from these foundational models but are tailored for specific tasks in various domains.

It is crucial to recognize that these specialized AI models are not isolated from the systemic biases of their foundational counterparts. They are immersed in a milieu of preexisting biases, absorbing and potentially amplifying the systemic prejudices embedded in the foundational models.

The study from Seyyed-Kalantari et al. (2021) sheds light on the underdiagnosis bias in AI algorithms, particularly in medical imaging, and how this can affect patient populations differently, in particular underserved patient populations, underscoring the systemic nature of such biases.

This immersion of specific AI models in systemic biases highlights the importance of understanding the deep-rooted nature of biases in AI development and underscores the need for a comprehensive approach to AI training that is mindful of both specific and systemic biases.

The Particular Biases Influence in Specific AI Models

Not only are specific AI models influenced by the systemic biases inherent in the foundational AI models on which they are built or refined, but they are also subject to more nuanced biases unique to their own application domains.

These specific biases arise from the particularities of the datasets or the contexts in which the AI is applied. Each dataset, with its unique characteristics and limitations, contributes to shaping the model's understanding and responses.

Consider, for instance, an AI model developed for medical applications using OpenAI's GPT. This model would inherently carry the systemic biases present in the OpenAI's GPT model.

However, it would also be influenced by biases specific to the medical domain, stemming from the clinical data it is trained on. These biases could be linked to various factors such as the demographic representation in the clinical data, the prevalence of certain conditions in the data, or even the manner in which the data were collected and processed.

Interestingly, the occurrence of these specific biases is not necessarily mitigated by the use of seemingly bias-free training data.

The learning process in AI is not a mere transfer of knowledge; it also involves the transfer of biases embedded in the foundational models.

Gichoya et al. (2023) in a paper in the *British Journal of Radiology* address real-world failures of AI systems in health care.

Their study showcases the varying levels of performance in AI systems, especially poor performance for historically underserved patients, illustrating how subgroup evaluations can reveal specific biases while underlining the multifaceted nature of biases in AI where specific biases are influenced by both systemic and application-specific factors.

The Particular Biases Influence in Foundational AI Models

Another intriguing aspect of AI development is the potential for specific AI models to influence their foundational models, thereby creating a unique feedback loop of biases.

These specific models, developed for distinct applications, can carry their own set of biases, which are shaped by the particularities of their training data and the contexts in which they are used. When the data generated by these specific AI models become widely published and accessible online, those data enter the vast pool of information that may be used to train or update foundational AI models.

This incorporation of data from specific AI models into the foundational models' training corpus introduces the possibility of a cyclical transfer of biases.

This feedback loop mirrors the interaction between systemic and specific biases found in society. In this AI context, the biases inherent in specific applications could start influencing the broader foundational models from which they were initially derived.

This phenomenon highlights a complex layer of interaction where biases are not just unidirectionally imparted from foundational AI models to specific applications but can also flow in the reverse direction.

The likelihood and impact of this scenario hinge on several factors, including the frequency with which foundational models are updated with new data and how representative the data from specific models are within the larger training corpus.

A study from Moor et al. (2023) discusses generalist medical artificial intelligence (GMAI) models. Their research illustrates how specific AI models developed for medical applications might influence foundational models, particularly in the way these models process complex medical information and learn from various data sources.

Just as societal biases evolve and are reshaped over time through new cultural inputs and changing norms, foundational AI models too are subject to continuous evolution influenced by the influx of new data and shifting contextual biases.

The Bias Perpetuation and Calibration in AI

The bias perpetuation and calibration within AI systems have been insightfully explored in research by Rohan Taori and Tatsunori B. Hashimoto (2022) from Stanford University. Their study sheds light on the pivotal role of calibration in learning algorithms, particularly how it influences the magnitude of bias perpetuation. The researchers found that consistent calibration of a learning algorithm—ensuring that the biases in samples annotated by the model closely mirror the biases present in the training distribution—plays a crucial role in controlling bias perpetuation.

This finding is particularly relevant in the context of specific AI models affecting foundational models, illustrating how biases, if unchecked, can be perpetuated through iterative learning processes.

This research underscores the importance of viewing "biases in AI" not as a static, intrinsic problem of AI technology but as a dynamic interplay of systemic and specific biases that evolve and propagate within AI systems.

The findings from Taori and Hashimoto's research also emphasize that merely attempting to "eliminate biases" from datasets through technical means, without a comprehensive understanding of the social dimensions and origins of these biases, is an approach destined for inadequacy. It fails to account for the complex, self-generating nature of biases within AI systems.

The Human Touch Reinforces AI's Biased Learning

A notable example is the reinforcement learning with human feedback (RLHF) method, which represents a complex interplay between technological capabilities and human input.

Prominently used in advanced AI systems like ChatGPT (Baum and Villasenor 2023), it involves meticulously tailoring the outputs of LLMs to align with a diverse array of human values, which are in turn shaped by the inputs from human interlocutors.

One of the most profound and elusive sources of bias in AI arises from the very nature of RLHF. The method's dependence on human feedback introduces an inherent variability, as the concept of "values" is not static but rather fluid, shifting with the diverse perspectives and interpretations of individuals.

Consequently, in its effort to refine and shape the AI model, this process inadvertently incorporates biases that are embedded in the human psyche, emerging from the thoughts, experiences, and judgments of the humans who interact with and guide its learning process.

While striving to create AI systems that resonate with human values, the RLHF method also encapsulates the intricate and sometimes contradictory nature of those values.

The Management of Biases in AI Is Much More Than a Technological Problem

Because machines are made by humans, they would not be perfect either.

Therefore, the commitment to address biases in AI systems necessitates a comprehensive approach that extends beyond the confines of machine learning algorithms and training data.

Experts at the National Institute of Standards and Technology (NIST) advocate for a broader examination into the origins of biases in AI. This expanded perspective encompasses not only the technical aspects of AI development but also delves into the wider societal factors that influence the creation and evolution of technology (NIST 2022).

Overall, beyond algorithmic fairness techniques, some nontechnical guiding principles are essential, ranging from regulation to education and organizational strategies.

This holistic perspective emphasizes the importance of understanding the dynamic interplay between technology and society. It encourages a multidisciplinary dialogue involving technologists, sociologists, ethicists, policymakers, and other stakeholders to collaboratively identify and address the root causes of biases.

About Regulation

Anchoring Mandatory Transparency Stances in AI Datasets

Every AI system should clearly disclose to users detailed information about the composition of the datasets it was trained on, including the collection periods, sources, content diversity, consent of use, and the methodologies used for their processing and selection.

Additionally, they should openly acknowledge potential limitations related to the geographical, demographic, and cultural diversity of the data.

Ensuring AI Responsibility Where It Should Be

Those responsible for foundational AI models should understand how the dissemination of data from specific AI models can influence their foundational AI model and be prepared to handle problems resulting from this interaction.

Those responsible for specific models should also understand how the characteristics of the foundational model influence their application and be prepared to handle problems resulting from this interaction.

Institutionalizing Independent Audits for Bias Detection and Regulation Compliance

Regular audits by independent third parties on AI systems are necessary to identify and correct biases before they become systemic. It should include a thorough analysis of the systems' transparency and explicability, while verifying their compliance with current regulations.

Auditors should consider the overall impact of the model on society, including privacy, data security, and human rights, as well as its influence on social and cultural norms.

About Education

Learning to Decode

Developers of foundational and specific AI models should be trained to understand and identify potential biases in vast datasets.

This training should cover how cultural and societal biases may manifest in diverse data and how to mitigate them.

Training must include modules on how specific models interact with foundational models and how adaptations or modifications can influence biases.

Enhancing Critical Thinking Education to Navigate AI Biases

Critical thinking education, including in-school curricula, should be strengthened to build the necessary skills to face modern information overexposure and reduce the negative impact of cognitive biases specifically related to AI.

These programs should teach how to scrutinize information sources meticulously, recognize potential media biases, differentiate credible from uncertain information, embrace skepticism as a crucial element of the scientific process, and develop an understanding of how our own biases and perspectives can influence our interpretation of information.

Advancing Interdisciplinary Education for AI Professionals

To grasp the specific challenges of foundational AI models, educational approaches should transcend traditional disciplinary boundaries, including an understanding of the environmental and legal impacts of these models that process massive amounts of data and can significantly affect resources and regulations.

The approach should also address these impacts in specific application contexts, highlighting how specific models may affect or be affected by laws and the environment in particular sectors.

About Organization

Establishing Diversity as a Core Principle in AI Development

Encouraging diversity among AI development teams is an asset in reducing specific and systemic biases. For example, a team composed of individuals from different ethnic backgrounds, cultures, genders, sexual orientations, and abilities is more likely to recognize stereotypes or biases in a dataset.

Moreover, establishing a continuous feedback process is crucial for continually improving AI systems and ensuring their fairness. This process should allow users and all relevant stakeholders to easily report bias issues they observe in AI systems.

Evolving Ethical and Holistic Decision-making

Sustainable decision-making practices must alter the framework of leadership practices to evolve the art of decision-making.

Leaders must integrate reflection on the long-term impact of their decisions, considering not only economic or performance benefits but also the repercussions on society, the environment, and individual well-being.

An AI That Serves Humanity

Whether it's our regulation, education, or management practices, one thing is certain: no so-called "responsible" AI will do the work for us.

AI makes human responsibility a paramount issue of our era.

Focusing solely on what needs to be improved in AI learning prevents us from looking at the bigger issue, which is human learning, a fundamental lever for self-improvement and thus the AIs we create.

Our era offers us a chance, not just to engage in the simple manipulation of data that feeds our AIs, naively hoping in doing so to extricate the prejudices from our world, but to refine our critical judgment. We are called to guide our choices by values deeply rooted in humanity, transcending mere algorithmic correction, to achieve a truer understanding of our collective being: our human touch.

In short, let's not just ask what AI can do for each of us—let's ask ourselves what we can do to ensure AI serves humanity.

Biography

Hamilton Mann is group vice president for digital marketing and digital transformation at Thales, a Doctoral Researcher at Ecole des Ponts ParisTech—Polytechnic Institute of Paris and a senior lecturer at INSEAD, HEC Paris, and EDHEC Business School. As a mentor at the MIT Priscilla King Gray Center and a host of the *Hamilton Mann Conversation* podcast, Hamilton actively participates in driving the advancement of digital technologies for positive societal change. He was named to the Thinkers50 Radar Class of 2024.

References

Baum, J. and Villasenor, J. (2023). *The politics of AI: ChatGPT and political bias*. Brookings. https://www.brookings.edu/articles/the-politics-of-ai-chatgpt-and-political-bias

Buolamwini, J. and Gebru, T. (2018). Gender shades: Intersectional accuracy disparities in commercial gender classification. *Proceedings of Machine Learning Research*, 81, pp. 77–91. https://proceedings.mlr.press/v81/buolamwini18a.html?mod=article_inline&ref=akusion-ci-shi-dai-bizinesumedeia

Ferrell, O.C. (2024). Understanding AI bias (and how to address it). *Ferrell Business in the News*. https://www.mheducation.com/highered/ideas/ferrell-business-in-the-news/understanding-ai-bias-and-how-to-address-it-january-2024

Gichoya, J.W., Thomas K., Celi L.A., Safdar, N., Banerjee, I., Banja, J. D., Seyyed-Kalanari, L., Trivedi, H., and Purkayastha, S. (2023). AI pitfalls and what not to do: Mitigating bias in AI. *British Journal of Radiology*, 96(1150). https://academic.oup.com/bjr/article/96/1150/20230023/7498925

Martinez, N., Agudo, U., and Matute, H. (2022). *Human cognitive biases present in Artificial Intelligence.* https://www.researchgate.net/publication/369185016_Human_cognitive_biases_present_in_Artificial_Intelligence

Moor, M., Banerjee, O., Abad, Z.S.H., Krumholz, H.M., Leskovec, J., Topol, E.J., and Rajpurkar, P. (2023). Foundation models for generalist medical artificial intelligence. *Social Neuroscience*, 616, pp. 259–265. https://www.nature.com/articles/s41586-023-05881-4

National Institute of Standards and Technology. (2022). There's more to AI bias than biased data. *NIST Report Highlights.* https://www.nist.gov/news-events/news/2022/03/theres-more-ai-bias-biased-data-nist-report-highlights

Norris, C.J. (2019). The negativity bias, revisited: Evidence from neuroscience measures and an individual differences approach. *Social Neuroscience*, 16(1), pp 68–82. https://www.tandfonline.com/doi/full/10.1080/17470919.2019.1696225?scroll=top&needAccess=true

Pagnini F., Manzey D., Rosnet E., Ferravante, D., White, O., and Smith, N. (2023). Human behavior and performance in deep space exploration: Next challenges and research gaps. *NPJ Microgravity*, 9(1), pp. 27. https://pubmed.ncbi.nlm.nih.gov/36997549

Seyyed-Kalantari, L., Zhang, H., McDermott, M.B.A., Chen, I.Y., and Ghassemi, M. (2021). Underdiagnosis bias of artificial intelligence algorithms applied to chest radiographs in under-served patient populations. *Nature Medicine*, 27(12), pp. 2176–2182. https://pubmed.ncbi.nlm.nih.gov/34893776

Taori, R. and Hashimoto, T. B. (2022). Data feedback loops: Model-driven amplification of dataset biases. *ARXIV.* https://arxiv.org/abs/2209.03942

10

The Case for Humanity in the AI Era

Stephanie LeBlanc-Godfrey
Founder of Mother AI

As a high-achieving, working mother, I find myself constantly torn between two worlds I deeply cherish: my family and my career. I yearn to be the present, engaged parent who knows every detail of my children's lives, while also striving to excel in my professional pursuits. I want to be involved in impactful projects, travel to industry-defining conferences, and be recognized for my contributions. This desire for validation exists not only in my career but also in my role as a parent. Balancing these competing priorities often feels insurmountable, leaving me wondering if there's a way to nurture both my personal and professional growth without the guilt and worry about the effect of my choices. As technology advances, I've explored the potential of artificial intelligence (AI) to serve as a powerful tool, enabling working parents like myself to alleviate the time-consuming tasks that often stand in the way of fully engaging in life's most meaningful moments.

Despite AI's potential, many view this technology with skepticism and fear, conjuring up images of cold, impersonal machines that threaten to replace human interaction. However, I believe that between these concerns and the untapped potential, a space exists where we can thoughtfully integrate AI to foster deeper, more meaningful connections and hold on to the human role in our AI interactions in both our personal and professional lives. AI has the power to collapse hours of effort into mere minutes, allowing us to approach each interaction with the ease, presence, and excellence we strive for—whether it's being fully engaged in our child's birthday celebration or delivering a game-changing presentation at work without the weariness that often accompanies extensive preparation.

In the realm of business, while it's enticing for some to turn to AI's promises of speed and ability that rivals humans, we must take a careful approach here. There can be no AI without HI (human intervention) to confirm accuracy, integrity, and the human touch that is not replaceable for a business to be functional and successful. AI helps us streamline the mundane tasks that often consume our time and energy, freeing us to focus on the activities that bring us closer to our loved ones. While AI is not a perfect solution, by prioritizing human connection and well-being in our approach, we can unlock its potential to support more fulfilling relationships and beneficial impact in our society.

AI in the Home

My journey to discover how AI can address the daily tasks of home life was the most intriguing because, like most parents, if AI doesn't provide us with our Rosey (the robot maid from the cartoon series *The Jetsons*), then what value can it bring? Meals need to be made, homework checked, laundry done, and schedules organized. When I started Mother AI in 2023, it was to address the lack of focus on the value of AI for parents. Business scale, automation, and a new world for creators were the prime areas of focus. As I methodically set out to see how AI could support me in four key areas—event organization, home organization, children's learning, and research-based tasks—I found incredible uses, from getting a list of local doctors who accept my insurance and are accepting new patients to site scrapes in a table form that gave me registration deadlines, dates, and costs for summer camps. However, the most profound impact AI had on my home life was in the way it strengthened my connection with my children and supported their learning journey at the same time.

It started with my sixth grader who was preparing for a test and wanted my help. I took the study guide she received from her teacher, uploaded it to an AI chatbot, and had it make me three more versions, including true/false, multiple choice, short answers, and essay questions (with an answer key). With that level of support, she continued to lean on me each time she had a test across all her classes. It became a ritual for us to engage for each upcoming test, create the exams, talk through the output, and identify areas she needed to focus on versus what she had nailed down—rinse and repeat for an entire school year. The benefits were multifold: it kept me close to her grades, what she was learning, what areas she excelled in versus found challenging, and how I could help her bridge the gap. This meant that instead of staying in her room to do homework, she came out and hung out in my office or on my bed doing homework while I did my own work or worked through topics and discussions with her. AI let me support her quickly to meet the moment, and I, not AI, was seen as the hero.

AI in Business

This technology can be effectively incorporated in four impactful ways while ensuring that human involvement remains central to the process. Despite the rush we've seen for companies to lay off entire departments in favor of AI, we've equally seen the backlash: throwing away humans doesn't quite lead to the desired results. I propose that we can thoughtfully and intentionally roll out AI in business only with human intervention (HI) at every step; in other words, AI and HI must go hand in hand.

1. Start Small

First, start small by implementing AI in a specific project, allowing for focused collaboration and iterative improvement based on employee feedback. This approach enables organizations to explore AI's potential in a controlled environment, gathering valuable insights and making necessary adjustments before scaling up. In a recent "AI in the workplace: How companies and workers are getting it right" report sponsored by Charter and the Innovation Resource Center for Human Resources (Goliogoski, Clemente 2024), they shared Cisco's approach to internal hackathons that gave employees the space to create and determine how AI is used. Knowing the distance between a developer who creates the program and the end user who ultimately uses the program creates a lot of room for error; the use of employee-led hackathons can solve real challenges quickly and efficiently. And this is even more important when it comes to AI since 65% of employees say they are anxious about AI replacing their job according to the Ernest & Young "AI Anxiety in Business Survey" (Hemmerdinger 2023).

2. Ensure clean data

Second, ensure clean data to align AI insights with business objectives and human needs. The quality and relevance of data are crucial for AI systems to generate meaningful outcomes. The desired flow of data connections across teams is often met with the reality of data silos, which means the pipes won't work. The crucial step here is to actively involve employees in the data creation, preparation, or clean-up process so that it can maximize the power of AI's data analytics tools. Organizations can and should leverage human expertise to guide AI toward solutions that truly benefit the workforce and the business as a whole.

3. **Retain human oversight**

Third, retain human oversight to foster a culture of collaboration between humans and AI systems. While AI can automate certain tasks and provide valuable insights, it's essential to keep humans in the loop to interpret results, make informed decisions, and ensure that AI is being used ethically and responsibly. The nascence of AI means that hallucinations, biases, and privacy issues are rampant and need the human oversight to detect and solve for it. Having employees dedicated to working alongside AI allows the strengths of both human and machine intelligence, leading to more creative problem-solving and innovation.

4. **Establish metrics**

Finally, establish metrics to measure AI's impact, prioritizing human values, well-being, and connection. By setting clear objectives and tracking progress, organizations can ensure that AI implementation aligns with their goals and values. This data-driven approach allows for continuous improvement and optimization, enabling organizations to make informed decisions about how to leverage AI in a way that benefits both the business and its employees.

By strategically integrating AI into the workplace, organizations can build programs, policies, and processes that effectively serve their intended end users. AI can help teams work more efficiently, freeing up time and energy for creative problem-solving and relationship-building. Beyond the realm of working parents, these principles can be applied across a wide range of industries and roles, enabling individuals and organizations to leverage AI in a way that enhances human potential and connection.

Shaping the Future

As we navigate an increasingly digital world, it's more important than ever to keep human touch at the forefront of our minds. By embracing AI as a tool to help us alleviate the time-consuming tasks that often stand in the way of fully engaging in life's most meaningful moments, we can cultivate a future where technology and humanity coexist fairly. Whether you're a working parent striving to balance family and career or an organization seeking to drive innovation, the principles of intentional AI integration and human-centered design can enhance your relationships and your work.

So let us approach AI with an open mind, a clear purpose, and a commitment to leveraging its capabilities to create more space for the things that truly matter: our connections, our passions, and our shared experiences. Together, we can shape a future where AI and human potential work hand in hand, enabling us to be fully present, engaged, and alive in the moments that define our lives. By keeping human touch at the heart of our efforts, we can ensure that the rise of AI serves to enhance, rather than diminish, the most valuable asset we have: our humanity.

Biography

Global Head of Inclusion Programs for Women of Color at Google, Stephanie LeBlanc-Godfrey began her career in infrastructure engineering at Lehman Brothers. From here she transitioned into the digital media industry, spending 10 years working on big data, forecasting, and inventory management for Forbes Media, FOX News Digital, and NBC News Digital.

Stephanie is the founder of Mother AI, a weekly AI learning journey series designed specifically for working parents and caregivers, and Parenting Backwards, which creates spaces and experiences for parents to develop parenting skills in the same way they develop their personal and professional skills. She is a member of the Thinkers50 Radar Class of 2024.

References

Hemmerdinger, J. (2023). *New EY research reveals the majority of US employees feel AI anxiety amid explosive adoption* [online]. EY. Available from https://www.ey.com/en_us/newsroom/2023/12/ey-research-shows-most-us-employees-feel-ai-anxiety

Goliogoski, E. and Clemente, J. (2024). *AI in the workplace: How companies and workers are getting it right – IRC4HR* [online]. Available at: https://irc4hr.org/projects/ai-lessons-from-companies-and-workers-getting-it-right/ [Accessed 12 Jul. 2024].

11

Human Against the Machine in Forecasting

Ville Satopää
Associate professor, technology and operations management, INSEAD

Forecasting is vital in business as it enables companies to anticipate future conditions and strategically plan their operations. By predicting sales trends, market demands, and economic shifts, businesses can optimize inventory, allocate resources efficiently, and adjust their production schedules accordingly. Forecasting can also help companies decide which new products to pursue and which to avoid, ensuring resources are invested in projects most likely to succeed and meet future customer demands. Forecasts are typically made by an artificial intelligence (AI) model or represent the judgment of an experienced human expert. Choosing the right approach to forecasting is crucial to its success and often depends on the context.

AI in Forecasting

Today's large language models (LLMs) are trained on a substantial portion of all text ever written by humans (Bernard 2023). At first this may seem like a lot, but to put this into perspective, Yann LeCun, a Turing Award–winning computer scientist, points out, "In 4 years, a child has seen 50 times more data than the biggest LLMs" (World Economic Forum 2024). This statement underscores the vast amount of data both machines and humans encounter throughout their lives. However, the critical difference lies in the processing capabilities. Whereas it might take a human years to manually analyze a spreadsheet with millions of numbers, an AI system can process the same data within seconds, without fatigue or complaint.

AI can also analyze data with a level of scrutiny unachievable by humans.

For instance, consider detecting COVID-19 based on a cough. To humans, two coughs may sound the same. However, AI looks at every detail and can identify even the most nuanced patterns that allow it to systematically detect COVID-19 cases in the data. While AI can still be susceptible to biases present in the training data, its predictions in forecasting tasks are generally less biased compared to human judgment. This reduction in bias results from AI's ability to objectively analyze data without the influence of human emotions or subjective experiences. The result typically is a noticeable boost in forecasting accuracy. Remarkably, in our COVID-19 example, it can detect positive cases with 99% accuracy (Chu 2020).

Human Judgment in Forecasting

A significant constraint of AI is its dependency on the quality and scope of the data it is trained on. Not all forecasting scenarios provide sufficient data for reliable AI predictions. One example is the 2016 Brexit referendum, where the United Kingdom faced a decision to remain in or leave the European Union. This event was unprecedented in modern political history, lacking any direct historical analogues that could have been used to train an AI model. In forecasting such events, the responsibility often shifts toward human experts.

Then, if AI requires data to make predictions, where does human expertise gather the information necessary for forecasting, and why can't this information be used to train AI models? As illustrated by the insights from LeCun, humans continuously absorb and process a diverse array of information throughout their lives. It is such life experience that allows humans to detect subtle "weak signals" within the broader context of events like Brexit and synthesize these signals into coherent predictions. Despite the richness of this human-processed data, it often remains uncaptured in datasets typically used to train AI, limiting the machine's learning potential. Of course, AI is trained on more data every day. As AI learns to absorb a bigger share of our digitized world, it is likely to make better predictions about unprecedented events, like Brexit. The field of AI is admittedly moving fast, but at least today AI is not outperforming humans in accuracy to predict future events without clear historical precedents (Schoenegger and Park 2023).

Even though human judgment can draw on the broader context to make predictions, it often suffers from bias (systematic error) and noise (random error; Satopää et al. 2021) and can be shaped by personal agendas other than forecasting accuracy. For example, in professional environments, individuals may sacrifice accuracy to make predictions that are likely to conform with the upcoming consensus of their group—a bias known as herding (Jia et al. 2023). Conversely, AI adheres solely to the objectives set during its training, that is, to generate as accurate predictions as possible.

The AI-human Hybrid in Forecasting

In 1997 IBM developed a chess-playing AI system called Deep
Blue that defeated the chess world champion, Garry Kasparov.
This historic event marked a turning point, leading Kasparov
himself to advocate for the synergy between human strategic
insight and AI's computational power. In chess competitions
where human and machine are allowed to collaborate, the combination often outperforms either alone. Kasparov highlights
that this success was not due solely to the computational strength
of the AI but was significantly enhanced by the *process* by which
the human strategically made use of the AI (Kasparov 2010).

If this is so, then what kind of processes can we use to pair AI
and humans in forecasting? One tried and tested technique is
known as "extremization" (Satopää et al. 2014). This begins by
collecting and averaging multiple human forecasts. The average
of many human forecasts is often more accurate than an individual forecast—a phenomenon known as the wisdom of the
crowd (Surowiecki 2005). Even though averaging can reduce
noise, it does not reduce bias because it cannot systematically
shift the forecasts up or down. For instance, if all forecasters are
overly optimistic and make predictions that are too high, averaging cannot correct this bias because it does not have the means to
systematically shift the forecasts down. The silver lining of biases
is that they are systematic, and AI offers powerful means to detect
such systematic patterns. This is why in the final step of extremization AI is allowed to shift the average forecast. The exact nature
of the shift (i.e., its direction and magnitude) is determined by
what works on data of past human forecasts of events whose outcomes are known.

During a multiyear forecasting tournament organized by
Intelligence Advanced Research Projects Activity (IARPA), we
used this technique to forecast challenging geopolitical future
events—the kind the intelligence agents would routinely predict

in their daily work life (Ungar et al. 2012). Each year we checked what shift of the average forecast would have worked the best on the forecasts of events that took place during the previous years of the tournament. Assuming that the human biases persist over the years, we then continued using that same shift to correct the average forecasts of the current year. This turned out to work extremely well. In fact, it allowed us not only to win the tournament but also to perform 30% better than intelligence officers with access to internal classified information (Spiegel 2014).

Extremization can help us realize the full potential of multiple human forecasts. In some cases, however, one may also have access to a machine forecast that uses information that is not captured in the human forecasts. How can we then integrate the collective information of the humans and machines into a single forecast? One idea is a machine-human-machine "sandwich" that, like extremization, uses AI to help humans arrive at predictions but also uses AI to help humans get started with forecasting. In short, we begin with the AI forecast. This is presented to the humans, who can adjust or update it according to their contextual information. However, as mentioned before, such human adjustments can be biased. Therefore, after the humans have adjusted the initial AI forecast, we apply a second AI step that corrects (if necessary) the human's adjustment of the initial AI forecast. This irons out any wrinkles in the human adjustment and ensures that the final product accurately represents both the human's and the machine's information.

This sandwiching approach allowed us to improve forecasts of the chances of a new drug passing through the different phases of a clinical trial at Eli Lilly and Company—a world-leading pharmaceutical company. Here the initial AI forecast was based on a data base of past trial outcomes of similar drugs. This forecast was then adjusted by a group of human experts with specific knowledge of the current drug. Finally, a second AI was used to correct any over- or under-reactions in the human adjustments.

The results were impressive: humans systematically improved upon the first AI, and the second AI further improved upon the humans. For instance, for the final phase, where research and development costs can reach hundreds of millions of dollars, the humans improved upon the first AI by 38% and the second AI further improved upon the humans by an additional 10%. This demonstrates that while AI alone can be powerful, it is the combination with human insight that creates a formidable tool in forecasting.

Final Thoughts

Our discussion on the merits and limitations of AI versus human forecasting underscores a crucial realization: neither is infallible on its own, yet each holds unique advantages that can significantly enhance decision-making when effectively combined. AI can process vast quantities of data with exceptional speed and rigor. Humans can complement this by drawing on information from the broader context. As seen in applications ranging from geopolitical analysis to pharmaceutical trials, such a hybrid approach not only addresses the limitations inherent in each method but also sets a new standard for predictive accuracy. This evolving partnership promises to revolutionize forecasting and offer more reliable, unbiased, and comprehensive tools to support decision-making in the future.

Biography

Associate professor of technology and operations management at INSEAD, Ville Satopää received his PhD and MA in statistics from the Wharton School of the University of Pennsylvania, and BAs in computer science and mathematics from Williams College.

He has received the Dean's Commendation for Excellence in Teaching multiple times and has also won the Best Teacher Award in the MBA program at INSEAD. Ville's research papers have been published in top statistical, management, and field journals, including the *Journal of American Statistical Association*, *Management Science*, and the *International Journal of Forecasting*. He was named to the Thinkers50 Radar Class of 2024.

References

Bernard, E. (2023). What are large language models? *The AI Edge*. https://newsletter.theaiedge.io/p/what-are-large-language-models

Chu, J. (2020). Artificial intelligence model detects asymptomatic COVID-19 infections through cellphone-recorded coughs. *MIT News*, 10, pp. 4811–4815.

Jia, Y., Keppo, J., and Satopää, V. (2023). Herding in probabilistic forecasts. *Management Science*, 69(5), pp. 2713–2732.

Kasparov, G. (2010). The chess master and the computer. *New York Review of Books*, 57(2), pp. 16–19.

Satopää, V.A., Baron, J., Foster, D.P., Mellers, B.A., Tetlock, P.E., and Ungar, L.H. (2014). Combining multiple probability predictions using a simple logit model. *International Journal of Forecasting*, 30(2), pp. 344–356.

Satopää, V.A., Salikhov, M., Tetlock, P.E., and Mellers, B. (2021). Bias, information, noise: The BIN model of forecasting. *Management Science*, 67(12), pp. 7599–7618.

Schoenegger, P. and Park, P.S. (2023). *Large language model prediction capabilities: Evidence from a real-world forecasting tournament*. arXiv preprint arXiv:2310.13014.

Spiegel, A. (2014). So you think you're smarter than a CIA agent. NPR.org. https://www.npr.org

Surowiecki, J. (2005). *The wisdom of crowds*. New York: Anchor.

Ungar, L., Mellers, B., Satopää, V., Tetlock, P., and Baron, J. (2012). The good judgment project: A large scale test of different methods of combining expert predictions. In *2012 AAAI Fall Symposium Series*.

World Economic Forum. (2024). The expanding universe of generative models. https://www.weforum.org/events/world-economic-forum-annual-meeting-2024/sessions/the-expanding-universe-of-generative-models

Inclusive Leadership

12

Four Simple Words to Help Connect with Others

Kirstin Ferguson
Adjunct professor at Queensland University of Technology Business School

"I don't know . . . yet."

These four words run counter to what most of us have been educated and trained to say. Yet these four words frequently represent reality and, importantly, can almost always help build connection with others.

When faced with not knowing something or ignorance we may have about a certain topic, there is a temptation to double down on how much we *believe* we know, even if only to ourselves. Our need to maintain a persona of competence and expertise, especially if you work in a blame culture where asking questions or not knowing is likely to be a career killer, means we can all fall victim to this common vice. In fact, research shows that the more expert we are in an area, the more likely we are to overstate how much we know (Lockhart et al. 2016).

Unfortunately, our ignorance is often invisible to us. It is a human blind spot.

The field of intellectual humility, an area of academic attention which has exploded over the past decade, can help us understand what drives our need to know and how being prepared to admit what we don't know can help build connection with others.

If you've never heard of intellectual humility, you're not alone. Simply put, intellectual humility is the willingness to admit that something you believe might be wrong.

Intellectual humility is a powerful way to become a more emotionally intelligent leader. This is because you will be prepared to own your mistakes and limitations. You won't have difficulty being open about how much you don't know, and you will engage with others openly and cooperatively to learn. You will also be grateful for the information and perspectives you gather and in doing so will help others feel seen, heard, and appreciated.

Intellectual humility allows us to willingly seek out and hear diverse ideas, collaborate with others different to ourselves, and engage in thoughtful discourse even on the most contentious issues. It is a way of thinking that enables us to maintain a positive perception of others, despite any disagreement on views we may have.

Research studies have shown that those who are high in intellectual humility show more empathy, are more concerned about the well-being of others, are less focused on accumulating power, and are more altruistic (Porter et al. 2022). The higher someone's intellectual humility, the more likely they are to report valuing and wanting to protect the welfare of others.

What We Experience

Intellectual humility enables us to think about the way we interpret and communicate how much we know. It has powerful elements that will help us to connect better with those around us and allow us to be emotionally intelligent modern leaders. Each of the following elements describes what we experience internally when we are intellectually humble and how thinking honestly about what we know, and don't, helps us connect to those we interact with.

We love to learn.

If we are intellectually humble, we are motivated by seeking information and learning something new. We get genuine pleasure or enjoyment from challenging tasks and effortful thinking as we learn about the world around us. We have an intrinsic motivation to acquire new knowledge and skills, simply for the joy of discovery and understanding. We persist with our love of learning despite setbacks and challenges because much of our love of learning comes through overcoming such intellectual hurdles.

We care about truth.

In a world of fake news, misinformation, and disinformation, we care about understanding the objective truth or facts of a matter, and we are motivated to find out what is true in any given situation. We apply all our critical thinking skills to understand why some apparent "truths" are not necessarily what they seem. We put in the effort to get to the bottom of complex issues to understand the truth of the situation. We are highly attuned to the strengths of different arguments and seek to gain insight into what may be motivating someone to maintain the position on an issue they hold.

We critically evaluate information.

We understand the pertinent information we need and are focused on seeking it out. We have the skills and abilities to critically think about the source of information we uncover and assess whether it is pertinent to our objective to learn and for truth. We can make creative connections between past ideas and new information. We can assess the credibility of the source of the information and question whether it is a reputable source for the topic at hand. We look for evidence to support the accuracy of information that is given, and we assess objectivity and balance in the material provided. We consider the logic and reasoning of the position being given and analyze whether it is valuable to the decision which needs to be made.

We accept we are fallible.

We are realistic and acutely aware we don't know everything—we have an accurate view of our strengths and opportunities for development. We are prepared to admit our limitations, even if only to ourselves. We also know, because we don't have all the answers, that the perspectives of others have value. We are prepared to be wrong because we know we probably don't have all the information, and we are comfortable with that because being fallible simply means we are human. Admitting our own fallibility helps keep our ego in check and makes us more open to following arguments wherever they lead rather than prejudging them based on our existing knowledge.

We know context matters.

We assess the situation to understand when we need to apply intellectual humility, and we know it is much easier to demonstrate in low-stake situations and much harder in a highly charged conversation when we feel personally challenged. We understand that when our strong convictions are challenged, we tend to hold on tightly to our existing beliefs and fail to recognize the views of others.

What Others See

There are important ways others experience us if we are being intellectually humble. Each of these helps build important connections with those we work with and help us become more effective leaders.

We own our limitations.

When we operate with intellectual humility, we are courageous enough to admit to others the limitations of our knowledge, and we don't see doing so as a weakness. We can see the world, and others in it, as it is and not as we might wish it to be. This allows us the opportunity to admit "I don't know" or "I was wrong." We are able to separate our ego from the extent to which we believe we fully understand something.

We respect others' views.

If we are intellectually humble, we are open to other people's points of view to help understand the gaps we need to fill in with our own information and knowledge. We are prepared to listen to others and respect their right to a different perspective, even if we disagree with them in important ways. We will seek to understand why another person may disagree with us, and we are sensitive to counterevidence because we respect and value the opinion of others. We are less likely to belittle, disparage, or criticize someone for the views they hold since we are also open to accepting the views of diverse people and ideas, free from prejudice.

We are curious.

If we are intellectually humble, we are genuinely inquisitive and able to confront information or challenges that are novel or different. We ask questions in a way designed to enhance our understanding of a topic, and we are not motivated by proving ourselves correct. We do not seek to win every argument, but instead we are curious as to why people might think the way they do. We are curious to learn from others what we might be missing. When we hear feedback, we are curious about why that person may think the way they do, and we can hear feedback without defensiveness.

We are open to new ideas.

We are actively open minded and flexible in our thinking, which means when we hear information from others that might be at odds with our own opinions or beliefs, we are able to engage with that information in a constructive way. We understand we can learn from new information we find, and we are open to rethinking our ideas which may have changed because of new information or evidence which has been uncovered. We believe allowing ourselves to have our mind changed by new evidence or an opposing argument is a sign of good character, not a weakness.

We can keep our ego in check.

We can separate our ego from what we know, which allows us to make discussions less personal. We are less likely to take offense when people question our point of view. Intellectual humility moves us away from ego to orient toward others, which includes being less defensive when confronted about our beliefs and less antagonistic toward the views of others different to our own.

These are all ways we can powerfully connect with others through being prepared to be intellectually humble and accept the limitations of how much we know.

Many of us would recognize people who are not intellectually humble. They remain fixed in their thinking and are determined to be right at all costs. They mistakenly believe they already have all the answers and are determined to hold firm to their views. They see any challenge to their opinion as a personal slight on themselves.

We can all fall victim to being inflexible in our thinking and believing we know the answer. We observe "know-it-alls" who need others to think they have all the answers but may understand, even if they only admit it to themselves, that they don't have the answer at all.

The more we can embrace intellectual humility as a mindset, the more likely we are to have an enduring impact in our teams and organizations. Intellectual humility creates a ripple effect of impact through our willingness to be open minded to the challenges we all confront.

Human connection is built by having the courage to be prepared to say, in those moments, "What am I missing here?" and hold our views a little more lightly.

Biography

Kirstin Ferguson is a writer, columnist, and company director. She is one of Australia's prominent leadership experts and is the author of *Head & Heart: The Art of Modern Leadership* (Berrett-Koehler, 2023), which featured on the Thinkers50 2023 Best New Management Booklist. In the same year, Kirstin was placed in the Thinkers50 Ranking, received the Thinkers50 2023 Leadership Award, and was appointed a Member of the Order of Australia for her significant contributions to business and gender equality.

References

Lockhart, K. L., Goddu, M. K., Smith, E. D., and Keil, F. C. (2016). What could you really learn on your own? Understanding the epistemic limitations of knowledge acquisition. *Child Development*, 87(2), pp. 477–493.

Porter, T., Baldwin, C. R., Warren, M. T., Murray, E. D., Cotton Bronk, K., Forgeard, M. J., Snow, N. E., and Jayawickreme, E. (2022). Clarifying the content of intellectual humility: A systematic review and integrative framework. *Journal of Personality Assessment*, 104(5), pp. 573–585.

13

How to Build Your Human Touch

Susie Kennedy
Founder and senior partner, KBA Solutions

Technological advances influencing social and cultural shifts, such as increased virtual working, mean human connections are more critical than ever. According to the UK Mental Health Foundation (2022), extensive studies have shown that positive connections to others are crucial for good physical and mental health. Poor relationships are associated with higher mortality rates, poor health, and unhappy lives. In these uncertain and turbulent times, successful leadership in the workplace requires the human touch—the ability to treat others in a personable and empathetic way, helping them feel connected and valued.

Some leaders are naturally gifted with the human touch, others less for various reasons. Fortunately, with the right mindset, leaders can develop human touch skills. But to build this critical leadership trait they need to understand what gets in the way and invest in practical techniques.

Why Develop the Human Touch?

There are many reasons for leaders to invest in developing their human touch, and retaining talent is one of them. A US Gallup Survey in February 2022 found that employees who strongly agree their employer cares about their overall well-being are 69% less likely to look for another job. This is significant given the current global skills shortage highlighted in the 2024 ManpowerGroup Global Talent Shortage survey, which reported that an average of 75% of employers had difficulty filling roles.

In addition to the benefit of retaining staff, various studies have shown that treating employees with a human touch makes them happier and increases their performance (Oswald, Proto, and Sgrio 2015). For example, in one study, Google, having invested in employee support, had an increase of 37% in employee satisfaction. Research by Professor Paul J. Zak found that people working in high-trust organizations reported being 50% more productive. The reverse is true, as research shows, when staff are subjected to rudeness and incivility, which results in reduced performance, deteriorating customer experience, and increased turnover (Brower 2021).

Trust is fundamental to successful relationships, whether personal, social, commercial, political, or economic. Without trust, it is difficult, if not impossible, to get things done in the workplace. By using the human touch, leaders can increase their ability to build trust. Research by Zak (2017) has shown that oxytocin, a hormone in the body that promotes positive feelings, increases trust in humans by reducing their fear of trusting a stranger. He identified eight key management behaviors that stimulate oxytocin production and generate trust.

Using a human touch makes a leader more likely to meet expectations and build a trustworthy reputation. Research shows that in the last 10 years, expectations about leadership presence have changed, with traits such as being physically present, inclusive, listening, and respectful now some of the most valued (Hewlett 2024). Similarly, the World Economic Forum *Future of Jobs Report* (2023) lists empathy and active listening, leadership, and social influence among the top 10 most important core skills.

What Gets in the Way?

A leader with a reputation for building trusting relationships is more likely to increase psychological safety within the team and create a culture of high performance. They are also more likely to find out about issues they must address. So, what stops some leaders from developing and using their human touch?

Over the last three decades, I have helped thousands of leaders develop leadership skills. I've noticed three key stumbling blocks that can prevent the human touch from being created. The first is a stereotypical belief that the individual is not a people person. The second is not prioritizing time for people; the third is a lack of confidence. Let's briefly examine each one.

I'm Not a People Person

Many of the leaders I work with are technical professionals. They typically have degrees in STEM-based subjects (science, technology, engineering, and math). I often hear individuals declare themselves technical people, not *people people*. This stereotypical belief about technical people can create a limiting mindset, especially when coupled with inaccurate generalizations about personality profiles, such as that *introverted thinking types don't do people*.

Some technical people may have greater strength in solving technical problems than people problems (and vice versa). Indeed, Dr. Valerie Patrick (2020), a specialist in leadership of STEM professionals, argues that technical people are attracted to and well trained in logical thinking, which is ideal for solving technical problems but not so good for solving people problems. She argues the brain has networks for logical thinking and social thinking and the more the logical network is used, the stronger it becomes. Likewise, the less the social network in the brain is used, the weaker it performs. This suggests that if leaders develop strength in dealing with technical problems, they can develop their people skills if they choose to.

I Do Not Have Time

There are several reasons why some managers do not prioritize their human touch skills and engage with their people, especially when transitioning to a more senior role. Some people feel pressured to prioritize time on tasks such as writing reports, preparing presentations, and problem-solving because this is what they believe their boss wants from them, rightly or wrongly.

Another reason could be that a manager feels comfortable and successful doing particular tasks they allow to dominate their diary, assuming that their people think the same way and don't need much contact from them. In some cases, a manager may find themselves in a leadership role they never intended and have little interest in but have no other route to increase their salary. This can happen in organizations that do not have technical career tracks or dual career paths that offer career progression without managerial responsibilities.

Some people may not prioritize the human touch because of the third stumbling block—they are unsure how to develop it, so they avoid trying.

I'm Not Sure How

Lack of confidence prevents people from trying new or different things. It is human nature to protect self-esteem and avoid doing something that might expose a perceived weakness. If managers believe they are not a people person, don't feel supported by their boss, have not made time to connect with the team, and see themselves as a manager rather than as a leader, and a shy one at that, they are unlikely to throw themselves into developing their human touch skills. So, the approach to developing human touch skills addresses these stumbling blocks using the following practical techniques.

Check Mindset and Purpose

The journey to developing one's unique human touch starts with intent and clarity of purpose—the desire to be a leader of people must be unequivocal. Coaching from a line manager or coach can provide the help and support needed to build confidence, dispel unhelpful stereotypes, determine priorities, and create clarity of purpose.

Some managers stepping up into a leadership role may need clarification about the difference between management and leadership and how best to allocate their time. A helpful tool is the classic *Harvard Business Review* article "What Leaders Really Do" (2001), in which Professor John Kotter explains the difference, making it clear that the role of the leader is to help their people cope with change by setting direction, engaging, inspiring, and motivating—skills that require the human touch.

Other leadership development techniques, such as those researched by Dr. Hitendra Wadhwa (2024) of Columbia Business School, can help leaders establish positive intention and focus on activating our five core energies: purpose, wisdom, growth, love, and self-realization. Blending the spiritual with the material, leaders learn to center themselves through contemplative practices. These and other human-centered leadership approaches, which include mindfulness techniques, enable leaders to be clear about their purpose, increase self-awareness, and better understand other people's needs.

Listen and Build Trust

Leaders who are clear about their purpose and want to build their human touch are more successful in listening. Being comfortable with themselves, they are more likely to be fully engaged and open to hearing what others say. The act of empathic listening shows people they are valued, feeling valued releases oxytocin, and this builds trust.

However, good listening requires practice, and leaders should routinely reflect on how to improve their listening skills. Are they hearing what they don't want to hear? Do they interrupt and finish others' sentences? Do they get distracted? Is their body language in listening mode? The rewards of good listening are substantial, and when people are listened to and given autonomy in their work, they feel trusted and more motivated.

Make Time for People

Spending time with and getting to know people is a great way to show you care about them, especially when starting a new role. Diary analysis and meeting cadence reveal what's important to a leader. For example, one senior leader I coach keeps a half hour in her diary every day for any team member who needs her. In setting a meeting cadence, focus on the purpose and goals of the meetings and involve the team in establishing a routine that works. Use one-to-one meetings to get to know your people well. Avoid canceling meetings other than in extraordinary circumstances, as it sends a message the team or individual is not important.

Make time for team members to get to know each other. When new members join the team, it is timely for everyone to introduce themselves again. Having regular check-ins, say at weekly meetings, allows everyone to share what's going on for them. Informal social gatherings help people get to know each other and connect in a relaxed setting, which helps build a caring, trusting culture. Spending time in person with the team is invaluable. In addition to body language cues, which improve communication, a leader can better read the mood and empathize when physically present.

Empathizing, however, can become exhausting, according to Professor Jamal Zaki. Leaders should recognize the need to balance empathizing with others with looking after themselves to avoid burning out with compassion fatigue. Zaki (2024) explains the multiple ways in which we can connect empathically with others. Two such ways involve *emotional empathy*, feeling what others feel, and *empathic concern*, wanting to help someone. To avoid burnout, leaders can learn to tune into one or other of these types of empathy depending on the needs of the other person and themselves in the situation.

Be Vulnerable and Get Feedback

As we have explored, a leader can use their human touch to create a culture where people feel valued and connected and express empathy for others—a psychologically safe environment. They can reinforce this culture by showing vulnerability, asking others what they think, and admitting they don't have the answers. According to Harvard Professor Amy Edmondson, the leading expert in psychological safety, "Being open about what you know and don't know builds trust and commitment" (Edmondson 2023, p. 106).

According to research, when leaders ask for help from their colleagues instead of telling them what to do, trust and cooperation increase. Leaders can make themselves vulnerable by seeking feedback, for example, asking how they can help their team feel valued and connected and what individual team members need from them.

Co-create the Vision

According to McKinsey, when people are involved in creating an outcome, they are much more committed to it by a factor of five (Dewar and Keller, 2009). As already mentioned, asking people for their help and opinions builds trust. Yet, leaders do not necessarily share strategic information or involve their teams in future planning. According to Zak (2017), only 40% of employees feel well-informed about company strategy, and uncertainty about the future direction leads to stress, which inhibits oxytocin and limits teamwork. A leader I coach wondered whether to involve his team in developing the department's strategic vision. He initially thought it was his job alone to set the direction but realized it was the ideal opportunity to build the team and use his human touch to gain commitment by co-creating the vision.

Expectations of leadership are changing. Globally, an estimated 2 billion people were born between 1997 and 2012, the so-called "Generation Z." They will soon overtake the number of baby boomers in the workforce, and they have different expectations from their postwar parents. Stanford University reported that Gen Z wants leaders to lead by consensus and involve them in decisions (De Witte 2024). They value mental health, work-life balance, trust, collaboration, and teamwork. Leaders need the human touch to meet these expectations.

Every leader can develop and improve their human touch. With the right mindset and skills, they can overcome stumbling blocks that may get in the way. With clarity of purpose and confidence, they can prioritize caring for their people, truly listen to them, and create a trusting, caring, connected culture of happiness and high performance.

Biography

Susie Kennedy is senior partner of KBA Solutions Limited, which she founded in 1993. KBA specializes in executive development and change leadership consulting. She is program director for KBA's Institute of Leadership and Management Strategic Leadership program for senior managers, with programs in the University of Cambridge, Premier Foods, and nationally for the UK Local Government at King's College London. Susie has contributed to a number of Thinkers50 publications.

References

Brower, T. (2021). Empathy is the most important leadership skill, according to research. *Forbes*. https://www.forbes.com/sites/tracybrower/2021/09/19/empathy-is-the-most-important-leadership-skill-according-to-research/?sh=56541873dc5b

De Witte, M. (2024). 8 ways Gen Z will change the workforce. *Stanford Report*. https://news.stanford.edu/report/2024/02/14/8-things-expect-gen-z-coworker/#:~:text=Having%20a%20work%2Dlife%20balance,than%20work%2C%E2%80%9D%20Katz%20said.&text=Because%20Gen%20Z%20grew%20up,a%20different%20perspective%20on%20loyalty.

Dewar, C. and Keller, S. (2009). The irrational side of change management. *McKinsey Quarterly*. https://www.mckinsey.com/capabilities/people-and-organizational-performance/our-insights/the-irrational-side-of-change-management

Edmondson, A. (2023). *Right kind of wrong: Why learning to fail can teach us to thrive*. United Kingdom: Cornerstone Publishing, p. 106f.

Hewlett, S. A. (2024). The new rules of executive presence. *Harvard Business Review*, January–February, pp. 134–139.

Kotter, J. P. (2001). What leaders really do. *Harvard Business Review*, 79, pp. 85–98.

McKinsey & Company. (2024). *It's cool to be kind: The value of empathy at work* [online]. Available from: https://www.mckinsey.com/capabilities/people-and-organizational-performance/our-insights/its-cool-to-be-kind-the-value-of-empathy-at-work [accessed March 30, 2024].

Mental Health Foundation. (2016). *Relationships in the 21st century: The forgotten foundation of mental health and wellbeing.* www.mentalhealth .org.uk/sites/default/files/2022-06/MHF-Relationships-21st-Century-Summary-Report.pdf

Oswald, A. J., Proto, E., and Sgroi, D. (2015). Happiness and productivity. *Journal of Labor Economics*, 33(4). pp. 789–822.

Patrick, V. (2020). *Why it's hard to manage technical people* [online]. Association for Talent Development. Available from: https://www.td.org/insights/why-its-hard-to-manage-technical-people [accessed March 29, 2024].

Wadhwa, H. (2024) Leading in the flow of work. *Harvard Business Review*, January–February, pp. 42–50.

World Economic Forum. (2023). *The future of jobs report.* https://www.weforum .org/publications/the-future-of-jobs-report-2023

Zak, P. J. (2017). The neuroscience of trust. *Harvard Business Review*, January–February, pp. 84–90.

Zaki, J. (2024). How to sustain your empathy in difficult times. *Harvard Business Review*, January–February, pp. 62–69.

14

Five Ways to Develop Your Meeting Intelligence

Soulaima Gourani
Cofounder, Happioh

Thomas Roulet
Professor of organizational sociology and leadership, Judge Business School, University of Cambridge

A lot has changed in the work world in the last few years, but one thing remains the same: most of us waste a great deal of time in not-so-useful meetings (Laker et al. 2022). Research shows that 70% of meetings prevent employees from being productive because they're long, tedious, and frankly, inefficient.

That said, meetings are not all bad. They serve an important purpose: they help people come together—in person or virtually—to work effectively and collaborate on projects. Productive meetings can create space for conversations and sharing new ideas. More importantly, meeting the same people regularly over time can actually foster a sense of trust and reciprocity (Swärd 2016) and belonging among team members and actually help create a "team culture."

Building a culture where meetings are productive and meaningful, rather than a chore, takes time and effort. This is especially hard when you're new to leading meetings. To better understand how new and first-time managers can lead more effective meetings, we combined our research expertise and working together with more than 300 firms to help them organize and deliver high-quality meetings. Here's what we found.

Introducing Meeting Intelligence

The authors conducted a review of the academic literature around what makes meetings effective and combined this with the practical experience of one (Soulaima), of collaborating with a wide range of firms through her software development startup, Happioh. Soulaima worked in particular with Danish pharmaceutical Novo Nordisk A/S to better understand the need of its employees to lead effective meetings and develop a technology platform that could support such process. From our review of academic research, quite a significant amount of this has focused on effective coordination (Okhuysen and Bechky 2009), but very little integrative work has connected the different skills needed to lead effective meetings—what we call Meeting Intelligence (MQ).

The biggest learning from our literature review is that managers play a crucial role in facilitating effective meetings. That means, their focus needs to shift from thinking of meetings as just a way to get work done but rather as a way to help their teams build meaningful relationships.

Indeed, there is no reason for all meetings to be bad. Junior employees, particularly, have been found to have an appetite for meetings (Subel, Stepanek, and Roulet 2022) because of their need to feel part of their organization. Well-conducted yet relatively informal meetings can boost engagement, improve the work culture, and boost collaboration among coworkers. However, the art is in getting the balance just right. That's when MQ kicks in. But learning how to lead an effective meeting takes time, skill, effort, and patience.

MQ—the ability to run effective, inclusive, and enjoyable meetings—differs fundamentally from established concepts of Emotional Intelligence (EQ) or Wellbeing Intelligence (WBQ; Roulet and Bhatti 2023) because it involves not only interpersonal but also organizational skills. Yes, leading a meeting requires not only the regulation and observation of our own emotions and those of others, but it also requires preparing and building up the content and the relationships beforehand, to effectively lead the interactions. It relies on a core set of skills that we uncovered from our review of research and discussions with large organizations on how they improve the quality of their meetings:

1. Fostering engagement

2. Getting to know your meeting attendees

3. Managing purpose and time

4. Diffusing the right information

Fostering Engagement During Meetings

One of the core takeaways from research on effective meetings highlights the importance of engagement during meetings and how this relies on efforts to build relationships. For instance, a bit of casual chat during team calls can help colleagues feel connected and engaged, provided this does not allow for inappropriate remarks, offensive humor, or microaggressions. This approach to leading genuinely enjoyable meetings takes time to develop and is learned from experience—and from getting to know a bit about the other attendees.

Excessive formality does not always work in fostering engagement, especially in a hybrid workplace. The lack of sharing a physical space can often be an impediment in forming genuine connections. Online, we tend to focus more on the task at hand rather than taking note of other peoples' body language or expressions.

Meetings are often used as a tool by managers to check in on people, delegate tasks, or seek updates on deadlines and assignments. However, ensuring that everyone—those in the office, those working remotely, as well as those working from a non-office workplace—feels included and valued begins by using meetings as a way to build connections between people.

Get to Know the People on Your Team

To lead effective team meetings, you have to know the people who report to you. Building meaningful connections with your team members is crucial to fostering collegiality during meetings (Bhatti and Roulet 2023). Collegiality is the positive spirit of companionship and the enthusiasm for collaboration around a common objective. Collegiality drives people's willingness to interact with each other and motivates them to engage in discussion and work together.

To get to know your team members beyond the context of the meeting you can set up weekly or bimonthly one-on-ones with your direct reports. Ask them about the work they do, what tasks they enjoy, which ones they find hard, and what they might need to stay motivated. You can also use this time to learn more about them outside of work. Learn about their passions, interests, and hobbies. Do they like reading? Perhaps seek some book recommendations from them. Do you follow the same soccer team? You can emphasize your similarities. Make an effort to learn more about the person who reports to you, not just the employee.

Similarly, don't hesitate to share your interests and passions too. This helps to create a genuine rapport with your team members that transcends the work context. The authenticity that arises from such connections has a positive impact on motivation and engagement levels (Gardner 2011). The goal is to get to know the people who report to you so that you can enable them to be their most productive, engaged, and authentic selves.

This might be harder if you have a big team or people dispersed across different locations. If that is the case, check with individuals on how they wish to connect. While some may prefer weekly check-ins, others may like to meet just once a month. Figure out a frequency and schedule that works for you, so you don't feel overwhelmed or burned out.

Find a Purpose to Meetings

We've all been in meetings that could have simply been an email! So, as a meeting facilitator, your role is to decipher the exact meaning and purpose of a meeting before setting it up. Ask yourself why you need the meeting. It might be that you want to set up a weekly team get-together in order to receive updates and check progress on a project. However, this may not require a separate meeting for each and every project with your team.

Understand the difference between the meetings that further your team's progress and those that sap their energy and concentrate solely on the ones that will enhance team productivity and morale.

To practice this, be transparent about the goals of the meeting, and send out an agenda in advance. This will help your team members stay on board and remain aligned with the purpose of the conversation. Setting a clear "why" will help to foster a strong feeling of belonging and boost engagement.

Understanding the three purposes of a meeting

1. **Motivating the team**

   Meetings play a central role in team identification and culture. Meetings can help maintain the team's stamina when an objective seems distant.

2. **Allocating tasks**

   A meeting can help get buy-in from a team and understand who can best execute a plan.

3. **Brainstorming or solving a complex problem or situation**

   Brainstorming sessions can be helpful to get a team to think creatively about an issue when solutions are not obvious or difficult to consider. Reduce "bounded rationality" or an individual's cognitive limits when making rational decisions. Let participants unveil a decision-maker's blind spots.

Finally, while it is important to understand and share the purpose of a meeting, it is equally vital to assess whether the purpose can realistically be accomplished within the scheduled time frame.

Get Better at Managing Your Time in Meetings

Meetings that ramble and overrun are not popular. One way to get better at sticking to the allocated time is to set a clear agenda in advance. This will help you plan for everything you want the meeting to accomplish. Share this agenda in the meeting invite where possible.

If you can't share a clear agenda with everyone beforehand, try taking 10 minutes at the start of the meeting to go over the specific points you want to cover. This will make your meetings more structured, efficient, and transparent. Mastering this skill might take time, but the more meetings you lead, the better you will become.

If you find that you're running out of time, then make people aware. Explain how you would love to hear more of their views but really have to move on right now due to time constraints and offer to continue the discussion offline. Then ensure that you do follow up with that team member afterward.

Invite the Right People to the Meeting and Feed Back to Them

Suppose you want to facilitate a brainstorming meeting with your team regarding a potential collaboration with another department, then it's worth considering inviting a few colleagues or key stakeholders from that department too. That way, you can keep all relevant parties in the loop from the outset rather than setting multiple meetings to convey the same information.

When deciding whom to invite, it is also crucial to establish in advance the input that you require. This means identifying the following people:

1. The best people to deliver or share inputs on specific information related to the agenda
2. The best people to be involved in the decisions that need to be taken during this meeting
3. The best people to implement the actions and decisions that arise

This way, all parties involved will understand why they are there, how they can contribute, and how they are involved. It will help you assemble the right participants for the purpose of meeting as well as for the subsequent actions that will need to be taken.

This practice requires knowing your organization inside out and building a sufficiently strong network across silos—particularly across departments. The one-on-one premeetings suggested previously can ensure that the less dominant voices, with relevant inputs, have an opportunity to express themselves.

After the meeting has concluded, the focus should shift to outcomes. Processing the information from the discussions and decisions reached during the meeting is critical for facilitating action. Create a concise yet comprehensive summary to disseminate to the relevant parties—the attendees as well as other stakeholders within and outside your organization. A well-structured meeting agenda and clearly defined purpose statement can aid in crafting a synopsis and formulating a clear follow-up plan.

Learning from Your Own and Others' Meetings

Identify colleagues renowned for their proficient meeting planning and ask to sit in on one or two of their meetings. This will help you observe how others structure and facilitate discussions. Often, the best way to hone your meetings skills is to pay attention to how your peers, boss, or someone with more experience leads meetings.

Soliciting participant feedback in your meetings can also help demonstrate that participants' points of view matter to you and makes them feel appreciated. This feedback can be combined with honest self-assessment—observing what subjects engaged your participants, what topics might have set off some triggers, and how they reacted to your input.

While practice makes perfect, developing your preparation, listening, and framing skills will transform your meetings into events that people look forward to, as channels for innovating, critical thinking, and fostering a positive work culture. This will ultimately benefit your personal career growth too. Moreover, if you share your learnings and best practices with the entire team, everyone will be able to access your valuable insights.

Now that you have an understanding of the core drivers of effective meetings and how to develop the associated skills, it is time to become the maestro of meetings. Think of it as conducting an orchestra—you are taking the central role of director and convener to give the musicians space for inspiration and ambition. Directing an orchestra, like conducting a meeting, is a skill learned from experience, a craft that can elevate your role and contribute to your success within the organization.

Biography

Soulaima Gourani is a Danish-Moroccan entrepreneur based in the Silicon Valley. She is the chief executive officer and cofounder of Happioh, a startup aiming to revolutionize how we run meetings. Soulaima was named to the Thinkers50 Radar Class of 2020.

Thomas Roulet is a professor of organizational sociology and leadership at the Judge Business School, University of Cambridge, and the cofounder of the King's Entrepreneurship Lab, at King's College, Cambridge. He was named to the Thinkers50 Radar Class of 2024.

References

Bhatti, K. and Roulet, T. (2023). Helping an employee in distress. *Harvard Business Review*, September-October, p. 38.

Gardner, W.L., Cogliser, C.C., Davis, K.M., and Dickens, M.P. (2011). Authentic leadership: A review of the literature and research agenda. *Leadership Quarterly*, 22(6), pp. 1120–1145.

Laker, B., Pereira, V., Malik, A., and Soga, L. (2022). Dear manager: You're holding too many meetings. *Harvard Business Review*. https://hbr.org/2022/03/dear-manager-youre-holding-too-many-meetings

Okhuysen, G.A. and Bechky, B.A. (2009). 10 coordination in organizations: An integrative perspective. *Academy of Management Annals*, 3(1), pp. 463–502.

Roulet, T. and Bhatti, K. (2023). Well-being intelligence: A skill set for the new world of work. *MIT Sloan Management Review*.

Subel, S., Stepanek, M., and Roulet, T. (2022). How shifts in remote behavior affect employee well-being. *MIT Sloan Management Review*, 63(3), pp. 1–6.

Swärd, A. (2016). Trust, reciprocity, and actions: The development of trust in temporary inter-organizational relations. *Organization Studies*, 37(12), pp. 1841–1860.

15

The UNITE Framework to Build Social Connection at Work

Constance Noonan Hadley
Founder, Institute for Life at Work and research associate professor at Boston University Questrom School of Business

Why Work Loneliness Should Be at the Top of Management Agendas

Work loneliness has been a widespread and growing issue for decades. An "epidemic of workplace loneliness" was declared in *Harvard Business Review* (Murthy 2017). In a study I conducted with Mark Mortensen in the fall of 2019, 76% of the global executives we surveyed reported having difficulty making connections with people on their team (Hadley and Mortensen 2021). Recent surveys continue to affirm the presence of loneliness in working populations (Cigna 2022; UK Government Department for Digital, Culture, Media & Sport 2023).

There are serious dangers to health and well-being associated with chronic loneliness as well as financial costs to employers (Bowers et al. 2022; Ducharme 2023; Holt-Lundstad 2018). In my research, I have found that loneliness is highly predictive of worse job satisfaction, lower engagement, and stronger intention to quit (Baym and Hadley 2023; Hadley, Marks, and Wright 2023). Other researchers have documented the damage to productivity and performance incurred by lonely workers (Ozcelik and Barsade 2018). From the medical community, we have learned about the dire physical consequences of loneliness, including increased rates of cardiovascular problems, diabetes, cancer, and dementia (Holt-Lunstad et al. 2015). The UK government estimated loneliness costs employers up to £9,900 per person per year (Peytrignet, Garforth-Bles, and Keohane 2020). In the United States, Cigna (2022) attributed a $154 billion annual price tag to the lost productivity caused by loneliness. It is no wonder that the US Surgeon General's Office has exhorted corporations to make addressing loneliness a strategic priority at all levels of the organization (US Surgeon General's Office 2023).

The Need for an Organizing Framework of Action

Given the extensive problems associated with work loneliness, it is critical to develop concrete and comprehensive solutions. In a literature review that Sarah Wright and I conducted for *The Cambridge Handbook of Loneliness*, we concluded that scholars have generated substantial knowledge of the measurement, antecedents, and consequences of work loneliness—but only fragmented clues as to effective interventions (Wright and Hadley in press). Books and articles aimed at managers, in contrast, contain more abundant advice for how to address loneliness in the workplace. For example, in *Harvard Business Review*, I described how gathering targeted data, cultivating psychological safety and inclusion, orchestrating empathy, redesigning team structures, and realigning incentives can reduce loneliness (Hadley 2021). However, none of the previous work we reviewed, including our own, offered a single comprehensive framework to guide an organization's human connection efforts.

Too often, attempts to build connectivity at work are done piecemeal, such as through ad hoc social events, or in an uncoordinated manner, such as initiatives emanating from human resources without business unit cooperation. Creating positive human connections at work requires a more holistic view and implementation strategy.

In this chapter, I introduce the UNITE framework, comprised of five primary actions to be led at the organizational and local levels: Understanding, Normalizing, Investing, Trialing, and Evaluating. I draw upon research to support these recommendations and point out potential pitfalls. Using this framework, I believe employers can bring their workforce together in a more coherent and sustainable manner.

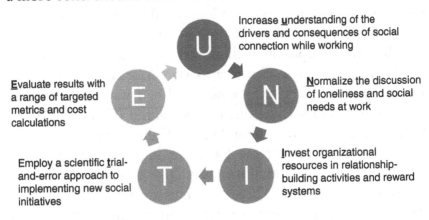

Increase understanding of the drivers and consequences of social connection while working

Normalize the discussion of loneliness and social needs at work

Invest organizational resources in relationship-building activities and reward systems

Employ a scientific trial-and-error approach to implementing new social initiatives

Evaluate results with a range of targeted metrics and cost calculations

Understanding

Given the prevalence of misconceptions about loneliness and social connectivity in a work context, the first step in the UNITE framework is to achieve accurate and nuanced *understanding* of these phenomena. To start building this knowledge base, employers can draw upon the references included in this chapter, starting with the UK Government's annual reports on loneliness and the US Surgeon General's advisory on social isolation and loneliness (UK Government Department for Digital, Culture, Media & Sport 2023; US Surgeon General's Office 2023). The key aspect of this step is to create a clear, evidence-based understanding of the problem and shared goals across the organization.

This step will likely involve some myth-busting. For example, we tend to think about lonely people as those sitting alone and looking miserable. In fact, lonely people often do not show their distress, especially in a work environment in which having unsatisfying relationships could be perceived as a sign of weakness or incompetence. Instead, coworkers may mask their loneliness under a veneer of cheerful smiles. Or they may mask in a different way, appearing disinterested in "useless" chitchat or socializing at work as a defense mechanism (Hadley and Wright in press). It is nearly impossible to tell who is lonely just by looking at them, especially because lonely individuals may not even recognize it in themselves (Hadley 2021).

Moreover, people often think assigning employees to teams will stave off loneliness. However, as Mark Mortensen and I found in our research, teams can be designed in a way that increases, rather than decreases, the threat of loneliness (Cigna 2022; UK Government Department for Digital, Culture, Media & Sport 2023). Factors that increase loneliness include teams that are short-lived or have shifting membership, modularized roles, and part-time contributors. These attributes are common in today's work teams (e.g., agile teams), yet they can undermine the sense of security and stability that facilitate personal relationships.

In addition to educating employees about the nature of work loneliness, it is critical in this step to establish a shared understanding of the value of coworker relationships. In my research with Nancy Baym, we found that connectivity to coworkers strongly correlated with job satisfaction in a sample of 836 office workers. In addition, higher connectivity predicted lower levels of burnout (Baym and Hadley 2023). In another article, my colleagues Katherine Kellogg, Erin Kelly, and I outlined the benefits of work relationships for innovation, productivity, and work-life balance (Kellogg, Kelly, and Hadley 2023). By the end of this first step in the UNITE framework, the organization should have established a common view on the drivers of high and low levels of social connection at work—and the importance of striving for positive relationships among colleagues.

Normalizing

The next step of the UNITE framework is to weave conversations about these issues into everyday work life to eradicate stigma, maintain emphasis, and collect robust data. This is the process of *normalizing* discussions about loneliness and social connection at work.

Loneliness is something that is rarely discussed in a work context because of the social stigma attached to it. Yet this is an experience that can affect anyone. For example, I have seen in my studies that people across industries and occupations experience a range of loneliness levels. Others have found that both entry-level positions and C-suite executives are prone to loneliness (Wright, Silard, and Bourgoin 2023). Despite its universality, people are unlikely to voluntarily disclose they are struggling to make connections at work. This is especially true for junior, new, and underrepresented minority employees, characteristics associated with higher levels of loneliness (Cigna 2020).

Normalizing conversations about loneliness and social connection requires the cooperation of leadership. If senior executives publicly share their personal experiences with loneliness as well as their commitment to prioritizing relationships, they will pave a path for others to follow. It can also be helpful to recruit workers from different levels and areas of the organization, employee resource groups, and external experts to communicate about these issues and facilitate open dialogue. Organizations may even choose to launch destigmatization campaigns, such as the "Let Us Talk Loneliness" initiative run in the United Kingdom (UK Government Department for Digital, Culture, Media & Sport 2023).

For the average employee, engaging in these conversations will require a high level of psychological safety—that is, a belief that they will not be punished or ostracized for taking an interpersonal risk. As I describe in an article with Mark Mortensen and Amy Edmondson, staying silent is rational in an environment characterized by fear or uncertainty (Hadley, Mortensen, and Edmondson 2023). Thus, it is critical to confirm that there will be no penalties for speaking up about being lonely or expressing dissatisfaction with relationships before encouraging employees to do so.

In this second step of the UNITE framework, organizations should make it a standard practice to discuss social experiences and preferences at regular intervals. If these conversations become part of the everyday discourse, then loneliness will become a shared and addressable problem rather than an individual experience shrouded in secrecy and shame.

Investing

Once the status quo and future goals have been established through open dialogue, action steps can be developed. Successful implementation will require *investing* time, effort, and money into targeted initiatives.

To provide some guidance to employers as to where to direct their efforts, Sarah Wright and I tested eight different ways companies could promote social cohesion, from happy hours to offsite retreats, in a sample of 1,000 office workers. Regardless of age, gender, job level, and many other characteristics we examined, we found the social opportunity favored by most people was a free communal lunch (Hadley and Wright in press). Ideally, these lunches would be offered on a routine (e.g., monthly) basis and be inclusive of all employees, including frontline and remote workers. Over time, hosting meals may constitute a significant investment on the part of employers, but our research indicates a funded lunch program would pay dividends in terms of building community. Many stories of connection told by our study participants involved the simple act of eating together with colleagues.

The second-most preferred option in our study was devoting the first 5–10 minutes of meetings to personal conversation. This practice is likely to be inexpensive monetarily, but it will require some sacrifice in time and short-term productivity. Meeting agendas would have to be adjusted and some additional planning may be necessary to structure and facilitate the chat time (e.g., use of ice breakers or games to prompt conversation). Yet here again, we believe the long-term gains are substantial.

If organizations are truly committed to reducing loneliness and increasing social connectivity, they must be willing to allocate resources toward these goals. This can take the form of setting up social opportunities, such as lunches and meeting chats, as well as providing rewards and incentives for people to participate. For example, in one study, Nancy Baym and I found that women reported giving social support to colleagues more often than their male counterparts did—yet men reported higher levels of organizational rewards (e.g,. promotions, bonuses) for their community-building efforts than did women (Baym and Hadley 2023). The best organizations will ensure there is equity built into the investments and returns associated with a socially connected workforce.

Trialing

Influencing the nature of relationships between adults in a work setting is complicated by the specific nature of the people and work environment involved. While existing research outlines some good general practices, *trialing* different options is likely to be necessary to achieve maximum success in any given organization. A growth mindset is core to the fourth step in the UNITE framework (Dweck 2006).

Unfortunately, many companies have declared rigid return-to-office rules under the guise of promoting collaboration and connection. Relationships, however, do not blossom simply from being in an office near someone. In a study with Sarah Wright, we found workers who worked full time in person were as likely to be lonely as those who only came to the office one or two days a week (Hadley and Wright in press). Thus, we encourage companies to treat their efforts to build connectivity as time-delimited trials rather than permanent mandates.

As important as it is to avoid permanent solutions without testing, it is essential to avoid too brief or one-off social experiments. Building relationships takes time and repeated touch-points between parties. A single lunch or happy hour is unlikely to generate high and widespread connection levels.

To guide the type and duration of trials to undertake, organizations should partner with their employees. Through surveys, interviews, and focus groups, new ideas and pilot tests can be co-developed. In addition to design principles, this process will elicit projections about the number of iterations or length of time necessary to see an effect of the pilot. Armed with these projections, organizations can prioritize and implement initiatives in a systematic manner.

It is important to accompany the experimentation process with senior sponsorship and blameless reporting to encourage widespread participation. Too often, culture-focused initiatives are relegated to the human resources department without the full knowledge or cooperation of the business units assigned to implement them. Again, if building a connected workforce is an organizational priority, then the entire organization should work toward achieving it. Accountability must be shared for community-building to work.

Evaluating

The final step in the UNITE framework is *evaluating* the impact of each social connection initiative. This is more difficult than it sounds because most organizations are not currently tracking loneliness or social connection at the level of precision required. To truly see progress against their goals, employers will likely need to pursue new metrics and monitoring systems.

For example, loneliness is a very particular phenomenon that cannot be captured with generic employee culture or engagement surveys. Organizations can use specific tools to assess loneliness levels in a population, such as the five-item Work Loneliness Scale (WLS) that Sarah Wright and I developed (Hadley and Wright in press). Conversely, organizations can ask about relational fulfillment and satisfaction with targeted questions that examine connections with different people and in remote versus office locations as we did in another study (Hadley, Marks, and Wright 2023). The key is to match the metrics to the hypotheses that underlie each experiment—these should be decided in advance to ensure data are properly collected.

Data collection can encompass a wide range of methodologies. The simplest tool is employee surveys, which can be a particularly useful way to capture the private sentiments and experiences of individuals. In addition, behavioral metrics can generate additional insight. For example, attendance at organization-sponsored events can be tracked to see if certain demographics and work groups are engaging in them. Employee retention, quitting, and transfer data can provide another form of feedback on the effectiveness of social initiatives. Artificial intelligence (AI) tools can be used as well. For example, AI meeting tools can unobtrusively evaluate participation in terms of turn-taking, social support gestures, and other forms of relational contributions.

Last, the evaluation step of the UNITE framework involves analyzing not only what is gained from trying something new but also what is likely to be lost if no action is taken. Research has shown us that the effects of loneliness worsen over time in terms of absenteeism, presenteeism, healthcare expenses, productivity losses, and turnover. For a fair estimate of returns on investment, it is critical to model those opportunity costs as well.

Final Thoughts

The UNITE framework is designed to provide a comprehensive and holistic approach to strengthening the social fabric of an organization. Each step builds upon the prior one, which means each step is essential for success and cannot be skipped. Yet the process of fostering relationships at work is more of a wheel than a ladder: there is no stopping point. As organizations and employees change, replenishment of energy and action is required at each step to keep up momentum. Moreover, the lessons from each trial initiative should be incorporated into the next one. Thus, the practices of understanding, normalizing, investing, trialing, and evaluating must continue for as long as the organization wants to shape and enhance the relational climate at work.

Biography

Founder and chief scientist of the Institute for Life at Work, Constance (Connie) Noonan Hadley is an organizational psychologist. She is also a research associate professor in the Management and Organizations Department at Boston University Questrom School of Business. Connie regularly serves as a consulting researcher at Microsoft Research Lab, working on projects relating to the future of work. Previously, she worked in management consulting at McKinsey & Company, and in marketing and operations at General Mills, Inc. Connie is a member of the Thinkers50 Radar Class of 2024.

References

Baym, N. and Hadley, C. N. (2023, May 15). The unequal rewards of peer support at work. *MIT Sloan Management Review.* https://sloanreview.mit .edu/article/the-unequal-rewards-of-peer-support-at-work

Bowers, A., Wu, J., Lustig, S., and Nemecek, D. (2022). Loneliness influences avoidable absenteeism and turnover intention reported by adult workers in the United States. *Journal of Organizational Effectiveness: People and Performance,* 9(2), pp. 312–335. 10.1108/JOEPP-03-2021-0076

Cigna. (2022). The loneliness epidemic persists: A post-pandemic look at the state of loneliness among US adults. *Cigna.* https://newsroom.cigna.com/ loneliness-epidemic-persists-post-pandemic-look

Ducharme, L. (2023, April 26). Why work friends are crucial for your health. *Time.* https://time.com/6274502/work-friends-health-benefits

Dweck, C. S. (2006). *Mindset: The new psychology of success.* Random House.

Hadley, C. (2021, June 9). Employees are lonelier than ever. Here's how employers can help. *Harvard Business Review.* https://hbr.org/2021/06/ employees-are-lonelier-than-ever-heres-how-employers-can-help

Hadley, C. N., Marks, B., and Wright, S. (2023, February 9). Research: How coworking spaces impact employee well-being. *Harvard Business Review.* https:// hbr.org/2023/02/research-how-coworking-spaces-impact-employee-well-being

Hadley, C. N. and Mortensen, M. (2021, Winter). Are your team members lonely? *MIT Sloan Management Review.* https://sloanreview.mit.edu/article/ are-your-team-members-lonely

Hadley, C. N., Mortensen, M., and Edmondson, A. (2023, April 25). Make it safe for employees to speak up—especially in risky times. *Harvard Business Review.* https://hbr.org/2023/04/make-it-safe-for-employees-to-speak-up-especially-in-risky-times

Hadley, C. N. and Wright, S. L. (in press). Overcoming loneliness at work: What managers need to know. *Harvard Business Review.*

Holt-Lundstad, J. (2018). Fostering social connection in the workplace. *American Journal of Health Promotion.* https://journals.sagepub.com/doi/ pdf/10.1177/0890117118776735a

Holt-Lunstad, J., Smith, T., Baker, M., Harris, T., and Stephenson, D. (2015). Loneliness and social isolation as risk factors for mortality: A meta-analytic review. *Perspectives on Psychological Science: A Journal of the Association for Psychological Science.* 10.1177/1745691614568352

Kellogg, K. C., Kelly, E. L., and Hadley, C. N. (2023, March 5). Why neglecting work relationships can sabotage innovation and productivity, according to research. *Fast Company.* https://www.fastcompany.com/90856240/managing-hybrid-teams-network-ties

Murthy, V. (2017). Work and the loneliness epidemic. *Harvard Business Review.* https://hbr.org/2017/09/work-and-the-loneliness-epidemic

Ozcelik, H. and Barsade, S. (2018). No employee is an island: Workplace loneliness and job performance. *Academy of Management Journal.* https://journals.aom.org/doi/abs/10.5465/amj.2015.1066

Peytrignet, S., Garforth-Bles, S., and Keohane, K. (2020). Loneliness monetisation report: Analysis for the Department for Digital, Culture, Media, & Sport. *GOV.UK.* https://assets.publishing.service.gov.uk/government/uploads/system/uploads/attachment_data/file/963077/Loneliness_monetisation_report_V2.pdf

UK Government Department for Digital, Culture, Media & Sport. (2023). Employers and loneliness report. *GOV.UK.* https://www.gov.uk/government/publications/loneliness-annual-report-the-fourth-year/tackling-loneliness-annual-report-march-2023-the-fourth-year

US Surgeon General's Office. (2023). Our epidemic of loneliness and isolation: The US Surgeon General's advisory on the healing effects of social connection and community. *US Department of Health and Human Services.* https://www.hhs.gov/sites/default/files/surgeon-general-social-connection-advisory.pdf

Wright, S. L. and Hadley, C. N. (in press). Work loneliness. In D. Perlman, D. W. Russell, and C. E. Cutrona (Eds.). *The Cambridge Handbook of Loneliness: Theory, Research and Interventions.* Cambridge University Press.

Wright, S., Silard, A., and Bourgoin, A. (2023). Publicly invulnerable, privately lonely: How the unique individual and structural characteristics of their organizational role contribute to CEO loneliness. In P. D. Harms and C.-H. Chang (Eds.). *Stress and well-being at the strategic level* (Vol. 21, pp. 65–79). Emerald Publishing Limited.

16

Devotion and Detachment

The Yin-Yang Equilibrium for Transformative Growth

Faisal Hoque
Founder of Shadoka and NextChapter

In my book, *Everything Connects: Cultivating Mindfulness, Creativity, and Sustainability*, I offer a comprehensive framework that integrates the principles of mindfulness, creativity, and innovation. The book details how Devotion, characterized by a deep commitment to one's continuous growth, and Detachment, the ability to maintain an objective perspective free from the constraints of preconceptions, are essential for transformational and sustainable growth.

Someone can be fully devoted to their work or purpose—investing time, energy, and passion—while also practicing detachment, which allows for adaptability and clear decision-making, while remaining open to new possibilities.

This balance of devotion and detachment is key to effective human connection.

Devotion

In Sanskrit and Bengali, devotion is referred to as "Bhakti" (ভক্তি) and "সাধনা" (sadhana), respectively. Bengali polymath and Nobel laureate Rabindranath Tagore defines "sadhana" as the spiritual practice or discipline aimed at the realization of life and attainment of infinite possibilities. True devotion involves a continuous, mindful effort toward growth and improvement, whether in personal capacities, leadership, or innovation. Devotion is about the journey of growth, whereas mindfulness plays a crucial role in understanding oneself and navigating challenges.

Detachment

Referred to as "Moksha" (মোক্ষ) in Sanskrit and "মোক্ষ" (mokkho) in Bengali. The philosophy of detachment, or nonattachment, has its origins in various Eastern religious and philosophical traditions. In Stoicism, a school of Hellenistic philosophy, detachment is primarily about emotional resilience and cultivation of an inner tranquility that remains undisturbed by external circumstances. Detachment is about making a conscious effort not to let adversity, pain, emotions, or attachments to outcomes control us. For leadership and personal growth, detachment is a pathway to fostering sustainable growth. It allows us to maintain a clear perspective, free from the biases and limitations that attachments can impose, thereby enabling more objective decision-making and resilience in the face of challenges.

True human connection happens when devotion's passion is balanced by detachment's wisdom.

Devotion provides the drive to impact humanity positively, while detachment offers the perspective to do so effectively. This integration allows us to be fully engaged yet adaptable, caring yet grounded, persistent yet embracing of change.

In essence, devotion fosters authentic engagement and service to others, while detachment provides the clarity and resilience to sustain those efforts amidst life's complexities. Balancing these forces enables a profound connection with the shared human experience.

Devotion and detachment are the yin and yang of sustainable growth. In mastering this delicate interplay, we unlock the power to lead our organizations fearlessly into the future.

This balance enables individuals and organizations to engage deeply with their work and life while also being able to handle the unpredictability and changes that inevitably occur.

Devotion as the Driving Force

Devotion in Practice
Example: Community Health Improvement

Context: A nonprofit organization focused on improving community health faced challenges in reaching underserved populations. The executive director, committed to a devotion-driven leadership approach, recognized the need for innovative strategies to engage with the community and address health disparities.

Actions: The executive director introduced a community partnership program, collaborating with local organizations, healthcare providers, and residents to identify key health issues and develop targeted interventions. This included mobile health clinics, health education workshops, and support groups for chronic disease management. The executive director's dedication to the community's well-being and her hands-on involvement in the programs served as a powerful motivator for the staff and volunteers.

Outcome: The partnership program led to improved health outcomes in the community, with increased access to health-care services and higher rates of disease prevention and management. The nonprofit's visibility and impact grew, attracting additional funding and support. The executive director's devotion to the mission and her ability to engage and mobilize diverse stakeholders showcased the effective-ness of devotion-driven leadership in achieving meaningful social change.

Devotion is synonymous with mindfulness—a deep, unwaver-ing commitment to one's work, personal development, and the collective mission of the organization (Hoque 2014a). It is the passionate pursuit of excellence, characterized by a con-tinuous mindset focused on learning and a relentless effort to achieve goals. Devotion in leadership manifests itself as the following:

- Engagement: Leaders who are devoted fully immerse them-selves in their roles, demonstrating genuine interest in their team's development and well-being (Salaman 2022).
- Persistence: Devotion equips leaders with the resilience to persevere through challenges, maintaining focus on the vision and objectives of the organization (Kempton 2021).
- Mindfulness: By being present and attentive, devoted lead-ers can spark creativity and drive innovation within their teams (Hoque 2022).

Detachment for Clarity and Adaptability

Detachment in Practice
Example: Crisis Management in a Multinational
Corporation

Context: A multinational corporation faced a significant crisis when one of its products was found to have safety issues, leading to public backlash and legal challenges. The chief executive officer (CEO), known for her detachment-driven leadership style, was tasked with navigating the company through this tumultuous period.

Actions: Instead of reacting defensively or letting emotions dictate the company's response, the CEO approached the situation with a calm and detached mindset. She assembled a cross-functional crisis management team, encouraging open dialogue and critical thinking to assess the situation from multiple perspectives. By maintaining emotional detachment, she was able to make difficult decisions, such as implementing a global product recall and launching a transparent communication campaign to address consumer concerns.

Outcome: The company's swift and thoughtful response helped to mitigate the damage to its reputation and restore trust with consumers. The CEO's ability to remain detached and objective under pressure enabled her to lead the company through the crisis effectively, demonstrating the value of detachment in crisis management and decision-making.

Detachment, on the other hand, is the ability to maintain an emotional distance from the outcomes of one's actions, allowing for a more objective and balanced perspective (Karaman 2021). It is not disinterest or indifference but a cultivation of a sense of objectivity, neutrality, and fairness. Detachment enables leaders to accomplish the following:

- Embrace change: Leaders who practice detachment can adapt to change with grace, understanding that outcomes are transient, and that true value lies in the journey and growth it fosters (Salaman 2022).
- Make informed decisions: Detachment allows leaders to view situations more objectively, making decisions that are not clouded by personal biases or emotions (Karaman 2021).
- Reduce stress: By not being consumed by the need for control, leaders can navigate pressures without becoming overwhelmed, contributing to better decision-making and well-being (Hoque 2014b).

The Synergy of Devotion and Detachment

The synergy between devotion and detachment is essential for leadership growth. Devotion provides the energy and commitment necessary to lead with passion and purpose, while detachment offers the perspective needed to lead with wisdom and adaptability. Together, they enable leaders to do the following:

- Balance commitment and objectivity: Leaders must be committed to their roles while also being able to step back and view situations with clarity. This balance allows them to lead with passion and adapt when necessary (Hoque 2022; Mattone 2023).
- Cultivate a supportive culture: By demonstrating both devotion and detachment, leaders can create a culture where team

members feel valued for their efforts and are encouraged to innovate and take risks (Salaman 2022).

- Lead authentically: The combination of self-awareness (devotion) and maintaining a broader perspective (detachment) enables leaders to act authentically, inspiring trust and loyalty among their followers (Kempton 2021).

To further illustrate the synergy of devotion and detachment in leadership, let's explore additional aspects of the hypothetical case study involving MedCorp and its CEO, Jane. By delving deeper into the practical applications and challenges faced, we can gain a more comprehensive understanding of how these two forces can be effectively integrated to drive organizational growth and transformation.

Fostering a Culture of Innovation

Jane recognized that encouraging a culture of innovation was crucial for MedCorp to stay ahead in the rapidly evolving health-care landscape. Her devotion to the organization's mission fueled her commitment to continuous improvement and her willingness to embrace new ideas and technologies.

However, Jane also understood the importance of detachment in the innovation process. She encouraged her team to approach challenges with an open mind, detaching from preconceived notions and traditional ways of thinking. This mindset allowed for more creative problem-solving and the exploration of unconventional solutions.

Jane implemented various initiatives to cultivate an innovative culture:

1. Idea generation sessions: Regular brainstorming sessions were held, where employees from different departments could share their ideas and perspectives without fear of judgment

or criticism. Jane's detached approach created a safe space for open dialogue and collaboration.

2. Innovation incubator: MedCorp established an innovation incubator, where cross-functional teams could work on developing and testing new healthcare solutions. Jane's devotion to the mission ensured that these initiatives remained aligned with the organization's core values and goals.

3. Partnerships and collaborations: Jane actively sought partnerships with research institutions, technology companies, and other healthcare organizations. Her detachment from traditional boundaries allowed MedCorp to tap into diverse expertise and resources, fostering a spirit of co-creation and shared learning.

Navigating Resistance to Change

Despite Jane's efforts, the transformational change process at MedCorp faced resistance from some stakeholders, including employees who were comfortable with the status quo and skeptical of the proposed changes. Jane's ability to balance devotion and detachment was crucial in addressing these challenges.

1. Empathy and understanding: Jane's devotion to her team and the organization's mission enabled her to approach resistance with empathy and understanding. She acknowledged the emotional impact of change and provided support and resources to help employees navigate the transition.

2. Clear communication: Jane's detachment allowed her to communicate the rationale for change objectively and transparently. She presented data-driven evidence and explained long-term benefits for the organization, patients, and employees.

3. Inclusive decision-making: While maintaining a clear vision, Jane remained open to feedback and input from stakeholders.

Her detachment enabled her to consider diverse perspectives and adjust change initiatives when necessary, fostering a sense of shared ownership and buy-in.

4. Leading by example: Jane's devotion to the mission and her commitment to personal growth inspired her team. She led by example, embracing change and continuously learning and adapting, demonstrating the value of detachment in the face of uncertainty.

Cultivating Resilience and Sustainability

The synergy of devotion and detachment also played a crucial role in cultivating resilience and sustainability within MedCorp. Jane's devotion to the organization's mission and her team's well-being drove her commitment to creating a supportive and nurturing environment.

1. Work-life balance: Jane recognized the importance of work-life balance and encouraged her employees to prioritize self-care and personal growth. Her detachment from the notion that success is solely defined by work allowed her to promote a healthy and sustainable work culture.

2. Continuous learning and development: Jane invested in professional development programs and opportunities for her employees, fostering a culture of continuous learning. Her devotion to personal growth and her detachment from rigid hierarchies empowered employees to take ownership of their development.

3. Succession planning: With a long-term perspective, Jane implemented a robust succession planning process. Her detachment from personal biases and emotional attachments ensured that the selection of future leaders was based on merit and alignment with the organization's values and goals.

4. Environmental sustainability: Aligning with MedCorp's mission of promoting well-being, Jane championed initiatives to reduce the organization's environmental footprint. Her detachment from short-term financial considerations and her devotion to creating a healthier future enabled MedCorp to implement sustainable practices and contribute to the broader community.

By integrating devotion and detachment, Jane was able to navigate the complexities of transformational change, foster a culture of innovation, address resistance, and cultivate resilience and sustainability within MedCorp. This balanced approach not only will enable the organization to thrive in the present but also lay the foundation for long-term success and impact in the healthcare industry.

Key Takeaways: Practical Application for Leaders

To integrate devotion and detachment in work and life, leaders should practice the following:

- Mindfulness: Engage in daily mindfulness exercises to cultivate devotion and presence in leadership activities (Hoque 2022).
- Reflectiveness: Regularly reflect on personal values and the impact of leadership decisions, fostering a deeper connection with oneself and others (Hoque 2014a).
- Emotional intelligence: Develop emotional intelligence to manage personal emotions and understand the emotions of others, enhancing detachment (Salaman 2022).
- Strategic prioritization: Prioritize tasks and responsibilities, focusing on what is most important while detaching from less critical issues (Echelon Front 2024).

The interplay between devotion and detachment is a powerful framework for transformative growth for any leader. By embracing these principles and practices, leaders can drive their organizations toward creativity, innovation, and sustainability, all while maintaining a sense of inner peace and adaptability in the face of constant change.

Biography

Faisal Hoque is an entrepreneur, technology innovator, and founder of Shadoka, NextChapter, and other companies. He also serves as an innovation leader for CACI, a company focused on US national security. Faisal is a three-time-winning founder and CEO of Deloitte Technology Fast 50 and Fast 500™ awards and a #1 *Wall Street Journal* bestselling author for his books: *REINVENT, Everything Connects,* and *LIFT*. He has developed more than 20 commercial platforms and worked with GE, MasterCard, American Express, Home Depot, PepsiCo, IBM, Chase, US Department of Defense, and the Department of Homeland Security. Faisal volunteers for several organizations, including MIT IDEAS Social Innovation Program. He is also a contributor at IMD, and in 2023 was shortlisted for the Thinkers50 Strategy Award.

References

Echelon Front. (2024). *The power of detachment.* https://echelonfront.com/the-power-of-detachment

Hoque, F. and Baer, D. (2022). *Everything connects.* Greenleaf Book Group.

Hoque, F. (2014a). *9 Essential principles to create, innovate, and sustain.* https://faisalhoque.com/9-essential-principles-to-create-lead-and-sustain

Hoque, F. (2014b). *Why connecting with yourself matters.* https://faisalhoque.com/why-connecting-with-yourself-matters/

Hoque, F. (2022). *How mindfulness cultivates creativity and innovation.* https://faisalhoque.com/how-mindfulness-cultivates-creativity-and-innovation

Karaman, P. (2021). *Detachment—A practice to unlock your leadership potential.* https://www.linkedin.com/pulse/detachment-practice-unlock-your-leadership-pinar-karaman

Kempton, S. (2021). *The five stages of detachment: Learning to let go.* https://www.yogajournal.com/yoga-101/spirituality/practice-detachment

Mattone, J. (2023). *The disciple leader: Balancing loyalty and independence for effective leadership.* https://johnmattone.com/blog/the-disciple-leader-balancing-loyalty-and-independence-for-effective-leadership

Salaman, R. (2022). *Faisal Hoque on transformational leadership: Expert interview.* https://www.mindtools.com/blog/faisal-hoque-transformational-leadership-expert-interview

IV

Connecting Culture

17

Win-Win-Win

When Human Purpose Meets Platform Thinking

Daniel Trabucchi
*Senior assistant professor of platform thinking at the
School of Management, Politecnico di Milano*

Tommaso Buganza
*Full professor of leadership and innovation at the
School of Management, Politecnico di Milano*

What Is Platform Thinking?

Platforms pervade our daily lives in the twenty-first century. We use them to support most of our daily activities, from listening to music through Spotify and renting movies on Prime Video, and from managing business relations through Microsoft Teams to looking for the best match on Tinder.

The word "platform" has entered our common language. We talk about "digital platforms," "institutional platforms," and even "political platforms," not to mention the "Big Techs" as platforms, and so on. In this chapter, we'll consider platforms as a specific value creation model, which means considering all those organizations that create value through mechanisms based on two main pillars: the presence of (at least) *two mutually dependent "sides" of customers* and the presence of cross-side *network externalities*. This last point, in particular, means that the more customers are on one side, the more value customers perceive on the other side (Parker and Van Alstyne 2005).

Let us make it clearer with an example. Airbnb is probably one of the flagship cases that supported this value creation model's diffusion (and awareness). Airbnb has two sets of customers: the travelers, representing the "demand side," and the hosts, representing the "supply side." The more travelers join Airbnb to find a place to sleep, the greater value hosts will perceive in joining the platform, having more possible "matches" and vice versa.

Airbnb represents a specific type of platform: a "transactional platform" (Cusumano et al. 2019). See Figure 17.1. Although other types of platform architectures exist (Trabucchi and Buganza 2022; Trabucchi and Buganza 2023), in this chapter, we will focus only on this type of platform.

The core mechanism of "transactional platforms" is the chance to reduce frictions in the market while enabling two sides to easily find each other by supporting the transaction, setting up a trustworthy environment, relying on data to enhance the matchmaking, and setting up a proper community feeling that

Travelers
(Demand side)

Airbnb

Hosts
(Supply side)

Figure 17.1   Airbnb as a "transactional platform."

facilitates the birth and exploitation of the cross-side network externalities (Trabucchi et al. 2022). Thinking back to Airbnb, for example, the platform manages the financial transaction and holds the money during the stay to protect both customers, sets up a review system to let the system award positive behaviors, uses data to suggest ideal prices, and pushes the idea of "belong anywhere" as a vision to create an engaged community.

Many other services we use almost daily share this value creation model: Uber, Booking.com, Deliveroo, eBay, and Amazon, to name a few. Not surprisingly (considering our society's tendency to oversimplify), their digital nature creates a simple (but wrong) equation in the minds of many: platforms = digital.

It is easy to prove this equation wrong; transactional platforms date back to when digital technologies were not even conceivable. As far back as 3000 years BC, Persian markets started aggregating sellers to convince more buyers to go to the same physical place. Unlike what we might think, digital technologies are not the enablers for transactional platforms but rather an incredible catalyst that accelerates and magnifies them. Platforms leverage the network's externalities and, thus, the number of actors involved. It is easy to see that a physical market can have thousands of customers, while in digital markets like Amazon, the customers can easily scale up to billions.

Platforms are mechanisms that allow people (and we stress people rather than customers) to meet each other and trigger a transaction between them. What if we shift the focus to the meaning they can perceive instead of focusing on the "transaction" they can have? What if we switch our attention from business to human connections?

We will examine this unexplored field, leveraging what we call "Platform Thinking": the ability to use platforms as glasses to read the reality around us and identify platform-based opportunities to foster innovation. Therefore, we will apply Platform Thinking to a human platform case: Thinkers50.

Thinkers50 as a Human Platform

Thinkers50 started in 2001 with a clear mission: to identify, rank, and share the leading management ideas of our age, with a hopeful undertone that these ideas could make a positive difference in the world.

The journey of Thinkers50 is a story of evolution, starting from a simple yet ambitious vision by Des Dearlove and Stuart Crainer. Des and Stuart, journalists specialized in management thinking, saw an opportunity in the late 1990s to sift through the torrent of management books flooding the market. Des recalls: "[For busy managers], *there was so much management literature that it was bewildering. Something else was going on, too—a creeping cynicism about management itself. Parts of the business press saw the new ideas as fads—smoke and mirrors. Some of them were, of course. But bracketing them all the same wasn't helpful. We wanted to shine a light on the good stuff to help managers tell the nuggets from the fool's gold.*"

They wanted to guide managers toward the most impactful ideas, akin to a consumer guide for management thinking. This was the inception phase, a time of building and nurturing a community driven by a shared sense of purpose, collaboration, and generosity. Over the years, it grew, moving from just the ranking to a set of initiatives—the awards, the business forums, special events with business schools, and much more—linked by the same goal: sharing leading management ideas.

The human quality of the people they attracted created a space where ideas could flourish and spread, and this was possible thanks to the early "Thinkers" who promoted and sustained a positive, virtuous culture of pure collaboration (see Figure 17.2). As Stuart says: "*We originally created the ranking to help managers identify the best management ideas, but what was becoming increasingly clear was how much people value being part of a community. In celebrating management thinking, we created a movement. We saw a*

Thinkers

Figure 17.2   Thinkers50 as a platform: Step 1

*huge appetite and excitement among the thinkers themselves to be part
of something bigger, something collegial and focused on helping society.
We had inadvertently tapped into something very powerful."*

As Thinkers50 grew, it naturally started attracting the attention of various partners like publishers. These early collaborators were drawn to the community for the opportunity to connect with thought leaders and because they shared the vision of making a meaningful impact through management ideas.

Thinkers50 added a new task to the community nurturing: Des and Stuart began to facilitate connections between Thinkers on one side and other stakeholders on the other. This shift morphed Thinkers50 into a platform that facilitates the matches between two sides. It is a strange kind of platform, though, not driven by transactional relationships but by a shared commitment to spreading impactful ideas. Such a strong community, sharing the vision of generosity, attracted partners keen to participate in the movement. The earlier partners, as mentioned, were mainly publishers and other players that could help amplify the Thinkers' ideas; we'll call them the "Amplifiers" of the emerging platform (see Figure 17.3).

Amplifiers   Thinkers

Figure 17.3   Thinkers50 as a platform: Step 2

Over the years, other players like speaking bureaus, agents, or publicists joined this side. This phase marked the beginning of Thinkers50's expansion beyond a community to a platform where interactions between thinkers and partners could happen more organically.

And it's not just Amplifiers; other types of actors started looking at the community. We are talking about companies looking to implement new, compelling management ideas. Their aim is not to spread Thinkers' ideas but to use those ideas to improve their businesses in real life, to make the world a better place for their employees and final customers. We call the leaders of these organizations "Doers": organizations, companies, consultancy firms, and even charitable foundations, committing to transforming ideas into practice.

This third phase in Thinkers50's evolution introduced a more formal approach, with emerging Amplifiers and Doers beginning to have a wider presence in the platform's life, by partnering, for example, on specific awards or lists, or creating new events within the Thinkers50 ecosystem (see Figure 17.4).

This phase is characterized by a concerted effort to bridge the gap between thought and action. The platform began to serve not just as a space for recognizing and sharing ideas but also as a meeting arena where thinkers and doers could come together to create

Figure 17.4 Thinkers50 as a platform: Step 3

real-world impact. This ecosystem, as it became, was built on the principles of generosity, trust, and a collective desire to drive positive change through management practices. Once again, the culture is driven by the most influential people in the community who open paths and lead by example, continuing to promote a virtuous culture. It's not just about the dissemination of ideas but about creating a tangible impact, making the principles and insights actionable in the corporate and organizational landscape.

Over the years, the Thinkers50 community—despite the limited number of spots up for grabs in a biennial ranking—grew significantly. Indeed, the introduction of the Hall of Fame in 2013 and the Radar List in 2014 promoted a virtuous dynamic cycle to keep the community alive, growing, and evolving with the world around.

Obviously, as the ecosystem gets wider, this creates an opportunity for some Amplifiers, Doers, or Thinkers to join it for predominantly transactional purposes. These opportunities are represented by the enlargement of the circles in Figure 17.5, with the outer rings representing the activity of people or organizations less aligned with the overall culture. This is creating a new challenge for the Thinkers50 Platform: building an ecosystem that maintains the culture of collaboration and generosity.

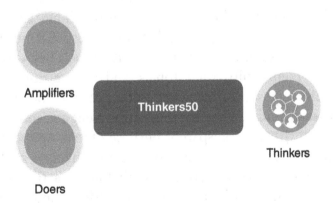

Figure 17.5 Thinkers50 as a platform: Step 4

Once again, the answer lies in the purpose and in the role of the human factor. Once a system is big enough, it can model the behaviors it wants to encapsulate, as we see with the role of the reviews on Airbnb. As Des said to us: "*It only works if it's win, win, win.*" There must be a valuable human connection between the Thinker and the Doer, but only if this human connection has channels to create a better world can the Thinkers50 Platform achieve its purpose, and the connection becomes meaningful: win, win, win. When this works, business transactions are a happy by-product of a healthy system and not its main goal.

Throughout these phases, the role of Des and Stuart has been pivotal. Monika Kosman, who joined in 2019, bringing a younger perspective and excellent marketing and commercial instincts to the team, has also been increasingly important in building the Thinkers50 community. The insights and stewardship of Des, Stuart, and Monika helped navigate Thinkers50 through its growth, ensuring that the community's foundational values—collaboration, generosity, and a noncompetitive spirit—remain intact.

Now, they act as a platform. On the one hand, they steer and help the community grow, while on the other hand, they connect with the Doers, facilitating collaborations and joint projects. In reality, however, they do a lot more than this. They are not just passive actors, making the matching frictionless and more probable. They act as human connection facilitators. They know people in the community, their topics, and their attitudes. They proactively suggest possible matches; they can facilitate meetings and suggest agendas. They are the platform engine, and they fuel this engine with the transparent purpose of making the world a better place. A match between Doers and Thinkers is a win-win. A purposeful match triggered by their human active role also fulfills the purpose of Thinkers50 as a platform and becomes a win-win-win.

Under the guidance of Des and Stuart, Thinkers50 hasn't just grown in size but also in influence, becoming a global beacon for those seeking to understand and implement the best management practices. The story of Thinkers50 is a testament to the power of ideas and the impact of a community united by a common goal: to improve the world through better management thinking and practice . . . indeed, possibly through platform thinking.

From Business Transactions to Human Connections

We usually link platforms and digital technology, but the reality is more complex. We are surrounded by multiple unconventional platforms that are based not on a digital flow but on physical exchanges of goods, services, knowledge, or relationships of which Thinkers50 is a perfect example. A pure community that evolved into a platform, an ecosystem of Thinkers, Doers, and Amplifiers, exchanging purposeful human connections that share the same view: management ideas can have a positive impact in the world.

This story of the comparison between traditional digital platforms and "human platforms" leaves us with three takeaways that we see emerging from comparing traditional digital transactional platforms and "human platforms":

1. *From "value proposition" to "culture"*
   One of the first critical elements of any successful digital platform is the proper design of multiple value propositions able to engage all sides in a coherent ecosystem (Muzellec et al. 2015). "Belong anywhere," the slogan of Airbnb, is a good example (Gallagher 2017). Moving onto human platforms, something changes. It's not just a proposition. When talking about people and not about customers, the right word is "culture."

Human platforms should nurture and model the culture they want to promote in their community. A culture is a set of norms, lived, not just written, that members of a community learn to recognize and promote, usually inspired by influential members like Des and Stuart, as well as leading Thinkers like Michael Porter, Clayton Christensen, C.K. Prahalad, and now Amy Edmonson. Even more, this culture has kept the community alive, welcoming the contributions, ideas, and energy of the "next generation" that emerged through the Radar classes, such as Ruth Gotian, with her work to nurture a real spirit of community for the newcomers.

Unlike a value proposition, though, cultures are lived, their purpose is more than transactional, and culture is subject to human beings' natural evolutions. This makes the system incredibly fragile, requiring many caring activities, as Des and Stuart continuously do, but also incredibly powerful because no rules can guide behaviors better than the social norms people truly believe in.

2. *From transactions to purpose*

Platform-based value creation models are mostly renowned for their ability to scale, gather gigantic financial evaluations, and generate incredible profits from mass transactions. This is one interpretation of platforms, but it is just one. We can have platforms with different purposes, like social impact or environmental sustainability (Gulati 2022). When entering a human platform, the purpose moves from a possible perspective to an essential element. "*To identify, rank, and share the leading management ideas of our age, with a hopeful undertone that these ideas could make a positive difference in the world*" is guiding the whole system. The direction is clear: to have a positive impact on the world. Money can be a happy by-product, not the engine. We move from a system that tends to maximize profit from a central perspective to a system so fragile that can exist and resist only if everybody wins: "win-win-win."

3. *From algorithms to human facilitation*

The core value driver of any (transactional) digital platform is matchmaking, which, given the numerosity of alternatives on both sides, is typically based on an algorithm (Parker et al. 2016). Numbers here are the key. (Traditional) platforms scale so quickly that possible matches become uncountable, requiring algorithms to manage them but also giving space to the perception of personalization within fixed variables. A typical example is Spotify, which built its early value proposition of getting you the best song given your mood rather than asking you what you want to listen to.

Well, human platforms are different. We cannot have, and don't want to have, algorithms to match humans in real life, like at the biennial Thinkers50 Gala. The game is just different. Numbers are different. But also, complexity is different. The variables to be considered are personality, area of expertise, talent, phase of the career, purpose drive, and many others. An algorithm cannot capture all the heterogeneity of the physical world of whispered words, sparkles in the eyes, and body language. If we want to stay true to the human dimension and the culture we talk about, we need humans to drive the match. We need humans to go more in-depth. Algorithms leave the space to people like Des and Stuart, who know the community in depth and can act as human facilitators, playing the role that is usually given to technology. See Table 17.1.

Platforms are lenses to view reality. Platforms are ways to read the value-creation mechanisms around us (Trabucchi et al. 2021). Platforms can also be a way to read (some) of the human connections around us. This story teaches us that when a platform is less

Table 17.1   From Digital (Transactional) Platforms
to Human Platforms

Digital (Transactional) Platforms	Human Platforms
From	*To*
Value Proposition	Culture
Transactions	Purpose
Algorithms	Human Connections

about numbers, less about scaling. When a platform, once the numbers decrease, moves from the digital to the physical space, we have one ultimate opportunity: the chance to have in-depth, meaningful human relations that brilliant platforms like Thinkers50 can nurture.

Biography

Daniel Trabucchi and Tommaso Buganza are the authors of *Platform Thinking: READ the Past. WRITE the Future* (Business Expert Press, 2023). They are members of the Thinkers50 Radar Class of 2024. Daniel is senior assistant professor and Tommaso a full professor of leadership and innovation at the School of Management, Politecnico di Milano. Daniel also serves as a senior researcher in the LEADIN'Lab, the Laboratory for Leadership, Design, and Innovation, which was cofounded by Tommaso.

Daniel and Tommaso are also joint founders of Symplatform, a yearly international conference on digital platforms that aims to match scholars and practitioners. They are cofounders and scientific directors of the Platform Thinking HUB, a community of innovation leaders focusing on platforms. Daniel is the scientific director of IDeaLs, a global research platform cofounded by Tommaso and the Politecnico di Milano.

References

Cusumano, M. A., Gawer, A., and Yoffie, D. B. (2019). *The business of platforms: Strategy in the age of digital competition, innovation, and power* (Vol. 320). New York: Harper Business.

Gallagher, L. (2017). *The Airbnb story: How three guys disrupted an industry, made billions of dollars . . . and plenty of enemies*. Random House.

Gulati, R. (2022). *Deep purpose: The heart and soul of high-performance companies*. Penguin UK.

Muzellec, L., Ronteau, S., and Lambkin, M. (2015). Two-sided internet platforms: A business model lifecycle perspective. *Industrial Marketing Management*, 45, pp. 139–150.

Parker, G. G. and Van Alstyne, M. W. (2005). Two-sided network effects: A theory of information product design. *Management Science*, 51(10), pp. 1494–1504.

Parker, G. G., Van Alstyne, M. W., and Choudary, S. P. (2016). *Platform revolution: How networked markets are transforming the economy and how to make them work for you*. WW Norton & Company.

Trabucchi, D. and Buganza, T. (2022). Landlords with no lands: A systematic literature review on hybrid multi-sided platforms and platform thinking. *European Journal of Innovation Management*, 25(6), pp. 64–96.

Trabucchi, D. and Buganza, T. (2023). *Platform thinking: Read the past. Write the future*. Business Expert Press.

Trabucchi, D., Sanasi, S., Ghezzi, A., and Buganza, T. (2021). Idle asset hunters—the secret of multi-sided platforms. *Research-Technology Management*, 64(1), pp. 33–42.

Trabucchi, D., Muzellec, L., Ronteau, S., and Buganza, T. (2022). The platforms' DNA: Drivers of value creation in digital two-sided platforms. *Technology Analysis & Strategic Management*, 34(8), pp. 891–904.

18

Organizational Purpose and Action

Who Sets the Table?

Weslynne Ashton
*Professor of environmental management and
sustainability at the Illinois Institute of Technology*

Introduction

In recent years, private companies have increasingly aligned their strategies and operations with societal-oriented purposes that transcend profitability and shareholder value (George et al. 2023). This shift responds to the growing awareness of how social and environmental issues impact long-term business success. Engaging a variety of stakeholders has become essential to build awareness of potential blind spots and risks and to develop lasting solutions. However, most engagement happens in superficial ways that perpetuate the status quo because they do not challenge fundamental beliefs or the distribution of power. To foster deep transformative change and go beyond window dressing, stakeholder partners must not only be "invited" to the table—on the terms and conditions set by the organization—but also have the opportunity to "set" the table and shape the agenda. This chapter explores the rationales and strategies for sharing power with stakeholders. Cases of climate and circularity related transformations that leverage authentic engagements and power sharing with key partners demonstrate how such approaches can lead organizations to achieve more impactful purposes and long-term success.

Shift in Purpose

Over the last half century, our understanding of the purpose of a business has evolved. Businesses are facing the increasingly visible environmental and social costs of operating in global market economies. They are being asked to contend with issues that were previously externalized, such as generating greenhouse gas emissions or impacting the health of communities through pollution.

At the same time, many business organizations are recognizing that shifting their purpose to create positive impacts on societies can lead to strategic and long-lasting advantages. The concept of creating shared value emphasizes that businesses can generate value for themselves and for society by addressing the latter's needs and challenges through their core competencies and offerings (Porter and Kramer 2011). More than being socially responsible, organizations benefit the most when these efforts are aligned around organizational purpose and values, leading to business transformation (Rangan, Chase, and Karim 2015).

In 1994, the carpet manufacturer Interface embarked on a journey to achieve zero environmental impacts by 2020. By orienting around this "Mission Zero" purpose, Interface employees and leaders successfully changed the way they thought about the business, what they produced, how they operated, and how they measured and communicated the value of what they were doing.

Engaging employees throughout the organization was critical for achieving this purpose. As the company expanded efforts beyond its factories and through its supply networks, engaging a variety of stakeholders in mutually beneficial ways became paramount. One notable partnership was with coastal communities in the Philippines who were interested stewarding their environment and clearing the marine plastic waste that ends up in their communities (Interface 2019). Interface collaborated with Aquafil, a fibers manufacturer, to empower community members to build new supply chains for recycled nylon, the main raw material for manufacturing carpets. Community cooperative businesses collected abandoned (ghost) fishing nets, processed, and sold these materials to Aquafil, which incorporated these materials into their recycled ECONYL. Interface purchases ECONYL, reducing the company's reliance on virgin nylon produced from fossil fuels and improving their business performance (Interface 2023; Coast4C n.d.).

Stakeholder Engagement

When businesses engage with their stakeholders, they can take different approaches. They must first decide the purpose of their engagement, which individuals or groups are relevant to that purpose, the distinct interests and relative importance of these people to the organization, and effective ways to engage them. In many cases, the purpose is to help achieve corporate goals, such as legitimizing actions, reducing risks, enhancing reputation, and improving financial performance (Crane and Ruebottom 2011). In these instances, the choice of partners is often "safe," those who are likely to confirm expectations (and biases) rather than disrupt ways of thinking or working. This approach maintains the existing relationships and ways of work, and more than likely results in superficial changes rather than substantive transformations (Landrum and Ohsowski 2017).

If the reason for such engagements is to more deeply understand and transform its organizational purpose and values, more authentic and deeper engagement is needed, with a coalition of more than the "usual players." In these cases, effective engagement requires moving beyond token gestures, and meaningfully involving stakeholders in decision-making process. Authentic partnerships require a shift from transactional to relational perspectives. The former is typically defined by "win-win" and "making the business case," where engagements conform to traditional business logic. Relational partnerships are characterized by mutual respect, shared decision-making, and "give and take" where commitments may not always have short-term positive financial returns because investments are required to build trust and establish completely new systems (Sungu et al. 2023). But they may lead to lasting positive impact for the company, such as through improving reputation, brand awareness, and customer and employee loyalty.

Chicago-based Rheaply is a purpose-driven enterprise that was launched in 2016 to help university labs repurpose equipment they no longer needed by selling to others within the same organization or outside of it, keeping those materials out of the waste stream. It has grown into a multimillion-dollar "circular asset management" service provider, with a wide variety of organizational clients (including multinational corporations) across the United States (Rheaply 2024). Like many companies during the COVID-19 pandemic, Rheaply faced a huge problem: its clients had stopped operating and no longer needed its services. But the leaders saw an opportunity where their resource exchange platform could assist the City of Chicago with supplying personal protective equipment to organizations and individuals. By deeply engaging with local government, not-for-profit, and small business partners, Rheaply temporarily pivoted around its purpose to focus on helping its home city solve an urgent problem.

While there were not any substantial financial returns for this effort, the company built important political capital and a compelling story that it has used to grow its public profile, attract clients, and raise substantial venture financing.

Truth, Power, and Equity

Organizations must also contend with how they hold power, and how hoarding it prevents transformative engagements with stakeholders. Organizations must learn to recognize the assets, strengths, and power of stakeholders, empowering them to have a more significant agency in how they participate—voicing their concerns, priorities, and ideas, collaborating to set the agenda for what issues must be prioritized, and verifying how these inputs are integrated into strategic decisions (Passetti et al. 2019). Acknowledging and working to share power necessitates hard conversations and reconciliatory actions because they challenge the status quo.

It is unlikely that organizations that have existed for a long time have done so without causing harm to people and planet, whether intentionally or inadvertently. As such, these organizations may need to acknowledge the impacts they have had on specific groups of people, for example, employees harmed by unfair policies or deep-seated biases, or communities harmed by earlier operations. It may also involve assessing their planetary impacts at local and global scales. Such truth seeking is necessary to repair harm and launch transformative, and not just performative, plans of action. Too often, organizations take short cuts and look to the future without acknowledging or trying to remedy past injuries or injustices. These are often uncomfortable truths. The modern, capitalist economy has been built on systems of patriarchy and white supremacy, which manifest in various ways, including gender and racial wage gaps, lack of representation in leadership roles, and discriminatory practices (Acker 2006; Calás, Smircich, and Bourne 2009).

Several public, private, and nongovernmental entities in the United Kingdom, including the Church of England, Lloyd's of London, and *The Guardian*, are grappling with how to repair the damages inflicted during their centuries of operation and participation in the Atlantic slave trade (Nevett, 2023). Some entities have committed to launching funds to compensate the descendants of enslaved Africans and invest in communities that continue to face structural racism and barriers to capital access. While investments are certainly called for, more critically, the recipients need to be involved in deciding where and how these investments might be made.

For organizations to thrive in the future, it is becoming increasingly apparent that the logic of what they do and how they do it needs to be more aligned with society's expectations of moral and ethical conduct. Aligning business purpose and action with societal goals provides a way for companies to improve both financial performance and stakeholder satisfaction. This process is not always going to be easy and will sometimes require difficult conversations and for organizations to cede power and share resources, in order to succeed in the long run. But deepening stakeholder engagement and increasing their agency enables mutual benefit and achieving more significant impact.

Biography

Weslynne Ashton is a sustainable systems scientist and associate professor of environmental management and sustainability at the Illinois Institute of Technology. She holds joint appointments at the Stuart School of Business and the Institute of Design and also co-directs ID's Food Systems Action Lab. Weslynne works with private enterprises and underserved communities across the United States and the globe to build capacity for just, sustainable, and circular practices.

References

George, G., Haas, M. R., McGahan, A. M., Schillebeeckx, S. J. D., and Tracey, P. (2023). Purpose in the for-profit firm: A review and framework for management. *Journal of Management*, 49(6), pp. 1841–1869. https://doi.org/10.1177/014920632110064

Porter, M. E. and Kramer, M. R. (2011). Creating shared value. *Harvard Business Review*, 89(1/2), pp. 62–77.

Rangan, K., Chase, L., and Karim, S. (2015). The truth about CSR. *Harvard Business Review*, 93(1/2), pp. 40–49.

Interface. (2019). *Lessons for the Future: The Interface guide to changing your business to change the world.* https://interfaceinc.scene7.com/is/content/InterfaceInc/Interface/EMEA/WebsiteContentAssets/Documents/25th%20anniversary%20report/English/wc_eu-lessonsforthefuture-en.pdf

Interface. (2023). *Asking for the "impossible can yield positive change."* https://blog.interface.com/asking-impossible-can-yield-positive-change

Coast4C. (n.d.) https://coast4c.com/products

Crane, A. and Ruebottom, T. (2011). Stakeholder theory and social identity: Rethinking stakeholder identification. *Journal of Business Ethics*, 102(1), pp. 77–87.

Landrum, N. and Ohsowski, B. (2017). Identifying worldviews on corporate sustainability: A content analysis of corporate sustainability reports. *Business Strategy & Environment*, 27(1), pp. 128–151. https://doi.org/10.1002/bse.1989

Sungu, A., Ashton, W., Shea, M., and Forlano, L. (2023). The un-common good making room for radical transition imaginaries. Ethnographic Praxis in Industry Conference (EPIC). Chicago, IL. October. https://www.epicpeople.org/uncommon-good-making-room-for-radical-transition-imaginaries

Rheaply. (2024). Available online: https://rheaply.com (accessed on 19 June 2024).

Passetti, E., Bianchi, L., Battaglia, M. et al. (2019). When democratic principles are not enough: Tensions and temporalities of dialogic stakeholder engagement. *Journal of Business Ethics*, 155, pp. 173–190. https://doi.org/10.1007/s10551-017-3500-z

Acker, J. (2006). Inequality regimes: Gender, class, and race in organizations. *Gender & Society*, 20(4), pp. 441–464.

Calás, M. B., Smircich, L., and Bourne, K. A. (2009). Extending the boundaries: Reframing "entrepreneurship as social change" through feminist perspectives. *Academy of Management Review*, 34(3), pp. 552–569.

Nevett, J. (2023). UK's £18tn slavery debt is an underestimation, UN judge says. *BBC*. Retrieved 6/24/2024 from https://www.bbc.com/news/uk-politics-66596790

19

The AI-powered Organization

Puzzles to Be Solved

Martin Gonzalez
Lecturer, Stanford University and author of
The Bonfire Moment

Hype cycles define how humanity engages with its new toys.

Excitement for magical, new technology is often followed by disappointment. We'll quickly learn that the sleight-of-hand trickery is unsophisticated, unhelpful, or unsustainable. We have seen many hype cycles: cryptocurrency, virtual reality, 3D printing, self-driving cars, and the expectation that work would forever go remote after the pandemic.

Artificial intelligence (AI) is different. And the hype is, for the most part, justified. It has two facets that put it in the same orbit as transformative innovations like the steam engine, the printing press, electricity, or the internet: general purpose and rapid diffusion. As a general-purpose technology, we are seeing it touch a wide range of tasks: from writing children's books to spotting unethical behavior by reading terabytes of emails; from diagnosing cardiovascular disease from retinal scans to predicting marine health from the acoustic monitoring of humpback whale songs. The range of use cases is dizzying to keep track of.

Having a broad set of uses is not enough. Rapid diffusion, aided by the right licensing paradigm and regulatory regime, is essential for transformative innovation. Generative AI exemplifies this.

Its rapid adoption can also be understood through a social psychologist's lens. Generative AI captured our collective imagination because it reflects our own humanity. Paradoxically, the sense of human connection makes it seem familiar. Instead of a science-fiction-like ball of pulsing light, we encounter human quirks: poems recited in a pirate's voice, the cringe-worthy humor of dad jokes, and the confident fabrications euphemistically termed "hallucinations."

We see ourselves. We all experience a *mirror encounter moment* with this technology. And this in turn creates both mass fascination and mass hysteria, against the backdrop of widespread layoffs in the tech industry and the resulting fears of further job displacement. This rapt attention helped ChatGPT reach 100 million users in just two months after launching in late 2022, an astonishing achievement compared to other platforms launched in the past 20 years.

Adoption into work is also happening at an unexpected rate. A May 2024 study revealed that 75% of knowledge workers use AI. It's not just recent graduates using it; millennials, Gen X, and baby boomers have usage rates of 78%, 76%, and 73%, respectively (Microsoft 2024). Despite concerns about AI taking our jobs, many are willing to delegate tasks to AI to avoid the drudgery of work.

Despite the rapid dissemination of AI tools, there are challenges to ensure that adoption in the workplace maximizes its benefits for everyone and adheres to the desired norm of "do no harm."

In this chapter, I will explore three puzzles we need to solve as AI integrates into organizations: selective upgrade, agentic preference, and the self-sufficiency spiral. All three relate to how AI might change organizational life. All three carry implications for how we will connect and collaborate with AI and with each other in the future. As public attention has largely centered on the narrative of substitution—fears about job displacement, bias, and misinformation in the models, or threats to students' foundational thinking and writing skills—the puzzles I uncover highlight the challenges of augmentation: What might occur as we integrate these technologies into our organizations without careful consideration?

Society and businesses aren't discussing these challenges enough. I hope highlighting them helps leaders maneuver around potential minefields when deploying generative AI in their organizations. To do this, I will lean on some of the most exciting social science research on generative AI and draw lessons from the widespread adoption of other work tools over the past decades. We are right at the base of this exciting technological mountain; many of these studies will need to be validated, challenged, and revised. Nonetheless, what we already know gives us the necessary footholds to carefully scale the heights of this new technology.

Selective Upgrades

There's no doubt generative AI endows users with new superpowers, but which users? Many people report significant benefits from this technology; in the study mentioned previously, 90% said AI helps them save time, 85% said it helps them focus on their most important tasks, and 83% said it makes their work more enjoyable. But opinion surveys like these can be biased—some respondents may have selective memories, others might view their experiences through an optimistic lens, and overall, we cannot accurately imagine what would happen if we did the same work under the same conditions without these AI tools. So to better understand causality and compare AI use with credible counterfactual scenarios, we rely on carefully designed randomized controlled experiments.

One of the earliest experimental studies on generative AI, conducted by researchers from Stanford University and MIT, analyzed three million chats by 5,179 customer service agents at a Fortune 500 software firm. They found that productivity increased by an average of 14%, with a remarkable 34% improvement for new and low-skilled agents (Brynjolfsson, Li, and Raymond 2023).

So, while the gains painted an optimistic picture, a couple more studies began to nuance our understanding of what tasks and who benefits from this upgrade.

Another pioneering experimental study by researchers from Harvard, MIT, Wharton, and the University of Warwick carefully studied management consultants at the Boston Consulting Group as they performed two types of work tasks: creative product ideation and business problem-solving. On the first task of creative product ideation, the study found that 90% of participants improved their performance, at a 40% improvement over those working on the same task without the AI tool. But when it came to business problem-solving, where study participants were asked to come up with recommendations to grow the revenue and profit of a fictitious client company, they did 23% worse than those who did not use the tool at all. Additionally, despite being warned about the potential for incorrect answers since this was a capability outside the model's frontier, participants did not challenge the tool's output (Dell'Acqua et al. 2023).

The same GPT-4 model was also used in another study on entrepreneurs participating in an accelerator program and also saw selective upgrade effects (Otis et al. 2024). The research team from Berkeley and Harvard discovered in their A/B test that founders with strong business performance (measured by profit and revenue) benefited by just over 15% from AI advice when seeking help on topics like expansion and growth strategies, operational improvements, or financial management. However, when lower-performing founders used the AI advisor for more challenging business tasks, they performed 8% worse than the control group that did not use it.

The finding that AI tools may not perform well at certain tasks is not new. Anyone can use an AI chatbot without discretion, apply it to a real-world task, and get poor results. These studies, however, suggest something different. Set up as randomized controlled experiments, where participants are given real-world incentives to perform well (BCG consultants, for instance, received more money during annual bonus time), these studies reveal that when people use their best judgment to extract value from these tools, some will unknowingly hurt their performance.

All this underscores the limitations of the popular adage "AI won't take your job but someone using AI will." We've seen through these studies that an individual using AI might not always outperform someone who is not using it in certain tasks. To ensure gains are a net positive for users, we need to understand which tasks AI tools can enhance and which they might hinder, even if these models are starting to appear universally helpful. To be clear: these studies tested the frontier models of 2023, the worst they'll ever be as advancements continue. As these models improve, we may see the complete elimination of selective upgrade effects—or we might not.

Here's the selective upgrade puzzle leaders need to resolve: extrapolating this variable performance across an entire organization over time, AI tools can create a significant divide between individuals who initially had much narrower performance gaps. As AI usage increases among teams eager to maximize productivity gains, how do we establish usage boundaries for tasks beyond the model's capabilities? And how do we support the subset of workers most vulnerable to performance declines by equipping them with the skills to make informed judgments?

Agentic Preference

In 2012, Knight Capital Group, an American financial services firm, lost $440 million due to a glitch in their high-frequency trading software, triggering trades that erased 75% of the firm's equity value overnight. Consequently, the firm was bought out to avoid bankruptcy, chief executive officer Thomas Joyce retired from his 35-year career in financial services, and distrust of algorithmic trading grew (Popper 2012).

It was the early years of this new technology, yet studies years later continued to suggest that humans remain averse to trusting algorithms.

Take for instance this widely cited study by Wharton researchers on algorithm aversion. In the study, subjects were given a choice between relying on a human forecaster or a statistical algorithm. Despite evidence showing that the algorithms were more accurate, the subjects chose the human forecaster more often. The aversion intensified when participants observed the algorithms making repeated errors, even though these errors were far fewer than those made by the human alternative. The researchers concluded: "Our studies show that this resistance at least partially arises from greater intolerance for error from algorithms than from humans. People are more likely to abandon an algorithm than a human judge for making the same mistake. This is enormously problematic, as it is a barrier to adopting superior approaches to a wide range of important tasks" (Dietvorst, Simmons, and Massey 2015).

Their research program then took an interesting turn: in trying to find ways to get people to trust the algorithms more, the study offered them the option to modify the imperfect algorithms. The researchers closely observed whether the respondents were more likely to select the algorithm they could control. And they did. In fact, it doubled their chances of adoption. Not only did adoption rates jump, but the users who could modify the algorithm "reported higher satisfaction with their forecasting process and thought that the algorithm performed better relative to themselves compared with participants who could not modify the algorithm's forecasts" (Dietvorst, Simmons, and Massey 2018).

What's most vexing about this result is that people will trust an algorithm more if they can exercise some control over it, even at the risk of tampering with its accuracy.

This is the second puzzle: we have a preference for agency, even if the choices we make aren't always better for the work. So leaders will need to decide to what extent is an increased error rate acceptable if it means increased adoption of these tools.

This puzzle has other facets. Another set of studies suggests we may fail to extract maximum value from AI tools due to overestimating our own capabilities. In lab studies conducted in Germany, the Netherlands, and the United States, participants worked with AI agents on various tasks, having the discretion to choose which tasks to delegate to the AI. The studies found that successful AI–human collaboration, with proper task delegation to the AI, led to a 25% performance boost over human-only teams. Conversely, poor delegation resulted in only a 7% increase. The study further explains that poor delegation decisions appeared to stem from human collaborators overestimating their abilities and opting to take on tasks themselves rather than seeking help from the AI agent. Researchers assert, "Although the AI accurately perceives its abilities, humans struggle to distinguish between tasks they can and cannot do" (Fügener et al. 2021).

Beyond these fascinating studies, a burgeoning body of research from the past two decades has produced upwards of 150 empirical studies in the fields of organizational behavior, human–computer interaction, information systems, and engineering exploring the broad topic of trust in AI. These studies reveal various other factors that enhance or erode trust in this emerging technology, such as the tangibility and human-like nature of interfaces, the transparency of the algorithm's workings, and the types of tasks assigned to the AI (Glikson and Woolley 2020).

As leaders consider enhancing their workforce with AI, they must understand that the issues highlighted in these studies can significantly reduce the value of these tools when scaled across the organization. Creating conditions that encourage teams to embrace and effectively use AI is crucial.

To ensure high fidelity and widespread adoption, leaders must invest time and resources in deploying AI tools that consider three types of fit:

- Technical fit: Evaluate whether the AI tools are compatible with existing systems and infrastructure to ensure seamless integration, prevent disruptions, and maximize efficiency. Often, technical fit is the primary focus for leaders when deploying new tools.

- Cultural fit: Equally important is addressing potential resistance due to agentic preference or overconfidence leading to poor delegation. To foster a positive reception, identify friction points the tools create in the workflow, encourage teams to adopt an experimental approach, and create a culture where feedback is quickly shared and acted upon.

- Political fit: Lastly, consider how your teams, cross-functional collaborators, or customers ask the question, "What do I stand to lose with the adoption of these new tools?" Many will struggle or even hesitate to articulate the true answer, but understanding this question deeply will help you implement these new tools effectively. When AI adoption shifts power dynamics and resource allocations, leaving people with a feeling of inadequacy or irrelevance, you'll find that people will use whatever power they have to resist these new tools.

Self-sufficiency Spiral

The third puzzle looks far beyond adoption and selective upgrade issues. It asks us to picture a world where these AI tools are in full swing. Then we wonder: What unexpected consequences could emerge?

It's useful to think of AI as helping people with two types of tasks: independent and interpersonal tasks. AI is useful for summarizing documents, thinking through a project plan, generating code, or tapping into the knowledge base of your company. These are independent tasks, where AI enhances productivity or supports strategic and creative thinking. Interpersonal tasks, on the other hand, include writing an email to a colleague, designing a presentation, consolidating performance feedback for a direct report, or setting up a *simulacrum*—a digital representation of a person's thoughts that others can interact with.

Two outcomes are expected to emerge from AI adoption: independent tasks increasingly take over interpersonal ones, and our ability to engage in interpersonal tasks gets dulled out by reliance on intermediated chatbots. Together, these effects could create a *self-sufficiency spiral* that reshapes work for future generations, and those results might not be entirely positive.

Let us consider the first outcome: independent tasks colonizing interpersonal work. With the usefulness and unlimited availability of AI tools, the number of tasks that used to be interpersonal get transformed into independent tasks. A new employee onboarding into a role can navigate solo. An entrepreneur who once needed a large team for product development, design, and strategy can now rely solely on AI. As Sam Altman, chief executive officer of OpenAI, put it, this could very well lead to the creation of the first "one-person, billion-dollar company" (the.reach 2024).

The colonization of interpersonal work is already underway. A Microsoft study revealed that after just 10 weeks of using Copilot, 37% of users attended fewer meetings (*AI Data Drop* n.d.). While I generally dislike unnecessary meetings, it's unclear if this trend is entirely positive.

Other interpersonal tasks will also get colonized. In January 2024, I abruptly ended my engagement with an executive coach after discovering an AI journaling app called Stilo.ai, which was surprisingly more capable and helpful. My new AI coach was better at asking thought-provoking questions, seemed to be a better listener, and did not require me to synchronize calendars to get into a coaching session. If I only needed a 5- or 10-minute chat, the coach did not have to ask unrelated questions to stretch it into a full hour. I also found myself being more honest with my new coach—my extrovert instincts that would "read the room" and chameleon my way through a conversation did not kick in. That made the coaching conversations even more useful.

The second outcome has to do with the dulling out of certain skills and intuitions as people become more reliant on AI. In a course at Stanford's Graduate School of Business that I lecture at called *The AI-powered Org*, Amir Goldberg and I offer students a fair warning: just as calculators have not made us mathematicians, AI tools for writing emails and presentations will not make us excellent communicators.

We believe it's primarily due to the erosion of what psychologists refer to as "theory of mind," the sophisticated ability to attribute mental states—like beliefs, intents, desires, and knowledge—to others. While perspective taking is psychologically costly, it helps us interact effectively. So if a machine takes over this role, it could atrophy our intuitions about reading people's needs and goals. This might lead to us becoming less skilled at considering how our actions affect others, which could in turn harm our ability to collaborate and the quality of our relationships. If perspective-indifferent decision-making becomes the norm across an organization, we can easily imagine the erosion of the collaborative quality that makes teams effective.

We know from previous technological waves that instant access to large amounts of digital media can develop certain skills while underdeveloping others. Over the decades since this digital media access was introduced, research has shown that while verbal IQ scores have risen, verbal SAT scores have fallen. This may be due to a boost in basic vocabulary thanks to the easy access to content, while reduced recreational reading limits the development of the abstract vocabulary needed for SATs (Dede 2009). Another fascinating study shows that when people detoxed from screen use for just 5 days, they exhibited a measurable improvement in their ability to read nonverbal emotion cues (Uhls 2014).

As interpersonal tasks become more solitary, and those that remain are increasingly mediated by AI, blunting our "theory of mind" skills, organizations may fall into the self-sufficiency spiral. This could in turn significantly impact fundamental aspects of organizational life.

Technology is humanity's tool to reach goals beyond our immediate grasp. The unfortunate irony I hope we do not face is achieving those goals only to find they no longer align with our original intentions. This phenomenon is evident in aspects of social media, where the promise of connecting the world has resulted in what MIT professor Sherry Turkle describes as being "alone together," where we "expect more from technology and less from each other" (Henry 1989).

While making unfounded predictions about the future would be risky, here are some aspects of work to which I will be paying close attention:

- **Collaboration.** How will the nature of collaboration change as teammates go down the self-sufficiency spiral? Will live, synchronous interactions become obsolete? If so, what does this mean for inherently interdependent tasks like strategy development? Does this signify the end or rebirth of informal networks? What will sustain these relationships if interaction frequency and substance change, with fewer casual questions and more substantial discussions?

- **The role of the manager.** Will organizational hierarchies become flatter and less dense? We know from the rise of personal computing in the 1980s that managers play less of a supervisory role and more of a player/coach role (Zhang 2023), and from the proliferation of enterprise software that improves self-management in the 2010s, hierarchies can afford to have fewer managerial layers (Gulati, Marchetti, and Puranam 2023). Will this trend intensify with the adoption of AI tools?

- **Organizational culture.** If we start with the premise that culture is a system of shared beliefs and behaviors reinforced through interactions, what will happen to a company's ability to create a strong culture with fewer interactions and more isolated work? How can companies build a sense of identity and connectedness within the team and organization in such an environment? Are we heading toward a future of impersonal, less culturally cohesive networks of individuals (Raab 2019) rather than entities with which individuals can strongly identify?

These puzzles of selective upgrade, agentic preference, and the self-sufficiency spiral represent a crucial starting point for leaders as they embed AI into the core of their organizations.

In my recent book, *The Bonfire Moment* (coauthored with Josh Yellin), we conclude from a review of decades of research on startup failure—including our own—that "teams are harder than tech" (Gonzalez and Yellin 2021). This reality seems to hold true for AI. We are just at the beginning of this evolution, and we can still shape how AI will influence our future.

Biography

Martin Gonzalez is a principal of organizational and leadership development at Google and is the author of *The Bonfire Moment: Bring Your Team Together to Solve the Hardest Problems Startups Face* (HarperCollins, 2024). He's spent his decade-long career at Google working closely with its senior AI engineering and research leaders and created Google's Effective Founders Project, a global research effort to decode success factors of entrepreneurs. Martin teaches at Stanford, Wharton, and INSEAD.

References

AI at work is here. Now comes the hard part. (2024, May 8). Microsoft. https://www .microsoft.com/en-us/worklab/s/43878f19ef5e48d9bc2c21de5476ea2d/

AI data drop: The 11 by 11 tipping point. (n.d.). Www.microsoft.com. Retrieved July 2, 2024, from https://www.microsoft.com/en-us/worklab/ai-data-drop-the-11-by-11-tipping-point

Brynjolfsson, E., Li, D., and Raymond, L. (2023). Generative AI at work. *National Bureau of Economic Research.* https://doi.org/10.3386/w31161

Dede, C. (2009). Immersive interfaces for engagement and learning. *Science,* 323(5910), pp. 66–69. https://doi.org/10.1126/science.1167311

Dell'Acqua, F., McFowland III, E., Mollick, E, R., Lifshitz-Assaf, H., Kellogg, K., Rajendran, S., Krayer, L., Candelon, F., and Lakhani, K. R. (2023). *Navigating the jagged technological frontier: Field experimental evidence of the effects of AI on knowledge worker productivity and quality* [Working Paper No. 24–013]. Harvard Business School Technology & Operations Mgt. Unit, the Wharton School. Available at SSRN: https://ssrn.com/abstract=4573321

Dietvorst, B. J., Simmons, J. P., and Massey, C. (2015). Algorithm aversion: People erroneously avoid algorithms after seeing them err. *Journal of Experimental Psychology: General*, 144(1), pp. 114–126. https://doi.org/10.1037/xge0000033

Dietvorst, B. J., Simmons, J. P., and Massey, C. (2018). Overcoming algorithm aversion: People will use imperfect algorithms if they can (even slightly) modify them. *Management Science*, 64(3), pp. 1155–1170. https://doi.org/10.1287/mnsc.2016.2643

Fügener, A., Grahl, J., Gupta, A., and Ketter, W. (2021). Cognitive challenges in human–artificial intelligence collaboration: Investigating the path toward productive delegation. *Information Systems Research*, 33(2). https://doi.org/10.1287/isre.2021.1079

Glikson, E. and Woolley, A. W. (2020). Human trust in artificial intelligence: Review of empirical research. *Academy of Management Annals*, 14(2). https://doi.org/10.5465/annals.2018.0057

Gonzalez, M. and Yellin, J. (2024). *The bonfire moment*. HarperCollins.

Gulati, P., Marchetti, A., and Puranam, P. (2023). *Digital collaboration technologies and managerial intensity in US corporations: An examination* [INSEAD Working Paper No. 2023/53/STR]. Available at SSRN: https://ssrn.com/abstract=4593374

Henry, S. (1989). *Alone together*. Heywood.

Otis, N., Clarke, R., Delecourt, S., Holtz, D., and Koning, R. (2024). *The uneven impact of generative AI on entrepreneurial performance*. Available at SSRN: https://ssrn.com/abstract=4671369

Popper, N. (2012, August 2). Knight Capital day trading glitch cost it $440 million. *New York Times*. https://archive.nytimes.com/dealbook.nytimes.com/2012/08/02/knight-capital-says-trading-mishap-cost-it-440-million/

Raab, J. (2019). Powell (1990): Neither market nor hierarchy: Network forms of organization. In B. Holzer and C. Stegbauer (eds.), *Schlüsselwerke der Netzwerkforschung*. Netzwerkforschung. Springer VS, Wiesbaden. https://doi.org/10.1007/978-3-658-21742-6_108

the.reach. (2024, February 2). *Sam Altman's prediction: The rise of a billion-dollar solo enterprise*. Thereach.ai. https://thereach.ai/2024/02/02/sam-altmans-prediction-the-rise-of-a-billion-dollar-solo-enterprise/

Uhls, Y. T., Michikyan, M., Morris, J., Garcia, D., Small, G. W., Zgourou, E., and Greenfield, P. M. (2014). Five days at outdoor education camp without screens improves preteen skills with nonverbal emotion cues. *Computers in Human Behavior*, 39, pp. 387–392. https://doi.org/10.1016/j.chb.2014.05.036

Zhang, L. (2023). The changing role of managers. *American Journal of Sociology*, 129(2), pp. 439–484.

20

Cultivating Active Allyship

Poornima Luthra
Associate professor (teaching), Copenhagen Business School

Imagine walking into work. The atmosphere is relaxed and welcoming. Colleagues greet each other warmly. A manager walks by and wishes you a happy Diwali. A colleague apologizes for forgetting it was a special day. A team leader asks a question and listens thoughtfully to the answers of everyone on the team. Another colleague shares a story about a time when they felt overlooked. Does this sound like a distant reality? Well, it doesn't have to be.

As humans, we know what difference genuine interactions make to our feelings of belonging and inclusion, positively impacting our well-being and satisfaction at work. These moments of *human touch* make us feel seen, heard, and valued, allowing us to thrive. This enables us to establish personal connections with others and interact in a way that makes others feel relaxed and safe. All of these behaviors are essential to leadership. After all, to lead people, collaborate effectively, and inspire others, we need to create thriving environments. We need this human touch.

While all of this sounds good, the question is: How do we cultivate human connection? One way is through the practice of active allyship. In my book, *The Art of Active Allyship*, (Luthra 2022), I define allyship as "a lifelong process of building and nurturing supportive relationships with under-represented, marginalized or discriminated individuals or groups with the aim of advancing inclusion." I also share the seven behaviors needed to be an active ally—someone who intentionally nurtures inclusion to create a sense of belonging where everyone feels that they can bring their unique selves to work; where they feel seen, heard, respected, and valued. That sounds very much like human touch, doesn't it?

Given the significantly overlapping scope of human touch and allyship, I draw on the seven behaviors to unpack tangible ways in which we can cultivate that human touch when leading others at work.[1]

1. Deep curiosity

Cultivating human touch begins with a deep curiosity to get to know and understand others—who they are, their backgrounds and life experiences, and what interests or motivates them. Everyone wants to be seen and heard, to be visible, to be recognized and appreciated. To cultivate human touch requires us to actively and intentionally seek out information to help us understand others. This could be learning more about a new team member's cultural or religious background to ensure that we engage in a way that is culturally intelligent and respectful, avoiding those awkward moments

---

[1] These behaviors are based on the knowledge-attitude-behaviour framework from the research on behavioral change. Schrader, P.G. & Lawless, Kimberly. (2004). The Knowledge, Attitudes, & Behaviors Approach: How to Evaluate Performance and Learning in Complex Environments. *Performance Improvement*. 43. 8–15.

that lead to feelings of exclusion. Deep curiosity is not an invitation to ask or expect others to educate us or to explain their culture or religious beliefs but rather satisfying our deep curiosity by making the effort to educate ourselves by exploring the wealth of available information in books, articles, and podcasts. Deep curiosity requires us to keep an open mind and listen without dismissing or getting defensive. In doing so, we gain know-how that enables us to engage with others in a way that makes them feel seen and heard.

Deep curiosity means learning about one another in a way that makes us feel valued.

2. Honest introspection

Our interactions with others are influenced by our biases, which are the mental shortcuts, heuristics, and algorithms we use to make quick decisions, form stereotypes, and even discriminate. Our brain receives an enormous amount of information every second, and we consciously process only a very small percentage of that. We rely heavily on our biases to help us make sense of the vast amount of information coming our way. Honest introspection of our biases is crucial to cultivating the human touch so that our interactions with others are fair and nondiscriminatory. What does honest introspection entail? It means coming to terms with the fact that as long as we have a brain, we are biased. Everyone is biased. Being biased does not make us "bad people," but our biases *do* influence our interactions with others, and consciously or unconsciously, they lead to acts of discrimination. To lead with a human touch, we need to introspect deeply on our biases, be aware of when and how they come into play and influence our interactions with others, and then make a conscious effort to block them from influencing those interactions.

Honest introspection means accepting that we have biases and being aware of how they influence our interactions.

3. Humble acknowledgment

Humble acknowledgment involves accepting that our workplaces and society are not experienced by everyone in the same way. We as human beings have a deep desire to assume that everyone's experiences of a particular context are the same. Acknowledging those experiences are not the same is uncomfortable. Humble acknowledgment is saying that "I don't know how someone different from myself experiences this context." Humble acknowledgment is recognizing the advantages that we have that others may not. It is recognizing there are worries, concerns, and obstacles that do not apply to ourselves but may apply to others. It is being aware that something may not be a problem for *you*, but can be a challenge for someone else. These advantages are our privilege, and they come from different sources—skin color, religion, gender identity, wealth, sexual orientation, educational opportunities, employment, and where we were born among many others. Leading with human touch requires us not just to acknowledge our privilege but to actively use our privilege to lift others to make them feel seen, valued, and heard. When we have privilege, we hold the power to give others who don't have those same privileges the opportunities they deserve and the space for their voice to be heard and respected. This is an integral part of leading with a human touch.

Humble acknowledgment means acknowledging our privilege and using it to amplify the voices and presence of those who do not have the same privilege.

4. Empathetic engagement

At the core of human touch is empathy, the ability to understand what others are experiencing or feeling and at times even to put ourselves in someone else's shoes to feel what they are experiencing. In fact, Wiktionary (2024) defines human touch as "the ability of a person to deal with others in a personable and empathetic way." We may never be able to fully understand or feel what others experience, but cultivating human touch requires us not only to try but to try hard. Engaging empathetically requires us to listen to others without getting defensive or dismissing their experiences simply because they do not match our own. It requires us to listen with the intention to understand and to do better. There are times that while our intention may be good, our actions or words cause harm. Empathetic engagement requires us to reflect deeply on how what we did or said could have impacted the other person, seen from their perspective and their life experiences.

Empathetic engagement means putting ourselves in someone else's shoes to better understand their experiences.

5. Authentic conversations

One of the ways in which we can demonstrate human touch is through engaging in authentic conversations that are open and honest. Human touch requires us to engage with people on the topics that matter to them, even if those topics make us feel uncomfortable. This is not easy. Human beings are creatures of comfort and stepping into uncomfortable conversations seems unnatural. Yet, it is in these moments of discomfort that we have the opportunity to grow, to unlearn and relearn the way we see the world and interact with others. As uncomfortable as it may be, engaging in authentic conversations on topics that matter to others in a spirit of growth and development is a key way to cultivate human touch.

Authentic conversations mean using uncomfortable conversations as a chance to grow and learn.

6. Vulnerable interactions

Human touch requires vulnerability. It requires us to share our fears, our stories, and our mistakes. To build rich human connections, we must show a side of ourselves that we may have previously masked. In doing so, we make it safe for others to do the same. So, how can we have these vulnerable interactions? We could share a personal story about an incident when we acted in a way that was not favorable and had a negative impact on others, focusing on what we learned from that incident and how we chose to do things differently from that moment. In doing so, we create an environment where people can step into their vulnerabilities, knowing that their leaders do the same. Another tool is to create a bias compass circle—a small group of people who can help us check our biases about others. They must be people whom we are comfortable getting vulnerable with. After all, we are unaware of many biases, and we need support to recognize them and their influence on what we say or do. In checking our biases with others in this circle, we ensure that we are being more inclusive in our interactions with others, making people feel relaxed and safe.

Vulnerable interactions mean sharing our mistakes and biases in a way that allows others to do the same.

7. Courageous responsibilities

To cultivate human touch requires us to take on courageous responsibilities. One concrete way to be courageously responsible is by using inclusive language that makes those different from us feel safe and relaxed in our presence. Many of the words and phrases we use are loaded with bias that favors some groups over others. Leading with a human touch requires us to use words and phrases that include others, not exclude some. For example, instead of using "hey guys," use "hey everyone." Instead of "mankind," use "humankind." The same goes for manmade or manpower. Instead of "blind spot," use "gap" or "oversight." Avoid phrases like "I am a slave to my work" or "This is my team's handicap." Another way in which you can be courageously responsible and ensure that others feel seen, valued, and heard is to ask yourself and others, "Who is missing from this room? Whose perspective, experiences, skills, and background are we missing to get a more complete picture and understanding of the issues at hand?" Then make a conscious effort to include those folks in those spaces by inviting them to meetings, recommending them to join decision-making bodies, and sponsoring them for promotions.

Courageous responsibility means being boldly inclusive with our language and actions.

As we look for concrete ways to develop workplaces where people can thrive; be seen, valued, and heard; feel relaxed and safe, the seven behaviors of active allyship provide us the blueprint we need to lead with the human touch and make workspaces for all a reality instead of a distant reality.

Biography

Poornima Luthra is an associate professor in the Department of Organization at Copenhagen Business School, where her primary areas of research are diversity and inclusion, inclusive leadership, and generational diversity. She is the author of *The Art of Active Allyship* (Talented Consultancy APS, 2022), which featured on the Thinkers50 2023 Best New Management Booklist, and *Diversifying Diversity: Your Guide to Being an Active Ally of Inclusion in the Workplace* (Independent, 2021). Poornima was named to the Thinkers50 Radar Class of 2023 and shortlisted for the Thinkers50 2023 Radar Award.

References

Luthra, P. (2022). *The art of active allyship: 7 behaviors to empower you to push the pendulum toward inclusion at work*. TalentEd Consultancy ApS.

Wiktionary. (2024). *human touch*. [online] Available at: https://en.wiktionary.org/wiki/human_touch#:~:text=human%20touch%20(uncountable),a%20 personable%20and%20empathetic%20way [accessed June 21, 2024].

21

Remote—But Not Disconnected

Malissa Clark
Associate professor of industrial-organizational psychology at the University of Georgia

In a creative business like ours, nothing can replace the ability to connect, observe, and create with peers that comes from being physically together, nor the opportunity to grow professionally by learning from leaders and mentors.
—Bob Iger, Disney CEO

In early 2024, IBobger defended his decision to require workers to return to corporate offices four days a week by stressing the importance of in-person collaboration. Disney is not alone in its pullback of remote and hybrid work arrangements that were established in response to the COVID-19 pandemic. In an open letter to employees explaining the new policy requiring employees to be in office three days per week, then–Starbucks chief executive officer Howard Schultz echoes this sentiment. According to Schultz, Starbucks' company culture is "rooted in human connection," and he argues it lost this due to remote work during the pandemic. In fact, many companies are pulling back the remote work policies implemented during the pandemic, including UPS, Boeing, Amazon, and Google, to name a few.

Needless to say, employees are not happy with these return-to-work mandates. A 2022 Gallop poll found that a whopping 94% of workers preferred a remote or hybrid work arrangement. Many workers prefer the flexibility and autonomy over work schedules that remote work offers, as well as the cost and time savings of not needing to commute into the office.

Putting aside the arguments that workers are more efficient in person (which the data do not support), common reasons provided for needing workers in the office include such things as, "The magic happens when we are all in the same room together;" "Our employees get so much out of water cooler conversations"; "We will lose the ability to pop into each others' offices for a quick chat"; and "Our in-person collaborations are critical to teamwork," to name a few. Indeed, it is true that it's physically impossible to casually bump into your colleagues in the hallway when you are at home. And, as I will discuss, these encounters are incredibly important. But are these impromptu conversations the only way coworkers can develop close bonds with one another? Absolutely not. With careful planning and implementation, remote environments can indeed foster the connections we build with one another in an in-person environment. Charles Duhigg, author of *Supercommunicators*, notes that many of our fears and worries about our ability to connect with others in a remote work environment are reminiscent of the concerns raised when telephones became popular a century ago. As he points out, we have learned how to effectively communicate over the phone, just as we will learn the best ways to navigate the new remote work environment. I agree, and add that it will just take dedication, creativity, and open-mindedness.

An initial barrier we need to overcome is the belief that being in the *same physical space* as our coworkers and supervisors is the only way we can build genuine connections with others.

In psychology, we have a concept called *psychological fidelity*, which refers to how closely a research study in an artificial setting (e.g., a laboratory) can induce participants to experience the same thoughts, feelings, and behaviors as the real world. Effective remote work designs are the ones that maximize their psychological fidelity.

Instead of digging in their heels and yanking employees back to the office (and at the same time, losing top talent), let's instead shift the conversation to understanding what key psychological processes are occurring during these office water cooler conversations and in-person team meetings and replicating those same psychological processes for remote work.

Fulfilling Our Need to Belong—Remotely

So, what psychological processes are at play during that random elevator or lunchroom chat with a coworker about our kids' soccer games or our recent vacations? Although they might seem trivial, these encounters help to fulfill our basic psychological need to belong. As humans, we have an innate desire to be connected with and accepted by others, and having these personal connections can improve our psychological as well as physical well-being. In fact, when our need to belong is thwarted, it can lead to detrimental health and well-being outcomes. Our need for human connection is also biological. Research shows when we communicate with another person, our breathing patterns and heart rates sync up, and our pupils start to dilate at the same rate. We consciously and unconsciously transmit emotional signals during conversation that synchronizes our brain activity with the other person's, a process called neural entrainment. We also engage in verbal mimicry when in conversation with another person, a process that involves unconsciously mirroring other people's syntax, language style, speech rate, and tone. We feel connected to that other person. Bonded with them.

Importantly, these connections can—and do—happen between people who have never physically met. There are countless examples of couples who fell in love long before ever meeting each other in person, simply through letters or phone calls, like the classic movie, *When Harry Met Sally*. Simply talking on the phone with someone, for example, can trigger the same psychological benefits and synchronized biological processes that occur when we are face-to-face.

Because these human connections are so important, organizations can begin by asking themselves two questions:

(1) Are my remote employees establishing meaningful connections with other individuals in the organization?

This question gets at the concept of building meaningful one-on-one connections with others. Feeling close to another person within the organization helps to fulfill our innate *need for personalized belongingness* (Baumeister and Leary 1995)—connecting with other individuals. In our nonwork lives, this could include our spouse, a close friend, or family member. In the workplace, it's equally important to have close connections. When we have these close relationships at work, research shows our own psychological well-being is enhanced. Moreover, when we feel connected to our coworkers, we are more likely to engage positively with them, offer help or advice, and empathize with them.

(2) Are my employees feeling connected to the organization and work unit/team?

We also desire to be connected to groups, to feel a sense of community—this is referred to as our *need for depersonalized belongingness* (Mael and Ashforth 1992). When remote employees feel truly a part of an organization, as opposed to outsiders or second-class citizens, they feel valued and included. In turn, they are more committed and less likely to leave the company, are more likely to support the organizational goals, and are more likely to go above and beyond to help other organizational members. The same goes for feeling connected to one's workgroup or team.

When employees say they feel "disconnected," it is important to get to the root of what they are referring to. They could feel disconnected from the organization as a whole—perhaps not feeling connected to the mission and vision of the organization, lacking a feeling that they are contributing to the organization's big-picture goals. However, maybe they are feeling disconnected from specific people within the organization, such as their immediate supervisor or coworkers. Or perhaps the lack of connection spans both of these areas. The specific nature of the disconnection will guide organizational change.

Designing Remote Work to Foster Belongingness

Organizations can take several actionable steps to redesign their remote work environment to ensure employees are connecting with others in ways that meet their fundamental need to belong. Before I get into this, I'd like to highlight the stories of Jacob and Carol, both remote employees. Even though neither Jacob nor Carol has met the vast majority of their coworkers and teammates face-to-face, they feel vastly different about how connected they feel to their organization and coworkers.

For Jacob, remote work has been very isolating and lonely. "I definitely feel detached, socially," fintech worker Jacob tells me. "I'm very accustomed to not communicating throughout the day. Sometimes it even feels like that loneliness feeds into my personal life. I'm by myself for 8 hours a day and not really communicating; just doing my work. It can get really hard sometimes." On the other hand, Carol reports having a very different experience. Even though she has never physically met any of her work colleagues—many are in fact spread out in locations around the world—Carol tells me she truly feels connected to her colleagues, that they genuinely were interested in what was going on in each of their personal lives.

It's not uncommon to hear vastly different remote work experiences from people. And to be fair, remote work isn't for everyone—some individual differences are at play too. But even small differences in the way in which remote work is designed and implemented can make a big difference in how connected your employees feel to others in the organization and to the organization as a whole. Let's dive into some of these differentiators.

1. *Remote environments need to create space for genuine personal connections.*

A long day of virtual meetings and emails not only can be draining, but if this is the primary (or only) way your remote employees are interacting with their coworkers, they are not truly connecting with anyone. This appears to be the case with Jacob. He describes his typical day at work as an endless string of virtual meetings, a multitude of emails, and a couple of brief calls or work-related IMs to his boss or coworkers when an immediate problem arises.

Sure, in-person work can look a lot like this too. But as I previously mentioned, we have more opportunities to seek out the proverbial water cooler conversations to serve as reprieves from this monotony. If your remote employees are not afforded those same opportunities, they will inevitably feel less connected.

Many platforms offer the opportunities for spontaneous nonwork conversations, and I encourage companies to explore the myriad options. Some commonly used options include a channel or feed on an existing platform that is reserved for personal conversations. Some of my favorite options resemble social media platforms such as Facebook or Instagram. Enterprise systems like this work well because they are designed to mirror the social experiences we have with our nonwork networks, thus maximizing their psychological fidelity.

In fact, Carol credits her company's social enterprise platform as the single most important factor driving her connections with coworkers. "Sure, we use it for communicating with each other about work," Carol tells me. "But what I love most about it is we truly use it professionally *and* personally. You learn about people and their broader interests and their families. So, you have starting points for conversations when you have those virtual meetings. We use it a lot like we would any other social media platform, where we can create a post, reply to a post, tag people, or have a private chat or conversation with someone." Carol also loves the built-in recognition tools and said her team uses it a lot to recognize each other's work by including #thanks in a post. For Carol, this enterprise system facilitated the development of both personalized and depersonalized belongingness.

2. *Proactively support your remote workers' psychological need to belong early and often.*

Remote employees should be set up for success from the start with comprehensive onboarding with an eye toward creating connections as well as learning the ins and outs of the new role. One approach is by implementing *structured unstructured time* for one-on-one introductions. Unlike typical onboarding meetings where the focus will be on learning the ins and outs of the new role or the company processes and procedures, structured unstructured time allows a designated amount of time for new employees to meet and get to know each other with no agenda items. In some organizations, existing employees will schedule themselves on the calendars of new employees. A variation of this is to arrange "donut meetings" for new employees—a concept inspired by the workplace communication platform "Donut" where new employees are randomly paired up with others in the company, regardless of function or level. The goal of donut meetings is to spark non-work-related connections between coworkers. Regardless of the specific platform or strategy, the goal is to allow your employees to spend time getting to know the people they work with on a human level. Through these interactions, coworkers have opportunities to discover common interests, passions, hobbies, and goals. These are the bonds that foster genuine connections.

Note that these efforts to build employee relationships should be on the company to initiate, not the new employees. I spoke with one man who was provided a list of names when he started his new remote job, with instructions to reach out to each person to set up an introductory meeting. Not only is this a daunting task for a new employee, but it also signals that the company doesn't care enough about these connections to ensure they are made. These efforts should be genuine, as employees can sense this too. Even though Jacob's company used the donut meeting approach, he sometimes felt that in these calls, the other person was uninterested in talking with him and that he felt like he was a bother.

Supporting connections doesn't stop at the initial onboarding, though. How can your organization facilitate additional opportunities for employees to interact? Distribute pulse surveys to assess how your employees are feeling and see what opportunities they suggest. You may be pleasantly surprised by their creativity. At some companies, virtual game nights are held. At others, workers are provided the occasional gift cards for local coffee shops so they can meet with others located in their area (or they can sip their coffee at a virtual coffee break).

It doesn't have to be an all-or-nothing approach, either. In-person social gatherings are a great way to enhance the connections that have already been formed in a virtual environment. This can include smaller events, such as a dinner or outing, as well as bigger events, such as an industry conference or an all-company retreat. Even though physical proximity is not required to foster strong interpersonal connections, in-person events can absolutely build upon existing relationships.

3. *Leverage technology to support your employees' relationships with each other and the company.*

When it comes to remote work, choosing high-quality platforms with solid user interface design is critical. If your platform is clunky or poorly designed, employees will not be motivated to engage with it. Enterprise systems with high psychological fidelity, like the social platform used by Carol's company, are great options for building connections among employees and also strengthening remote employees' connection to the organization. High-quality tech also helps to ensure remote and in-person employees can equally contribute to meetings and discussions (the last thing you want is a glitchy or poor-quality system that doesn't allow remote employees to hear or be heard).

Leverage technology to mirror the synchronous work that we may be more likely to experience in an in-office environment. If you are unable to physically pop into someone's office to give feedback on a document, try using screen casting to provide recorded comments instead. If your in-person strategy meetings include writing on whiteboards or sharing handouts, instead use a shared screen allowing everyone to edit documents and slides in real time. If working together in real time is critical, designate specific times of the day where all team members work on virtual documents together to replicate the same "temporal burstiness of activity" that facilitates team performance (Riedl and Woolley 2017).

Conclusion

Organizations can't simply switch from in-person to remote—and change nothing else—and expect remote employees to feel connected. In order for your employees to build genuine human connections virtually, forward-thinking organizations are figuring out how to maximize the psychological fidelity of the remote environment so that employees are able to experience the same positive interpersonal benefits working remotely as they would get in a face-to-face interaction.

The organizations that successfully create high-quality remote work environments that facilitate personal connections among employees will have a leg up when it comes to recruiting and retaining the ever-growing number of workers who desire to work remotely. And by taking these intentional steps to enhance workers' remote work experience, who knows, you may realize that this remote-work thing is not so bad after all.

Biography

Associate professor of industrial-organizational (I-O) psychology at the University of Georgia, Malissa Clark is also associate head of the department of psychology and director of the Healthy Work Lab. She is the author of *Never Not Working: Why the Always-On Culture Is Bad for Business—and How to Fix It* (HBR Press, 2024), which has been recognized as a top management book of 2024 by numerous outlets including Adam Grant's 12 New Books to Launch, *People Management,* and *Management Today.* Malissa's work has been published in premier outlets, including the *Journal of Applied Psychology,* the *Journal of Management,* and *Journal of Organizational Behavior.* She has also been featured on various podcasts and in outlets including *Time, US News and World Report, New York Times,* and *The Atlantic.* Malissa is a member of the Thinkers50 Radar Class of 2024.

References

Baumeister, R. F. and Leary, M. R. (1995). The need to belong: Desire for interpersonal attachments as a fundamental human motivation. *Psychological Bulletin*, 117, pp. 497–529.

Mael, F. and Ashforth, B. E. (1992). Alumni and their alma mater: A partial test of the reformulated model of organizational identification. *Journal of Organizational Behavior*, 13, pp. 103–123.

Riedl, C. and Woolley, A. W. (2017). Teams vs. crowds: A field test of the relative contribution of incentives, member ability, and emergent collaboration to crowd-based problem solving performance. *Academy of Management Discoveries*, 3(4), pp. 382–403.

V

Open Minds

22

Making Human Connection Neuroinclusive

Ludmila Praslova
Professor of industrial-organizational psychology at Vanguard University of Southern California

Human connection is deeply interwoven with the concept of belonging. For example, the US Surgeon General (2022) defines *belonging* as the sense of being an accepted group member or of *connectedness* stemming from one's interpersonal relationships. Although belonging is more likely to refer to the feeling of being a part of larger groups, and connection to interpersonal experience, human connection can serve as the foundation of belonging. Meaningful interactions with others contribute to a sense of being understood, accepted, and valued for who we are—key components of belonging.

Connection and belonging are crucial to our psychological well-being, social functioning, and our very survival. Research has consistently shown that strong social ties are associated with lower levels of anxiety and depression, better cardiovascular health, and longevity (Fiske 2018; US Surgeon General 2022).

Conversely, a lack of human connection can lead to feelings of isolation and loneliness—threatening our physical and mental health. The human brain is hardwired to seek out connections with others, and when this need isn't met, it can lead to a sense of alienation and existential dread, and even illness.

While developing belonging and a sense of community is crucial to supporting the health and well-being of individuals, it is also necessary for the functioning of human systems. The success of groups and organizational prosperity is built on the diversity of talents within these groups unlocked by the will and the skill of the group to create an environment where people can belong and thrive (Ely and Thomas 2020). However, supporting human thriving and belonging must consider that while human connection is a shared need, the forms it takes differ. Understanding this diversity is crucial to individual and organizational success.

Human Connection and Neurodiversity: One Size Does Not Fit All

The foundational human need for connection is experienced and expressed in ways shaped by our cultural backgrounds, experience, personality, and hard-wired neurobiological differences, such as the need for stimulating versus calm environments. While all of these are important facets of our identities, here I will mostly focus on the often forgotten but crucial to who we are neurobiological differences: neurodiversity.

What Is Neurodiversity?

The idea of neurodiversity emerged in the late 1990s with the initial goal of depathologizing differences such as sensory sensitivities, intensity of interests and emotions, a need for direct and transparent communication, and other characteristics often associated with autism. Soon it also encompassed variability in attention, learning, and movement characteristic of attention deficit and hyperactivity disorder/difference (ADHD), learning differences such as dyslexia or dyspraxia, and other neurobiological differences, such as Tourette syndrome (Praslova 2024).

Neurodiversity-related terminology is continuing to develop, but there is relative agreement on some of the key terms. *Neurodiversity* refers to the biological fact that there is a limitless variety in human neurodevelopment, which is just as essential to humanity as biodiversity is essential to life. The *neurodiversity paradigm*, then, is a view that stresses this diversity as one of the important aspects of human intersectional identities. There is not one "correct" type of thinking and being in the world—however, some types have been privileged and others disadvantaged. A reaction to these privileges and disadvantages is the *neurodiversity movement*—a social justice movement aiming to counteract prejudice and pathologizing based on neurobiological differences and to promote the interests of people and groups that have been disadvantaged and excluded due to their neurobiology (Walker 2021; Praslova 2024).

Some find the idea that there is not one "correct" or "normal" type of mind surprising. After all, most of us have been socialized to "know" what the "normal" is—paying attention in class, getting along—and going along—with others, moderating one's emotions to fit social circumstances. And yet, there are situations when rapidly scanning the environment, nonconformity, and action propelled by emotional intensity are not only advantageous to the person but potentially lifesaving to that person's group. Still, we label, shame, suspect, and shun those who are different. The shaming and shunning reflect *neuronormativity*—a set of ideals, actions, and functions seen as "normal" by prevailing cultural and societal standards. Anything out of the range of "normal"—including extraordinary abilities, creativity, and unconventional thinking of some neurodivergent people—is suspect.

While "normal" is culturally defined within specific societies, *neurotypical* people's neurodevelopment matches prevailing standards. They naturally enjoy and prefer neuronormative behavior, or at least can meet neuronormativity requirements without fighting their nature so hard that it breaks them and makes them sick. On the other hand, *neurodivergent* people's natural wiring does not align with neuronormative expectations. In some cases, conforming to these expectations is extremely costly or even impossible. For example, some people can be precluded from participating in traditional networking activities when these activities do not accommodate sensory sensitivities, social anxiety, or nonverbal forms of communication, such as using communication devices.

The term *neurodivergent* could apply to a wide range of differences, from inborn sensory sensitivities to acquired PTSD (post-traumatic stress disorder), trauma related to brain surgery, or long COVID. A more specific term, *neurominority* group, refers to specific populations of neurodivergent people who share a similar form of innate neurodivergence inseparable from who they are, and experience some degree of prejudice or exclusion because of it (e.g., members of ADHD, dyslexia, or Tourette syndrome communities; Walker 2021). An example of such exclusion is the 30–40% unemployment rate among all neurominorities and the 80–85% unemployment and underemployment among autistic people with college degrees (MyDisabilityJobs 2022). Addressing these disadvantages is necessary to make sure workplaces are as *neurodiverse* (a collective term for groups including mixed neurotypes) as humanity overall, and that neurodivergent people are not subject to discrimination that limits opportuneness and cuts short their lives.

Currently, the prevailing societal contexts for human connection typically reflect neuronormativity. This means that people from neurominority groups face many barriers, including the barriers to (1) fulfilling the need for social connection in ways that align with their neurobiological needs and (2) fully exercising and being rewarded for their talents.

Barriers to Connection

A Google search for images of "people connecting" brings up photos of individuals socializing in groups, in close physical proximity, hi-fiving, hugging, clinking glasses, and in busy social settings such as restaurants and bustling open offices. Fewer images depict one-on-one interactions in quieter places or being present with each other without talking. And yet, to some people, the sense of being understood and accepted for who they are comes from the quieter forms of connection, and from others respecting their privacy, need for quiet, and physical boundaries/bodily autonomy.

A sense of connection and belonging is not one-size-fits-all, and treating it as such means that people from some groups may face systemic barriers to meeting their need for connection. Specifically, neurotypical people are more likely to have social opportunities that align with their preferences. Conversely, some people from neurominority groups may have to pay for the connection and social approval by sacrificing authenticity, investing extra energy, and endangering their health, while others might be excluded altogether. As one example, autistic people and sensory-sensitive people are often left with no good options for socializing. We can try to abandon authenticity, put extra effort into masking to fit in, force ourselves to endure the sensory overwhelm of busy venues, and risk burnout. Or we act authentically and risk social exclusion or bullying.

In addition to social struggle, the lose-lose choices faced by many neurodivergent people in neurotypical contexts likely contribute to drastic levels of unemployment of neurodivergent talent and the loss of their unique perspectives and innovative contributions.

Barriers to Talent

Organizations and societies benefit when every member has opportunities to fully develop and exercise their abilities, and suffer when prevented from doing so. Neuronormative social expectations that serve as a barrier to professional opportunities are a form of preventing neurodivergent people from exercising their talents. Neurodivergent people are often excluded from professional opportunities aligned with their talents because they are deemed "too fidgety," "lacking in eye contact," "too emotional," "too nerdy," and generally because they elicit a vague "different from me" feeling from evaluators who are likely to be neurotypical. Even being unable to wear certain fabrics or clothing styles due to sensory sensitivities or high heels because of coordination challenges can lead to being labeled as "unprofessional" and result in social and professional exclusion. Too often, job interviewers and other gatekeepers use neurotypical behavior standards as requirements for hiring and promotion, regardless of the actual job expectations. Bosses and coworkers use these characteristics as a justification for social exclusion. When this happens, neurodivergent people lose, and organizations and societies lose.

It is important that the business case for inclusion is not taken to mean that economic utility is a measure of human value. Human dignity and value are not determined by whether someone has "special" or any kind of talents; humans should not need a business case for existence and well-being. Nor should expectations based on statistical averages be applied to individuals. On the group level, however, the members of the often-excluded neurominority communities possess unique sets of strengths that can greatly benefit organizations and society. Their tendency to think differently often leads to innovative problem-solving and creativity, offering fresh perspectives that challenge conventional approaches.

On average, autistic people tend to have high levels of intrinsic motivation, intense focus, and persistence in mastering subjects of interest. This can result in developing deep expertise in specific areas. Research also shows that autism is associated with attention to detail, patterns, and anomalies that may result in identifying threats and suggesting improvements that others might overlook. Contrary to stereotypes, autistic people also demonstrate high levels of both nonverbal and verbal creativity. Moreover, their high levels of honesty and integrity, a strong sense of fairness and justice, and resistance to bystander apathy can support transparency and ethical practices within organizations (Kasirer and Mashal 2014; Grove et al. 2016; Hartman et al. 2023).

Likewise, ADHD has been shown to correlate with a heightened sensitivity to justice. It is also associated with remarkable creativity and divergent thinking resulting in innovative ideas and solutions. Despite the stereotypes, ADHD can also be associated with the ability to hyperfocus on tasks that align with one's interests, leading to extensive explorations of topics and innovative outcomes (Sedgwick et al. 2018; Ashinoff and Abu-Akel 2021).

While no neurodivergent people are alike, many other skills and strengths are associated with neurodivergence. People with dyslexia often excel in seeing the big picture and can be highly creative and entrepreneurial. Members of Tourette syndrome, dyslexia, dyspraxia, dyscalculia, and other neurominority communities often develop strong problem-solving skills as they find alternative ways to approach tasks that challenge their coordination or cognitive styles in environments not designed for them.

The evidence of the exceptional achievements of neurodivergent people is abundant. For example, findings from the autism hiring program at JP Morgan suggest that autistic employees properly matched to work can be up to 140% more productive than the average employee. Much success is documented by the Israeli Army's Roim Rachok program, which recruits and trains autistic analysts. Research also demonstrated that 40% of self-made millionaires are dyslexic. Moreover, organizations designed with neurodiversity in mind have shown that not only is neuroinclusion good for business, it supports all forms of diversity (Flanagan 2003; Kushner 2019; Ossola 2021).

Case Study: Ultranauts

Founded in 2013, originally as ULTRA Testing, Ultranauts Inc. is an engineering firm that offers a range of services including software testing and analytics. Ultranauts' employment model is designed to be inclusive of neurodiverse talent and is majority neurodivergent.

The company's founders, Rajesh Anandan and Art Shectman, wanted to demonstrate that neurodiversity—early on, autism specifically—can be a competitive advantage in the business world. The company then expanded this mission to include a commitment to developing inclusive and trauma-informed work environments. Ultranauts has made significant strides in creating an inclusive organization that accommodates the needs of all employees. This includes flexible work arrangements, clear and transparent communication, and an environment that respects individual work preferences, potential psychological triggers, and sensory sensitivities.

The commitment to flexible and remote work contributed to the company's resilience and profitability during the COVID-19 pandemic, as it did not need to reimagine its processes and avoided a disruption. Ultranauts has created meaningful, neuroinclusive employment opportunities and built a strong and competitive business in the quality engineering sector (Walker 2021).

Toward Neuroinclusive Human Connection

My model of holistic (neuro)inclusion, which calls for honoring social, cognitive, emotional, and physical/sensory differences as a foundation of belonging (Walker 2021), can provide a framework for building neuroinclusive norms for human connection.

Social Inclusion

Social inclusion calls for reducing stigma, stereotypes, and social exclusion and creating neuroinclusive cultural norms. Following are some of the important steps:

1. Educating all leaders and employees about neurodiversity and addressing misconceptions and misinterpretations of neurodivergence

2. Facilitating varied forms of social connection, including socializing in quieter, less crowded spaces, small group, one-on-one, and virtual interactions, and not placing excessive value on one form of socializing, such as traditional networking

3. Ensuring that employees are welcomed but never pressured to participate in social activities

4. Supporting various forms of communication as foundation of social inclusion. People who are comfortable expressing their thoughts verbally and on the spot and those who communicate best in writing and prefer to think carefully before making statements should have equal opportunities to express themselves

5. Ensuring direct, straightforward organizational communication and transparency (Communication based on implicit cues and "mind reading" is exclusionary.)

6. Ensuring participation and leadership of neurodivergent people in shaping more neuroinclusive social norms and cultures

Social inclusion is supported by cognitive, emotional, and physical/sensory inclusion.

Cognitive Inclusion

Cognitive inclusion requires a variety of communication methods that align with different thinking and processing styles. For example, respecting the need for different schedules (e.g., by limiting meetings to the most essential), communication mechanisms, and work environments allows more people to thrive, succeed, and enjoy the social benefits of participating in meaningful work.

Emotional Inclusion

Emotional inclusion means addressing rigid and judgmental attitudes toward differences in emotional intensity and expression, such as removing stigma and exclusion faced by people who express normal human emotions such as sadness or what is deemed as "excessive" joy.

Sensory Inclusion

Sensory inclusion means designing social spaces that support a range of sensory needs. Do "social spaces" need to be noisy and crowded? When they are, sensory-sensitive people are excluded. Designing social spaces for sensory safety also supports the social inclusion of neurodivergent people and access to developing meaningful connections and belonging.

In essence, supporting neuroinclusive human connection requires a departure from conditional "inclusion" that forces neurodivergent people to "fit" into rigid social norms, expectations, and requirements associated with neuronormativity. It calls for replacing the demand to "fit" with more welcoming and inclusive norms for socializing, communication, and overall being in the world, including attention to sensory needs. It calls for developing new, more flexible, compassionate, and belonging-oriented cultures.

Biography

Ludmila Praslova is professor of industrial-organizational psychology at Vanguard University of Southern California. She teaches how to design healthier work environments and helps organizations create cultures where people of all backgrounds understand each other and thrive. Ludmila is the author of *The Canary Code: A Guide to Neurodiversity, Dignity, and Intersectional Belonging at Work* (Berrett-Koehler, 2024). She is a member of the Thinkers50 Radar Class of 2024 and *The Canary Code* was named to the Thinkers50 Best New Management Booklist for 2024.

References

Ashinoff, B.K. and Abu-Akel, A. (2021). Hyperfocus: The forgotten frontier of attention. *Psychological Research*, 85, pp. 1–19. 10.1007/s00426-019-01245-8

Ely, R.J., and Thomas, D.A. (2020). Getting serious about diversity: Enough already with the business case; it's time for a new way of thinking. *Harvard Business Review*. https://hbr.org/2020/11/getting-serious-about-diversity-enough-already-with-the-business-case

Fiske, S.T. (2018). *Social beings: Core motives in social psychology*. 4th ed. Hoboken, NJ: Wiley.

Flanagan, B. (2003, October 4). Who wants to be a millionaire? *Guardian*. http://www.theguardian.com/uk/2003/oct/05/benflanagan.theobserver

Grove R., Roth I., and Hoekstra R.A. (2016). The motivation for special interests in individuals with autism and controls: Development and validation of the special interest motivation scale. *Autism Research*, 9(6), pp. 677–688. http://doi.org/10.1002/aur.1560

Hartman, L.M., Farahani, M., Moore, A., Manzoor, A., and Hartman, B.L. (2023). Organizational benefits of neurodiversity: Preliminary findings on autism and the bystander effect. *Autism Research: Official Journal of the International Society for Autism Research*, 16(10), pp. 1989–2001. 10.1002/aur.3012

Kasirer, A. and Mashal, N. (2014). Verbal creativity in autism: Comprehension and generation of metaphoric language in high-functioning autism spectrum disorder and typical development. *Frontiers in Human Neuroscience*, 8, pp. 615. https://doi.org/10.3389/fnhum.2014.00615

Kushner, D. (2019) Serving on the spectrum: The Israeli Army's Roim Rachok program is bigger than the military. *Esquire*. https://www.esquire.com/news-politics/a26454556/roim-rachok-israeli-army-autism-program

MyDisabilityJobs. (2022). *Neurodiversity in the workplace | Statistics | Update 2023* [online]. Available from: https://web.archive.org/web/20230315021851/https://mydisabilityjobs.com/statistics/neurodiversity-in-the-workplace/

Ossola, A. (2021). Neurodiverse applicants are revolutionizing the hiring process. *Quartz*. https://qz.com/work/1981466/neurodiverse-applicants-are-revolutionizing-the-hiring-process

Praslova, L.N. (2024). The canary code: A guide to neurodiversity, dignity, and intersectional belonging at work. Berrett-Koehler.

Sedgwick, J.A., Merwood, A., and Asherson, P. (2018). The positive aspects of attention deficit hyperactivity disorder: A qualitative investigation of successful adults with ADHD. *Attention Deficit and Hyperactivity Disorders*, 11(3), pp. 241–253. 10.1007/s12402-018-0277-6

US Surgeon General. (2022). *The US Surgeon General's Framework for workplace mental health & well-being*. Washington, DC: Author. https://www.hhs.gov/sites/default/files/workplace-mental-health-well-being.pdf

Walker, N. (2021). *Neuroqueer heresies: Notes on the neurodiversity paradigm, autistic empowerment, and postnormal possibilities*. Fort Worth: Autonomous Press.

23

Inclusion Is the Foundation for Human Connection

Mita Mallick
Wall Street Journal *best-selling author and workplace transformation expert*

It was one of the toughest career assignments I had ever had. I was leading one of the most challenging portfolios for a Fortune 100 company. All the brands in this particular portfolio were in double-digit decline. Because the brands weren't growing, our funding and support kept getting cut. Our targets didn't change; the pressure to grow kept intensifying. This vicious cycle continued for months.

And yet, it was one of the happiest moments in my career. I had never felt more included at work. And I had never felt more connected to my colleagues.

This would seem counter to what so many of us have seen in our careers: when the business is struggling, the seeds of toxicity can be planted. Teams can be in a constant state of overwork, reworking initiative over and over again, with tensions running high. The pressure to perform can be unrelenting. And the strongest of connections with colleagues can start to fracture.

243

The environment can become one of finger pointing, placing blame on each other, with many embracing a survivor game show mentality: who will outwit and outlast each other to be the last one standing to get the recognition, glory, and in some cases, still have a job. Survival of the individual can become more important than survival of the team, shattering the once-strong connections colleagues may have had. And as a result, a revolving door appears, as colleagues move on to escape the toxicity and join organizations where they will be valued and recognized.

And during one of the toughest moments of my career, I experienced some incredible moments of inclusion. As a team, we spent three days together in a business war gaming workshop, where we stepped into our competitors' shoes, thinking about how they might respond to our new strategies. We thought about what they do and what our countermove might be. As a team, we traveled together to a retailer who was interested in a new innovation we wanted to launch. We stayed up the night before finalizing the deck at a local bar as we had nachos and wine. As a team, we would show up in the mornings with Starbucks coffee for each other every Monday and Wednesday for our team meetings. And no matter how intense the work was, we paused to celebrate birthdays, work anniversaries, and other special occasions. Over the next 18 months, we set the portfolio of brands on a path to go from double-digit decline to single-digit growth.

Every single step of the way, each member of this team ensured others were included. We gave each other a seat at the table. We listened to different perspectives and different solutions we had never thought of. We didn't judge and shut each other down. We gave each other credit for the work we were doing and showed up as one team. The more we included each other, the more we became invested in the work together.

We didn't turn on each other and blame each other for the current state of the business. We relied on each other, we depended on each other to turn the business around together. Because we felt included, we felt more connected to the work and to each other. We stayed together, on that very team. Without inclusion and connection, we wouldn't have been able to turn the business around.

The intense DEI (diversity, equity, and inclusion) backlash has been felt across the United States, from legislation being passed locally and nationally, to companies defunding DEI initiatives, to leaders like Elon Musk saying things like "DEI must DIE." Now, many are questioning the future of DEI work (Mallick 2023; Risi 2023).

And yet despite this backlash, now is not the time to abandon our efforts to create more inclusive and connected organizations. Once again, we need leaders to understand that inclusion is a driver of the business (Moore 2024).

Inclusion is a competitive advantage, and those who harness the power of inclusion will outpace their competition in the marketplace. Inclusion in the workplace is essential to human connection. Inclusion is the foundation for human connection. And those who choose to ignore the power of inclusion will ultimately be left behind.

What does inclusion look like in our workplaces?

Many of us come to work to collect a paycheck. Some of us have come to work because we have found our purpose. Inclusion started with being recognized and valued for our contributions at work. We want our voices to matter. We want our colleagues to see how we are making an impact every single day. And when we feel like we are included in our workplaces, we are more likely to trust and build meaningful relationships at work. We don't stay for the fancy perks and benefits; we stay when we feel connected to the people we work with.

As an employee who has worked for small companies and big companies, across many different sectors, one thing has remained constant: the more I have felt valued and included at work, the more I am engaged and committed to making an impact. Feeling included is directly related to how productive I am on any given day (Olson 2022; Carucci, Opie, and Scott 2023).

According to *Harvard Business Review*, microaggressions can impact our careers in a multiple of ways, including increased burnout and decreased job satisfaction (Washington 2022). It can take significant emotional, physical, and sometimes financial resources to recover from the impact of repeated harm in the workplace. In fact, 7 out of 10 employees say they would be upset by a microaggression, and 50% of employees would consider resigning.

Many of us are hired for our expertise and our track record of success. We want to come to work and be at 100% capacity; we want to make meaningful contributions. But imagine if the environment you are in doesn't allow you to do this. For instance, if you are kept off meeting invites, if colleagues make fun of your accent, if you keep having your work stolen, if colleagues exclude you from lunch outings, if you are taken off an initiative you put hours into with no explanation. Given these factors in the environment, your 100% capacity to contribute can drop to 75%, to even 50%. Rather than being able to focus on the work you were hired to do, your energy is instead spent worrying about whether or not you actually belong at this organization.

If this happens to multiple individuals over time, this can be a huge drop in productivity for an organization. Individuals feel less connected to others and less connected to the work. Imagine the hours lost and wasted that can't be recovered. This can negatively impact the bottom line. The work of inclusion is designed to stop productivity-killing microaggressions like these. When employees feel valued, respected, and recognized for their contributions at work, they are able to unlock their potential. And in turn, they can help the company unlock its potential.

Finally, when talent walks out the door, the cost is higher than we might think. According to *Gallup* (McFeely and Wigert 2019), the cost of replacing an individual employee who resigns can be anywhere from one-half to two times their annual salary—and that's a conservative estimate. In totality, US businesses lose close to $1 trillion every year to employees quitting.

According to a *FlexJob report* (Rearick 2023), some of the top reasons employees quit their companies include unfair pay, toxic workplace culture, feeling undervalued, limited advancement, bad boss, and misaligned values (Zara 2022; Taffet 2023; Crowle 2022; Deutschendorf 2019; Gnozzo 2023; Humphrey2022; Levitt 2023). Many of these reasons and more can be traced back to a lack of an inclusive and connected culture.

Many leaders underutilize insights from employee exit interview surveys, where people say exactly why they are leaving. In exit interview surveys workers often say that they don't feel valued for their contributions or their work, they feel excluded, and move on to find places that will include and recognize their impact.

In my experience, it's not the endless supply of free snacks, that meditation app and room, the ping pong table, or the laundry list of fancy perks that get employees to stay at an organization. When individuals feel that they are included on their teams and in their workplaces, they are less likely to look elsewhere for career opportunities. When workers feel included, they are more likely to be motivated, engaged, and happier at work. Inclusion is the most powerful retention tool available to leaders. When we feel included, we feel connected to our colleagues, to the work, and to the company. It's more difficult to walk away from those connections and start again somewhere else.

Ultimately, inclusion is a driver of the business. Those leaders who accept and harness the power of inclusion and connection will set themselves and their organizations apart from competition in the years to come.

Here's a starting list on how to make your colleagues feel more included and connected to the work and each other:

1. Invite individuals to meetings when their work or projects are being discussed.
2. Create an environment where everyone listens to all ideas. Stop each other when you see an idea being shut down, ridiculed, or questioned. When brainstorming, consider giving people dedicated quiet time to write down ideas on sticky notes. You can go around and share individually and then place the ideas on the wall to review at the end of your brainstorm.
3. Allow individuals to share their own work and their ideas. Always credit them if they are not in the room; you can create a contributors section on any documents being shared and verbally acknowledge them.
4. Thank each other for the hard work and hours that are being spent on projects. Even if a project fails, consider sending handwritten notes of appreciation including gift cards to their favorite local bakery or pizza shop.
5. Keep colleagues informed of all changes and updates to the business as soon as possible, especially if it's something they contributed to. If a customer cancels its contract, the budget is cut, or an innovation is delayed, don't put off sharing the bad news. If they are part of the team and part of the work, they deserve to know as soon as you do.
6. Ensure individuals are being paid fairly and equitably for their contributions. Work with your human resources team to close the pay gaps, which includes reviewing base compensation and stock grants.

7. If you are giving out spot bonuses as a token of appreciation, make sure you keep a list of who gets these spot bonuses and when. Rotate this monetary recognition every quarter, ensuring everyone gets a chance to receive this award.

8. Nominate different team members to present on behalf of the team, particularly if it's a division or company-wide forum or a business update.

9. When mistakes are made, don't point fingers, place blame, and publicly or privately humiliate people. Work together to understand what happened and coach each other with kindness. This is an important learning opportunity to avoid these missteps again.

10. Interrupt your bias when it comes to who your "go to," reliable individuals are on the team. Why do you go to the same individuals to ask for help? Why do you nominate the same individuals to help with a special project? Why aren't you including and considering the other people on the team?

Biography

Mita Mallick is the author of *Reimagine Inclusion: Debunking 13 Myths to Transform Your Workplace* (Wiley, 2023), a *Wall Street Journal* and *USA Today* Best Seller. She is a LinkedIn Top Voice and a contributor to the *Harvard Business Review, Adweek, Entrepreneur,* and *Fast Company*. Mita has been featured in the *New York Times, Washington Post, Time* magazine, and the *CBS News* documentary, "Women in the Workplace and the Unfinished Fight for Equality." She was named to the Thinkers50 Radar Class of 2024.

References

Carucci, R., Opie, T., and Scott, K. (2023). Want to bring out everyone's best performance? Learn to lead with fairness. *Fast Company*. https://www.fastcompany.com/90964556/want-to-bring-out-everyones-best-performance-learn-to-lead-with-fairness

Crowley, M. C. (2022). It's not just money. This is what's still driving the Great Resignation. *Fast Company*. https://www.fastcompany.com/90727646/its-not-just-money-this-is-whats-still-driving-the-great-resignation

Deutschendorf, H. (2019). What you should do when you feel unappreciated at work. *Fast Company*. https://www.fastcompany.com/90309224/what-you-should-do-when-you-feel-unappreciated-at-work

Gnozzo, C. (2023). 3 work red flags that mean it's time to quit. *Fast Company*. https://www.fastcompany.com/90847660/3-work-red-flags-that-mean-its-time-to-quit

Humphrey, J. (2022). Bad boss? 5 things to keep in mind when quitting. *Fast Company*. https://www.fastcompany.com/90817159/bad-boss-consider-quitting

Levitt, D. (2023). How to address the misalignment between company values and product design. *Fast Company*. https://www.fastcompany.com/90989949/address-misalignment-between-company-values-and-product-design

Mallick, M. (2023). What's next for chief diversity officers? *Fast Company*. https://www.fastcompany.com/90967182/whats-next-for-chief-diversity-officers

McFeely, S. and Wigert, B. (2019). *This fixable problem costs U.S. businesses $1 trillion* [online]. Gallup. Available at: https://www.gallup.com/workplace/247391/fixable-problem-costs-businesses-trillion.aspx

Moore, C. (2024). Mark Cuban just schooled Elon Musk on DEI with a clear-eyed explanation for why it's good for business. *Fast Company*. https://www.fastcompany.com/91005329/mark-cuban-elon-musk-dei-diversity-equity-inclusion

Olson, J. (2022). Companies perform better if they're more inclusive: Take these 3 steps to increase diversity. *Fast Company*. https://www.fastcompany.com/90753499/companies-perform-better-if-theyre-more-inclusive-take-these-3-steps-to-increase-diversity

Rearick, B. (2023). Why 62% of workers want to quit their jobs (or already have). *Money*. https://money.com/why-workers-quit-jobs-reasons [Accessed 12 Jul. 2024] https://money.com/why-workers-quit-jobs-reasons

Risi, J. (2023). Elon Musk is wrong: DEI needs to remain front and center in 2024. *Fast Company*. https://www.fastcompany.com/91000694/op-ed-elon-musk-wrong-dei-needs-remain-front-center-2024

Taffet, D. M. M. (2023). Keep winding up in a toxic workplace? Here's how to break the cycle. *Fast Company*. https://www.fastcompany.com/90886566/keep-winding-up-in-a-toxic-workplace-heres-how-to-break-the-cycle

Washington, E.F. (2022). Recognizing and responding to microaggressions at work. *Harvard Business Review*. https://hbr.org/2022/05/recognizing-and-responding-to-microaggressions-at-work

Zara, C. (2022). The Great Resignation: Here's a simple reason why your employees want to quit. *Fast Company*. https://www.fastcompany.com/90716203/the-great-resignation-heres-a-simple-reason-why-your-employees-want-to-quit

24

Beyond the Individual

The Power of Community

Neri Karra Sillaman
Professor of practice and entrepreneurship expert,
University of Oxford

In an era marked by volatility and unpredictability, resilience has become a buzzword synonymous with personal grit and perseverance. From companies striving to stay ahead in rapidly changing markets to individuals facing life's myriad challenges, resilience is often touted as the key to success and survival. A recent study (Bond and Shapiro 2014) found that 90% of workers think that resilience comes from within themselves. Yet this prevailing narrative, which glorifies resilience as a solitary pursuit, overlooks a crucial element: the transformative power of community. As Rosabeth Moss Kanter (2013) once put it, "[r]esilience thrives on a sense of community—the desire to pick oneself up because of an obligation to others and because of support from others who want the same thing."

In an age of heightened connectivity, paradoxically the sense of community has diminished. Technological advancements and evolving workplace norms, while facilitating constant communication, have also fostered a pandemic of isolation. This not only affects personal well-being but also poses significant challenges to organizational health. In fact, research focusing on why employees are dissatisfied and unproductive found that 65% of them reported experiencing a lack of community in their workplaces (Porath 2022). Another recent study (Brucks and Levav 2022) revealed how a lack of connection also inhibits creativity: virtual teams generate fewer ideas overall and fewer good ideas relative to their colleagues who meet face-to-face. This growing disconnect has been shown to dampen creativity and productivity, with studies highlighting a universal craving for more communal connections in professional settings.

My exploration into the significance of community is not purely academic; it's deeply personal and rooted in my life's narrative. My journey from a persecuted minority in the 1980s communist Bulgaria to becoming a refugee and then forging a new life as an academic and entrepreneur has imbued me with a firsthand understanding of community's transformative potential. This experience underlines my research, driving me to explore how community can be harnessed as a strategic asset in business and society.

Companies like my own (Neri Karra), LEGO, DBS Bank, as well as nonprofit organizations like Bridges to Prosperity, have demonstrated that understanding the value of community can significantly enhance profitability and transform businesses (Richardson, Huynh, and Sotto 2020; Suqi 2023). Through interviews with various organizations and individuals who have successfully integrated community into their operations, I've gained valuable perspectives on this topic. In this chapter, I will illustrate the indispensable role of community within organizations and demonstrate how leveraging this often overlooked factor can be a key driver of success. Additionally, I will provide practical guidance on how to effectively cultivate and harness the power of community to achieve organizational goals and create lasting impact.

Cultivating Trust

Community cannot be built without trust—it is the foundation upon which all else stands. Therefore, business leaders seeking to create resilient and successful firms should prioritize forging trust-based relationships that develop into deep connections. Trust is vital for creating healthy, equitable relationships, ensuring safety, and enabling transparent communication, and its importance needs to be recognized across all aspects of the organization: from internal dynamics to partnerships with suppliers or distributors, to customer interactions. Yet our grasp on how to prioritize trust in enhancing the sense of community, including how to identify key trust elements for effective engagement and determining supportive practices, remains limited (Lansing 2023).

Building trust with internal stakeholders—i.e., your employees and personnel—is clearly an essential element of creating the sort of strong work community in which resilience flourishes. A sense of community can be rekindled through relatively simple exercises, like arranging for staff to attend memorable, fun events together, cooking and eating together at work, and creating opportunities for staff to enjoy shared experiences and teach each other non-work-related skills that align with their areas of mutual interest. Such approaches produce tangible benefits in terms of stress reduction, improved retention, and increased job performance—all crucial components of organizational resilience (Porath and Piñeyro Sublett 2022).

In the early days of building our own business, my family and I also built trust by emphasizing our commonalities with business partners, employees, and customers. We focused on the shared experience of having lived in communism, being immigrants, and wanting to provide a better life for oneself and others. When we first opened our store in Istanbul, we had put up a sign that said, "Please come in for a homeland cup of coffee." Our business initially began by us selling t-shirts from a factory whose owner provided them to us on credit because he recognized my parents as "immigrants like himself." When we moved into producing leather goods, we similarly demonstrated trust when we provided them "for free" to entrepreneurs from former Soviet countries, allowing them to pay us only after they had sold the goods. More recently, when Russia's invasion of Ukraine devastated the two markets upon which our business primarily depended, the chief executive officer of a leading Italian luxury brand that we produce for exemplified exceptional trust and community by telling us, "We are in this together, and we will increase our orders to you because we know the challenges you are facing."

Establishing a Solidarity-driven Culture

It's easy for companies to talk about their purpose, values, and culture, but such words will only forge a strong community and a resilient organization when they are substantiated by actions. Actions that create a culture of solidarity not only enhance employee morale but also align everyone toward common goals, thus strengthening collective spirit and organizational resilience. Examples of tangible actions that can generate solidarity include sharing profits more equitably with employees, such as was done by Hermès when it paid a €4,000 bonus to every member of its staff based on 2023 results (Garnier 2023).

Creating a culture of solidarity is not, however, just about awarding financial bonuses or realigning pay differentials. Listening to employees' voices and giving everyone a chance to be heard is equally important. Recent research by McKinsey (Catalino et al. 2022) has shown the value of employee resource groups—"internal communities of workers with shared identities and interests"—as a means of making people feel more included within an organization, with consequent benefits for the recruitment and retention of diverse talent. When I interviewed Roman Rodomansky, cofounder and chief operations officer of Ralabs, a Ukraine-based software development company, he told me how they revamped their hiring process during the COVID-19 pandemic to make sure they hired people who fit with the culture of the company: one where every voice is heard, there is unity among the team, and they work toward shared goals, which sustains them during the uncertain and challenging times that Ukraine has certainly faced.

In our own company, Neri Karra, we do not use the title "usta," which means "master" in Turkish and that most traditional manufacturing companies use. The idea is to create solidarity, collectivism, and unity among employees so that they feel they are on equal footing and have equal opportunities for advancement. It is also aimed at keeping people motivated toward the overall objective of preparing the highest quality leather goods possible. We have found that individuals focused on collective success and advancement thrive in these circumstances, whereas those seeking individual titles and advancement do not last long.

Redefining Metrics of Success

In today's business landscape, redefining success metrics involves broadening a company's focus from traditional financial measures to include celebrating progress, learning, and adherence to core values and purpose. This perspective emphasizes the importance of long-term sustainability over immediate financial gains. Recognizing achievements that contribute to building a healthy, thriving community within a firm is crucial. This approach fosters a holistic view of success, aligning with the ethos of a resilient and enduring business.

However, the rise of "community" as a marketing buzzword brings with it the risk of insincerity, especially when community-building efforts appear solely aimed at driving sales. It's vital to ensure that such efforts resonate authentically with the intended audience and contribute genuinely to the community's welfare. Put simply, if you try to build a community simply to monetize it, it will not work.

LEGO's transformation from the brink of bankruptcy to being heralded as one of the world's most recognizable brands showcases an unparalleled business resurgence. Central to this revival, as Chief Executive Officer Jørgen Vig Knudstorp highlights, was a commitment to authentic community engagement, focusing on delivering unparalleled value to children, suppliers, and employees alike.

> We want to be an irreplaceable but also irresistible brand for children. . . . [W]e view financial value creation as the result of being highly recommended by children, highly value creating for our business partners, and having creative and engaged employees. If we have those three things, we cannot help but actually make a profit at the end of the day. (Knudstorp 2017)

By excelling in these areas, LEGO demonstrated that profit naturally follows when a company invests in its community.

Similarly, Ralabs, under Chief Operating Officer Roman, redefined success amidst the Russia–Ukraine War by prioritizing community well-being and resilience. This strategic shift, which balanced growth with the imperative to support local and internal communities, led Ralabs to support significant initiatives like the BoycottRussia campaign and aid for Azovstal defenders. Through these actions, Ralabs illustrates how businesses can extend their impact beyond conventional metrics, affirming that true success encompasses the welfare of all stakeholders.

Enhancing Empathy and Understanding

To build a resilient and innovative organization, it's essential to cultivate a culture of empathy and understanding across all levels and departments. This approach involves more than just collaboration; it requires a deep appreciation of the diverse roles and challenges within the business. During my research on managing creative people (Sillaman 2023), I interviewed the chief executive officer of an Italian leather company who emphasized the importance of teamwork in bringing designs to life. He noted how the various departments, especially design and manufacturing, collaborate and shadow each other, in order to increase empathy and understanding of each other's work, which eventually leads to even more creativity and innovation. Regular cross-team meetings, job shadowing opportunities, and joint celebrations of success are effective ways to bridge gaps between different teams, ensuring that everyone is aligned and respects one another's workflows and resources.

Echoing this sentiment is DBS Bank's approach (Hurry et al. 2021) under Paul Cobban, chief data and transformation officer. DBS ran 250 Process Improvement Events involving cross-functional teams from various departments to collaboratively map and reinvent processes. These teams presented their proposals directly to their managers, ensuring almost complete buy-in and cultivating a culture where empathy and collaborative innovation thrived.

Both examples illustrate the power of creating a community within the workplace that respects and understands each member's role and perspective. This approach not only strengthens team bonds but also drives innovative thinking and problem solving. In environments where empathy is a cornerstone, teams can develop more effective, empathetic solutions to business challenges, leading to a more cohesive and resilient organization.

Promoting Transparent and Inclusive Communication

Community-based resilience in any organization derives its strength from open channels for communication that encourage transparency and inclusivity. Such channels require leaders to establish safe spaces where employees can voice their ideas, concerns, and feedback without fear of judgment or retribution. Regular town hall meetings, anonymous suggestion boxes, and open-door policies can be effective. When I interviewed Roman, it struck me how extensively he emphasized open and transparent communication at Ralabs, which it views as essential in building a resilient organizational culture. By implementing diverse channels like emails, virtual meetings, and an intranet for feedback, Ralabs has fostered a welcoming environment for dialogue.

Amid the war, Ralabs' commitment to transparency intensified. The firm adapted its communication strategy to maintain constant contact, offering frequent updates and direct engagement through Q&A sessions. Efforts to support employee relocation and emergency preparedness, including the distribution of backup packages, highlighted the organization's dedication to staff welfare and operational continuity. Roman's focus on inclusive communication has not only helped Ralabs navigate challenges but also reinforced its community, demonstrating the power of open dialogue and collective support in ensuring organizational resilience and success.

In concluding, exploring the power of community in building resilience reveals a profound truth: resilience transcends the individual, flourishing within the collective strength and unity of communities. The stories of organizations like LEGO, DBS Bank, and nonprofits such as Bridges to Prosperity, as well as insights from leaders like Roman at Ralabs and my own experiences as a business owner illustrate this beautifully. They show that when businesses prioritize trust, solidarity, and a shared sense of purpose, they not only survive challenges but emerge stronger, more connected, and more successful.

The essence of this exploration underscores that true resilience is not a solitary endeavor but a communal achievement. It is nurtured in environments where open communication, empathy, and inclusivity are valued and practiced. This shift toward viewing success through the lens of community engagement, well-being, and collaborative innovation marks a departure from traditional metrics focused solely on financial outcomes. It challenges us to redefine what it means to be successful, urging us to consider the broader impact of our actions on the people and communities we serve.

By fostering environments where every member feels valued, heard, and connected, we can build organizations that are not only resilient in the face of adversity but also thriving centers of innovation, creativity, and shared success. In doing so, we affirm the indelible truth that together, we are stronger.

Biography

Nerri Karra Sillaman is a professor of practice and entrepreneurship expert at Saïd Business School, University of Oxford. She is also founder of a multimillion-dollar sustainable leather goods and accessories brand, Neri Karra, which has been recognized both as a B-Corp and a Positive Luxury venture, and Moda Métiers, a fashion and luxury business consultancy. Her research on entrepreneurship, family business, and strategy has been published extensively in top-tier academic journals. Neri is the author of *Fashion Entrepreneurship: The Creation of the Global Fashion Business* (Routledge, 2021). She was named to the Thinkers50 Radar Class of 2024.

References

Bond, S. and Shapiro, G. (2014, November). *Tough at the top? New rules of resilience for women's leadership success.* Retrieved from https://www .genderportal.eu/sites/default/files/resource_pool/tough_at_the_top_1.pdf

Brucks, M. S. and Levav, J. (2022). Virtual communication curbs creative idea generation. *Nature,* 605, pp. 108–112.

Catalino, N., Gardner, N., Goldstein, D., and Wong, J. (2022). *Effective employee resource groups are key to inclusion at work. Here's how to get them right* [online]. McKinsey & Company. Retrieved from https://www.mckinsey .com/capabilities/people-and-organizational-performance/our-insights/ effective-employee-resource-groups-are-key-to-inclusion-at-work-heres-how-to-get-them-right

Garnier, J. (2023, February 17). Hermès grants €4,000 bonus to all employees. *Le Monde.* Retrieved from https://www.lemonde.fr/en/economy/ article/2023/02/17/hermes-grants-4-000-euro-bonus-to-all-employees_ 6016291_19.html

Hurry, S., Ayodeji, O., Conti, M., and Goswami, E. (2021, February). This world-leading bank in Singapore successfully reinvented itself as a start-up. *IMD.* Retrieved from https://www.imd.org/news/finance/updates-this-world-leading-bank-in-singapore-successfully-reinvented-itself-as-startup

Kanter, R. M. (2013, July 17). Surprises are the new normal; resilience is the new skill. *Harvard Business Review.*

Knudstorp, J. V. (2017, February 9). *At LEGO, growth and culture are not kid stuff* [online]. Boston Consulting Group. Retrieved from https://www.bcg .com/publications/2017/people-organization-jorgen-vig-knudstorp-lego-growth-culture-not-kid-stuff

Lansing, A. E., Romero, N. J., Siantz, E. Silva, V., Center K., Casteel, D., and Gilmer, T. (2023.) Building trust: Leadership reflections on community empowerment and engagement in a large urban initiative. *BMC Public Health,* 23, 1252. 10.1186/s12889-023-15860-z

Porath, C. (2022). *Mastering community: The surprising ways coming together moves us from surviving to thriving.* Balance.

Porath, C. and Piñeyro Sublett, C. (2022, August 26). Rekindling a sense of community at work. *Harvard Business Review.*

Richardson, B., Huynh, K., and Sotto, K. E. (2020, January 16). Turn your customers into your community. *Harvard Business Review.*

Sillaman, N. K. (2023, October 4). Leading creative people is hard—here's how to do it. *Harvard Business Review.*

Suqi, R. (2023, October 5). How a network of bridges is connecting 1.7mn isolated people. *Financial Times.*

25

Empathy

Kai Anderson
*Partner, head of executive advisory
and transformation at Mercer*

We can imagine the beginning of humanity as a rather grim affair. The constant search for shelter, for food without becoming food yourself, determined the arduous everyday life of our ancestors 300,000 years ago. They soon discovered that survival worked better in larger groups than alone or in smaller families. They began to hunt together, look after their offspring together, and distribute tasks within the community.

It is highly likely that they were helped by a characteristic that we now call empathy. Empathy enables us to put ourselves in another person's shoes. Not rationally, but emotionally, we feel what the other person is feeling.

Recognizing the needs and requirements of others in the early stages of human development helped better group coordination—to hunt more successfully and distribute tasks. It also created social cohesion, building trust and developing mutual respect. And just as importantly, empathy was used to resolve disputes and find fair solutions.

This characteristic gave our ancestors an evolutionary advantage that is still effective today.

The biological foundations for this phenomenon are so-called "mirror neurons," which enable us to understand and imitate the actions of others. Mirror neurons were originally discovered in primates, but further research has shown that they are also present in humans. These special nerve cells become active when a person performs or observes the same action as another person. Early humans used learning-by-imitation to develop essential survival techniques, such as tool making and hunting.

If we skip about 12,000 generations, we still find empathy as an essential survival trait in hunting communities today, such as the !Kung San from the Kalahari or the Ache from Paraguay. Studies show that empathy and egalitarianism make the sharing of food and resources and collective decision-making possible in the first place.

And so welcome to the modern age. Humanity has been on an amazing journey, during which the growth of knowledge has continuously accelerated. This knowledge has enabled us to develop technologies that rival humans in many respects.

However, we cannot be sure that humanity's self-image and self-confidence is not being damaged in the process. Sigmund Freud proposed the theory of three existential insults to humanity. The first insult arose from Galileo Galilei's discovery that the earth is not the center of the universe. We owe the second insult to Charles Darwin, who proved that humans are descended from apes. Freud himself was responsible for the third insult, proving that man is not the master of his own consciousness but is dominated by his subconscious. Some psychologists add a fourth insult to this—being beaten by artificial intelligence (AI) in what is probably humanity's most important domain: thinking.

While it is undisputed that AI is already far ahead of humans in various disciplines (and in the future will be light years away), we can be optimistic about the further development of our species. After all, AI is ultimately an amplifier of our own abilities.

However, the further development of AI is forcing us to recognize and develop our strengths as humans. Empathy plays a central role in this.

Before we look at how empathy is already changing our everyday working lives, one thing should be made very clear: AI will never be able to develop authentic empathy. It is only capable of mimicking empathy. It will never be able to make complex moral decisions that consider the welfare of others on its own. It will never build emotional bonds, not long term, not even short term. Have you ever lain on a stretcher in a cold room waiting for an operation? Have you experienced a nurse or doctor taking your hand and telling you that everything will be fine? Then you will know that no artificial being will ever give you a comparable feeling.

Genuine empathy makes us feel compassion, and we can confidently adopt this characteristic as uniquely human.

Let's think back just a short time and remember the horror of the COVID-19 pandemic that began in spring 2020. Suddenly, the question, "How are you?" was no longer a cliché, but a serious attempt to understand how the other person was really feeling. We shared our worries and hardships with others—we sympathized and showed genuine empathy.

With this traumatic event, empathy also found its way into business life on a broad front. Suddenly, managers were concerned about the health of their team members. They tried to understand, to help, and to balance work and private life as best as possible. Despite, or perhaps because of remote working, which forced half of the working population into their homes, we began to really listen to each other, show consideration, and keep our teams together. Without empathy, we would have failed miserably.

The discovery of empathy as a leadership competency was not made during the pandemic, however. As early as 1970, Robert K. Greenleaf described empathy as one of the principles of servant leadership in his groundbreaking essay, "The Servant as Leader." Around 40 years later, marketing folks discovered the topic for themselves in order to better empathize with their customers, and it was another 10 years after that when the pandemic gave empathy a critical boost.

There has been much discussion in recent years in the context of personnel development as to whether empathy can be learned or is more innate. We can assume that both are the case. Evidence suggests that some people naturally have a greater capacity for empathy than others. This innate predisposition can be influenced by genetic and neurological factors, as mentioned previously.

However, empathy is also a skill that can be developed through experience and learning. By consciously learning and training empathic communication and behavior, people can improve their empathy skills, which include active listening, changing perspectives, and understanding the emotions of others.

We can noticeably increase our empathy skills with a few consistent activities.

Active listening

Take time to listen carefully to your team members and be aware of the personal context as well as the professional one. Focus on understanding their needs, concerns, and ideas rather than just responding or judging. Show interest in their concerns and ask questions to deepen your understanding.

Change of perspective

Try to put yourself in your colleagues' shoes and understand their perspective. Ask yourself how you would feel if you were in their situation. This can help you to develop empathy and find appropriate solutions.

Sensitivity to emotions

Pay attention to the emotional signals of your counterpart. Be attentive to nonverbal communication such as body language and tone of voice. Try to recognize feelings and react to them appropriately.

Open communication

Create an open and trusting atmosphere where your team members feel safe to express their thoughts and feelings. Encourage them to share their opinions and listen to them carefully without interrupting or judging.

Show empathy in actions

Show your empathy not only through words, but also through actions. Offer support when employees have difficulties—both in their jobs and in private. Recognize their achievements. Be flexible and willing to consider individual needs.

But be careful: empathy is not pity, although there is a fine line between the two. Pity is not constructive; it devalues the person being pitied rather than helping them. Empathy, on the other hand, is constructive in nature and aims to find solutions.

If we take this kind of behavior to heart, we will significantly improve the culture of our teams. Furthermore, the soft skill of empathy can be translated into hard results. According to a 2024 study by Businessolver,[1] 88% of employees say they would be willing to stay with their organization if it empathized with their needs. In times of demographic change, where retention is the new recruiting, this is a real competitive advantage.

A study by Catalyst (2021) found that when employees perceived their managers as empathetic, engagement increased by 76%. Innovation increased by 61%. And here is where we should have the chief executive officers' and chief financial officers' attention: Harvard Business Publishing found that the top 7% of high-performing companies emphasize empathy in

[1] https://www.businessolver.com/resources/2024-state-of-workplace-empathy-executive-report-part-1/

their organizational culture (Bonterre 2023). Do we need more arguments for a new style of leadership and interaction?

Perhaps one more thing: empathy enables us to perceive other people in all their facets and accept them as individuals. Empathy is therefore the basis of true inclusion. An inclusive organization values and promotes diversity, in which different perspectives and experiences can be brought to bear and in which all employees feel respected and accepted. Genuine inclusion is a prerequisite for diversity—the goal of most companies beyond regulatory requirements. According to a study by EY (n.d.), the presence of empathy leads to increased efficiency (88%), creativity (87%), job satisfaction (87%), idea sharing (86%), innovation (85%), and even company revenue (83%).

So if we want to get to the roots of diverse organizations and not just address symptoms, we should make empathy a cornerstone of our corporate cultures.

Do we need to see AI as part of diversity in our companies? Should we even feel empathy for AI? We can answer this question in the negative just as confidently as we should not be offended by AI. As long as AI has not developed its own consciousness, such considerations are superfluous. When and whether it ever will is written in the stars. If we manage to survive as humanity for another 300,000 years, our descendants will hopefully look back and pity our current efforts to save ourselves and our planet as much as we pity the fate of the first humans. But one thing is certain: if humanity still exists in such a distant future, it will only be as deeply empathic beings worthy of the name *human*.

Biography

Kai Anderson is a partner and head of executive advisory and transformation at Mercer. Previously, he was a partner at Promerit AG, a people management company he founded in 1999, which joined the Mercer group in 2018. After studying industrial engineering and founding a software company, Kai was involved as vice president in setting up a spinoff of the University of St. Gallen. Today, he heads Mercer's executive advisory and transformation in Europe. Collaborating with forward-thinking clients and colleagues, Kai continues to shape emerging trends in the people management sector. Throughout his career, he has received multiple accolades as one of Germany's "Leading Heads of HR." Kai was named to the Thinkers50 Radar Class of 2024.

References

Bonterre, M. (2023, November 30). Empathetic leadership: How to go beyond lip service. *Harvard Business Publishing: Corporate Learning.* https://www.harvardbusiness.org/empathetic-leadership-how-to-go-beyond-lip-service/

Businesssolver. (2024). *2024 state of workplace empathy* [online]. Available at: https://www.businessolver.com/workplace-empathy/

Catalyst. (2021). *Empathic leaders drive employee engagement and innovation* [online]. Available at: https://www.catalyst.org/media-release/empathic-leaders-drive-employee-engagement-and-innovation-media-release/

EY. (n.d.). *Empathic leadership and the Great Resignation* [online]. Available at: https://www.ey.com/en_us/empathic-leadership-and-the-great-resignation

VI

People Pleasers

26

How to Avoid Burnout Through the Power of Human Connection

Kandi Wiens
Senior fellow at the University of Pennsylvania

In a 2023 report titled "Our Epidemic of Loneliness and Isolation," US Surgeon General Vivek Murthy declared social disconnection an urgent public health concern. Among its many negative effects are a greater risk of anxiety, depression, suicidality, sleep disturbances, dementia, impaired immune function, heart disease, type 2 diabetes, and stroke—not to mention a higher likelihood of premature death from any cause. The harms aren't confined to individual health outcomes, either. Loneliness and isolation are also associated with lower academic achievement, worse performance at work, and lower community resilience and economic prosperity. "[T]he harmful consequences of a society that lacks social connection," Murthy observed, "can be felt in our schools, workplaces, and civic organizations, where performance, productivity, and engagement are diminished" (US Surgeon General, 2023).

The full report is a worthy read, and I along with many others eagerly await the recommendations of the World Health Organization's Commission on Social Connection, co-led by Murthy and set to run through 2026. But as a researcher and professor who studies burnout, emotional intelligence, and resilience, what especially piques my interest is that the consequences of social disconnection are identical to those of burnout.

The similarities are no coincidence. But before we get into why, let's get some clarity on terms. According to social science and psychology, loneliness is the feeling of being alone, no matter where you are or with whom, and social isolation is the lack of connection with others. You can be in a crowded room and still feel lonely, while isolation means you're without adequate social support or interaction. Meanwhile, *burnout*—a term that's often used casually to indicate a state of extreme stress at work or just being fed up with your job—is a specific phenomenon recognized in the World Health Organization's International Classification of Diseases. It's an occupational syndrome caused by chronic, unmanaged workplace stress and characterized by three symptoms: (1) feelings of energy depletion or exhaustion; (2) increased mental distance from one's job or feelings of negativity or cynicism toward one's job; and (3) a sense of ineffectiveness and lack of accomplishment (World Health Organization 2024). In short, if your workplace stress is unrelenting, you feel exhausted and disengaged, and your performance is suffering, there's a strong likelihood you're in a state of burnout or at high risk of developing it.

Burnout, like loneliness and social isolation, has reached epidemic proportions. Rates of incidence vary according to research methods and study cohort, but a study of more than 10,000 knowledge workers found that 7 in 10 employees were burned out (Asana 2022), while a Gallup survey (2023) found that 77% of employees were experiencing low engagement and a record-high 44% reported being under high stress on a daily basis. Any way you cut it, this is a lot of unhappy, disengaged, and overly stressed workers who are less likely to be innovative and productive, more likely to make errors, and less likely to be collaborative and socially connected (American Psychological Association 2023). All of which impacts the bottom line: worldwide, burnout costs organizations up to $190 billion per year in lost productivity, absenteeism, and turnover (Weiss 2020).

Why are loneliness, social isolation, and burnout so harmful, affecting everything from our mental health to our cardiovascular health to our performance and productivity at work? The common denominator is chronic stress.

Burnout experts Christina Maslach and Michael Leitner posit that burnout occurs when employees experience "chronic mismatches" between what they need to support their performance and well-being and what their work environment provides. One of the key areas where a mismatch can occur is *community*, which refers to any of the ongoing relationships employees have at work (coworkers, supervisors, clients, customers, other stakeholders). When these relationships are characterized by insufficient support and trust or are marred by conflict, employees experience deep stress and strain on a daily basis, which makes them feel isolated and makes work feel more demanding. The cumulative effect is a much greater vulnerability to burnout (Maslach and Leiter 2016).

Recent data bear this out. In a study of more than 3,000 workers, those who scored low in social connection and belonging at work experienced 158% more anxiety and depression, 153% more loneliness, 109% more burnout, and 77% more stress than their highly connected peers. All of this individual distress affects teams and organizations as well. Workers with weak social ties were more likely to be disconnected from their organization's goals, with 73% less engagement than their highly connected colleagues and a 313% stronger intention to quit (BetterUp 2022). Lonely employees are also more than twice as likely to miss work due to illness and more than five times as likely to miss work due to stress (Cigna Group 2022).

Given our fundamental need for belonging and connection, it's no wonder that social stressors are so painful and trigger such an extensive array of ills. Research in neuroscience has revealed that an experience of social rejection, exclusion, or loss activates the same neural pathways as an experience of physical pain and can be every bit as distressing (Eisenberger 2012). In fact, loneliness and social isolation are such deeply stressful experiences that our brains perceive them as threats, quite literally hazardous to our health. Thus when our sense of connection is threatened, whether it's due to social isolation (for example, lockdown or remote work), loneliness (we feel we don't fit in at work or have few connections), or conflict (we work with a toxic colleague), our brains launch the fight-flight-freeze response to deal with the threat. And when those stressors are ongoing, the stress response gets stuck in the "on" position, leaving our bodies and brains revved up and overtaxed, with no chance to recover and return to baseline.

"What we think happens," explains Dr. Robert Waldinger of the Harvard Study on Adult Development, "is that relationships help our bodies manage and recover from stress. We believe that people who are lonely and socially isolated stay in a kind of chronic fight-or-flight mode, where, at a low level, they have higher levels of circulating stress hormones like cortisol, higher levels of inflammation, and that those things gradually wear away different body systems" (Saner 2023). This is a beautifully succinct description of what happens when stress becomes chronic. While short bursts of stress provide us with the energy and focus to deal with a challenging situation, unrelenting stress causes systemic problems in the body, in the mind, and in performance. As overall well-being and performance suffer we become even more stressed, leaving us stuck in the proverbial vicious cycle and moving ever closer to burnout.

As dire as all of this sounds, this is a case where the malady suggests the cure. Every ill effect of disconnection can be counteracted with reconnection. With the right mindset and tools, we can not only manage stress, but leverage it for our benefit. Perhaps best of all, just as the effects of disconnection and burnout are systemically harmful to individuals and organizations, the healing effect of strong, supportive relationships contributes to comprehensive well-being and success for workers as well as organizations.

Researchers and management professors Emma Seppälä and Marissa King affirm that positive relationships with coworkers—ones in which employees feel connected, valued, supported, respected, and secure—are the most important factor in happiness at work, and significantly promote workplace engagement. Feeling socially connected results in greater psychological well-being, which translates into higher productivity and performance. "This is true in part," they explain, "because social connectedness leads to higher self-esteem, which means employees are more trusting, empathic, and cooperative—leading others to trust and cooperate with them" (Seppälä and King 2017). This is the power of human connection, and it creates work environments where burnout can't take hold. As Maslach and Leiter put it, "A lively, attentive, and responsive community is incompatible with burnout" (Leiter and Maslach 1999).

In my own research, I found that people with what I call burnout immunity—employees who rate their daily stress at a 7 or above on a 10-point scale but show no signs of burning out—rely on their social connections at work to help them manage their stress. It's long been established that social support acts as a buffer between stressful events and their negative outcomes and can also increase our resilience, enabling us to bounce back more quickly after challenges and setbacks. Similarly, having supportive relationships at work mitigates the stress associated with our job demands by providing us with a support system that can help us solve problems and navigate challenging situations

(Cross, Dillon, and Greenberg 2021). Without exception, every person I've known who has burnout immunity enjoys close connections at work (even if it's with just a few trusted colleagues), they make a habit of seeking others' input and working collaboratively, and they are vulnerable enough to ask for help when they need it. Together, these healthy habits decrease their likelihood of burning out.

Luckily for those of us who weren't born with burnout immunity, it's a condition that can be acquired. Here are some of the social connection strategies I observed in those with burnout immunity, and which any of us can learn and practice.

Join a Professional Group of Likeminded, Trusted Supporters

Find confidantes in your network who get where you're coming from and who can skillfully help you manage your work-related stress. The Major Cities Chiefs Association (MCCA) is an organization that provides a supportive forum for police executives from the 79 largest cities in the United States and Canada. It gives these "top cops," who must protect a significant amount of sensitive information, a safe environment to candidly share their challenges with others who have the background and experience to understand them. If you don't have access to an organization like the MCCA, other outlets include networking groups, professional organizations, or a few trusted colleagues. Simply sharing your experiences can be a stress reliever, and others may have coping strategies or tips you wouldn't have thought of.

Identify and Form Relationships with Resilient Role Models

One of the best ways to become adept at any new skill is to learn from those who excel at it. Who among your coworkers is steady, reliable, and coolheaded in the midst of high-stress situations? Who is able to bounce back quickly after a challenging situation? Who views stressful situations as challenges rather than threats and has grown and become stronger due to successfully overcoming setbacks? These are your resilient role models. Not only can you learn from their example, you can enjoy and benefit from the social support they offer. "Seeking proximity to other adults when we are an adult is a productive way to continue to scaffold our [ongoing] development," physician and human development expert Dr. Peter Loper told me. "Having an 'experienced other' like a mentor, a boss or colleague we look up to, or other role models helps us learn how to navigate stressful situations."

Ask for Help

All of my research participants and coaching clients with burnout immunity don't hesitate to ask for help when they need it. I've also never known anyone who's recovered from burnout (including myself) who did so without strong support from others. Asking for help didn't come naturally to all of them, but each one has learned the value of *proactively* reaching out before they get into the danger zone of chronic stress and burnout. They gain strategies and solutions for whatever challenge they're facing, plus all the positive benefits of social interaction.

Offer Help

One of the most powerful ways to lower your own stress is to help relieve the stress of others. That's right; extending a helping hand not only benefits other people, it can trigger what's known as the tend-and-befriend response to stress. Rather than the usual fight-flight-freeze response, tend-and-befriend occurs when we engage in prosocial behaviors such as volunteering, cooperating, sharing, and helping. It's mediated neurochemically by a trio of "feel good" hormones, namely oxytocin, dopamine, and serotonin. Oxytocin, aka the love or bonding hormone, is released during any positive social interaction. Dopamine is released when we experience a reward (in this case the pleasure that comes from an altruistic act), and it works to dampen fear while increasing optimism, motivation, focus, and pleasure. Serotonin, meanwhile, is a natural mood booster and stress reliever.

Align Yourself with Positive, Optimistic Colleagues

Through a phenomenon known as emotional contagion, we tend to mirror the emotions and emotion-based behaviors of those around us. It happens in milliseconds, usually without our conscious awareness. If you're in a work environment that's "infected" by high stress, cynicism, disengagement, and low morale, you're likely to absorb and act out those same negative states (Barsade 2002). This is why stressed-out employees stress out other employees, and why you're more likely to become burned out if you interact frequently with a burned-out colleague. Fortunately, emotional contagion works both ways, and some researchers think positive emotions are more communicable than negative ones. Do whatever you can to decrease your exposure to negative coworkers who drain your energy—an important burnout prevention strategy all on its own—and to increase your time with positive, stress-resilient coworkers who boost your mood and increase your sense of belonging.

Seek One-on-one Support

Sometimes, it's necessary to seek more intensive social support that is dedicated to you and your unique situation. This can occur through friends or other loved ones, but support from trained professionals includes a therapist or counselor, an executive coach, or a mentor.

Regularly Connect with People Outside of Work

We all need to fully unplug from work at regular intervals to interrupt the stress cycle and recover from the demands of work. There are few more restorative and enjoyable ways to do so than to spend time with those you esteem. Whether these social ties are loose (acquaintances) or close (friends and family members), as long as the relationship is characterized by trust and support and is not beset by unresolved conflict, engaging in non-work-related activities with others offers all the benefits of social connection, increases your resilience to stress, and counteracts the negative effects of stress. You just might have a little fun too.

Having supportive social relationships at work vastly decreases the risk of chronic stress and burnout and offers a host of advantages for both individuals and organizations. Supportive coworkers can reduce the burden of our workplace stress by listening to us, by offering new ways to solve problems, and by simply helping us feel less isolated, all of which translates into greater engagement and job satisfaction, more productive collaboration, and real gains for teams and organizations. But the benefits of human connection run much deeper. As a fundamental need as essential for our well-being as sustenance, shelter, and security, human connection is a basic building block for leading a happy, healthy, and fulfilling life, at work and everywhere else.

Biography

Kandi Wiens, EdD, is a senior fellow at the University of Pennsylvania Graduate School of Education and the author of

Burnout Immunity: How Emotional Intelligence Can Help You Build Resilience and Heal Your Relationship with Work (HarperCollins, 2024). She is also a member of the Thinkers50 Radar Class of 2024. A nationally known researcher and speaker on burnout, emotional intelligence, and resilience, Kandi developed the *Burnout Quiz* to help people understand if they're at risk of burning out.

References

American Psychological Association. (2023). *Employers need to focus on workplace burnout: Here's why.* https://www.apa.org/topics/healthy-workplaces/workplace-burnout#:~:text=%E2%80%9CWhen%20workers%20are%20suffering%20from,and%20the%20bottom%2Dline.%E2%80%9D

Asana. (2022). *Anatomy of work global index 2022.* Author.

Barsade, S.G. (2002). The ripple effect: Emotional contagion and its influence on group behavior. *Administrative Science Quarterly*, 47(4), pp. 644–675. 10.2307/3094912

BetterUp. (2022). *The connection crisis: Why community matters in the new world of work* [online]. Available from https://grow.betterup.com/resources/build-a-culture-of-connection-report (accessed November 9, 2022)

Cigna Group. (2022). *The loneliness epidemic persists: A post-pandemic look at the state of loneliness among US adults* [online]. Available from: https://newsroom.cigna.com/loneliness-epidemic-persists-post-pandemic-look

Cross, R., Dillon, K., and Greenberg, D. (2021). The secret to building resilience. *Harvard Business Review.* https://hbr.org/2021/01/the-secret-to-building-resilience

Eisenberger, N. I. (2012). The neural bases of social pain: Evidence for shared representations with physical pain. *Psychosomatic Medicine*, 74(2), pp. 126–135. 10.1097/PSY.0b013e3182464dd1

Gallup. (2023). *State of the global workplace 2023.* Author.

Leiter, M. and Maslach, C. (1999). Six areas of worklife: A model of the organizational context of burnout *Journal of Health and Human Services Administration*, 21(4), pp. 472–489.

Maslach, C. and Leiter, M. P. (2016). Understanding the burnout experience: recent research and its implications for psychiatry. *World Psychiatry*, 15(2), pp. 103–111. 10.1002/wps.20311. PMID: 27265691; PMCID: PMC4911781.

Saner, E. (2023, February 6). Forget regret! How to have a happy life—according to the world's leading expert. *The Guardian*.

Seppälä, E. and King, M. (2017). Burnout at work isn't just about exhaustion. It's also about loneliness. *Harvard Business Review*. https://hbr.org/2017/06/burnout-at-work-isnt-just-about-exhaustion-its-also-about-loneliness

US Surgeon General. (2023). *Our epidemic of loneliness and isolation*. Washington DC: Author. https://www.hhs.gov/sites/default/files/surgeon-general-social-connection-advisory.pdf

World Health Organization. (2024). *ICD-11 for mortality and morbidity statistics*. https://icd.who.int/browse/2024-01/mms/en#129180281

Weiss, L. (2020). Burnout from an organizational perspective. *Stanford Social Innovation Review*. https://ssir.org/articles/entry/burnout_from_an_organizational_perspective

27

Leading Gen Z

Jenny Fernandez
Adjunct professor of marketing at Columbia University and New York University

The landscape of leadership is undergoing a profound transformation with the entry of Gen Z into the workforce. These individuals, born roughly between 1997 and 2012, are currently between 12 and 27 years old. They began entering the workforce in 2018. Generation Z has grown up amidst unprecedented times, marked by macro-social movements, systemic issues, income disparities, and missed learning opportunities due to the global pandemic. These factors have played a pivotal role in shaping their identities and unique leadership values. While we don't fully understand the impact of their experiences, we have some indications.

Major Trends Impacting Gen Z

1. **Digital native generation.** Generation Z grew up as the first fully digital cohort, having access to social media and smartphones since the age of 12. With this access, they felt pressured

285

to document every aspect of their lives, exposing themselves to heightened levels of anxiety, FOMO (fear of missing out), and online bullying. These experiences led to social comparisons that impacted their self-esteem and contributed to feelings of depression. The United States is facing what Surgeon General Vivek Murthy calls a decade-long youth mental health crisis. According to the Centers for Disease Control and Prevention, one in three students (44% of teens) consistently feels sad and hopeless, with suicide rates steadily increasing since 2007 (Walensky et al. 2023). The McKinsey Health Institute's (MHI's) 2022 Global Gen Z Survey further confirms that mental health issues among Gen Z are a global phenomenon (Coe et al. 2023).

2. **Economic uncertainty.** The United States has witnessed what economics professor Tyler Cowen called the "death of the American dream," citing the disruptive effects of automation from the technology breakthroughs of the internet age ("Third Industrial Revolution"). Homeownership now appears elusive and out of reach for many, with 50% of Gen Zers believing they would need to win the lottery to afford a house. In addition, upward mobility in the United Sates has been cut in half in the past 40 years, particularly impacting the middle class. Therefore, Gen Z recognizes that there is a high probability they will not be economically better off than their parents. According to the IMF's World Uncertainty Index, the global economic uncertainty remains high since 2016 due to UK Brexit, US elections, US-China trade tensions, the global pandemic, ongoing conflicts, and widespread financial instability (Ahir, Bloom, and Furceri 2023).

3. **New parenting styles.** Another significant trend influencing Gen Zers is the rise of "helicopter parenting." Social psychologist and New York University Stern Professor Jonathan Haydt described it as the overprotection of our youth (Honestly Podcast n.d.). While this approach is often well intentioned,

it may have hindered their ability to adapt and be resilient to confront life's challenges. Failure is part of our success journey, and experiencing sadness is a natural part of the path to happiness. Embracing "healthy friction" is essential for learning, adapting, and fostering personal growth.

4. **Lack of institutional trust.** Gen Z has seen the trust in government, media, business, and religion, once guiding pillars of a meaningful life, steadily decline. Although these institutions are not without their flaws, they historically served as stable and constructive conversation partners—places where younger generations could get reliable feedback on their ideas and "healthy friction" learning experiences.

5. **Technology advancements.** Generative artificial intelligence (AI) technologies are poised to revolutionize industries and reshape the global workforce at an unprecedented pace. A McKinsey Global Institute report projects that AI automation could displace up to 800 million jobs worldwide by 2030, particularly impacting developed markets like the United States and Western Europe (Manyika et al. 2017). This accelerated automation will require the workforce to acquire new skills, with estimates suggesting that between 12% and 33% of workers globally may need to transition to new occupations. The World Economic Forum warns that by 2027, "Businesses predict that 44% of workers' core skills will be disrupted, because technology is moving faster than companies can design and scale up their training programmes" (Masterson 2023). As we usher in the Fourth Industrial Revolution, Gen Z is poised to experience the greatest impact of automation.

Gen Z in the Workplace

These trends have given rise to a generation that is highly conscious of societal issues but disillusioned by the inability of institutions to effectively solve them. In the workplace, Gen Zers are disengaged, struggling to "fit in," and lack a strong sense of connection with their coworkers, managers, or employers. Gallup research highlights that Gen Z exhibits the highest level of disengagement at work compared to any other generation, at 54%. Consequently, many of them experience undue stress and a quarter report symptoms of burnout (Pendell and Vander Helm 2022).

Nevertheless, this generation is on the cusp of assuming leadership roles. According to Deloitte, with one-third of the global population identifying as Gen Zers, they are poised to surpass millennials as the largest demographic. By 2029, Gen Z is projected to comprise one-third of American workers. As highlighted by BBC and Bloomberg, Gen Z commands an estimated $450 billion in buying power worldwide, with $360 billion in the United States alone (Noenickx 2023; Pollard 2021). They are known to leverage this purchasing power to support businesses that align with their values.

Addressing these evolving leadership dynamics requires managers and organizations to redefine their paradigms and toolkits. Empowering and supporting Gen Z employees is crucial for fostering their full engagement, finding meaning in work, and igniting their motivation.

Cultivating Human-centric Mindsets and Essential Skills

In my 2022 *Harvard Business Review* (Fernandez, Les, and Landis) article, "Helping Gen Z Employees Find Their Place at Work" I highlighted three key areas that carry significant meaning and motivate Gen Z to engage in culture, business, and the economy. These intrinsic motivators have a profound impact on personal satisfaction and enjoyment. They are autonomy, mastery, and purpose. These motivators can serve as guiding principles for businesses.

Autonomy

The first motivator is autonomy. We all require the freedom to create, fail, and do so within a supportive environment. Gen Z highly values the freedom to self-direct aspects of their work experience. It gives them the flexibility they need for work-life integration and to manage their mental health. Supporting autonomy in the workplace, as advocated by self-determination theory, enhances engagement, satisfaction, and productivity while fostering stronger relationships between employers and employees.

New Leadership Paradigm in Action

In practice, self-direction can take many forms. One prominent example is flexible work arrangements. I recently interviewed "Maria," a successful Gen Z professional in a Fortune 500 company in the financial services industry. She began her career working remotely during the pandemic. She excelled and was promoted. However, when her company mandated full-time in-office work, she considered quitting.

Gen Z has cultivated work habits they want to preserve, such as taking breaks to recharge, preparing meals at home, or walking their pets. Gen Z values the ability to manage their schedules and prioritize quality of life over traditional perks. According to Jabra's 2021 Global Hybrid Ways of Working Report, "59% of respondents reported that 'flexibility' is more important to them than salary or other benefits." Thus, businesses offering options and flexibility are taking steps to build trust with Gen Z, resulting in happier employees, reduced turnover, and increased productivity.

Another manifestation of self-direction is work autonomy, where employees choose passion projects. Atlassian, a global software company, exemplifies this with its "ShipIt" days initiative. Employees select projects to work on for 24 hours, fostering creativity and innovation. This allows employees to explore new ideas and initiatives outside of their regular responsibilities, promoting a culture of experimentation and autonomy. This is also akin to Google's "20% Time" policy that allows employees to dedicate up to 1 day a week to self-selected projects. This policy has led to the development of many innovative products, including Gmail and Google News. When Gen Z feels inspired by their work, they become engaged in the company. Therefore, organizations that empower employees with passion projects will thrive with Gen Z.

Innovative companies may consider piloting a compressed workweek, such as the four-day workweek. This not only frees up time and shifts focus from hours to output but also encourages leaders to delegate more tasks to early career staff, fostering upscaling and cross-training. In the United Kingdom, nearly 90% of the original pilot companies continued the four-day workweek (see Andrew Barnes insights on page 17), with half making it a permanent arrangement. This change led to increased employee satisfaction, lower turnover, and increased productivity. Following this trend, several prominent global companies, including Panasonic Japan HQ, Lamborghini, Buffer, and Airbnb, have adopted similar practices.

Mastery

The second motivator is mastery, reflecting Gen Z's desire for personal growth. They pursue mastery for two main reasons. According to the Workforce Institute at Kronos Inc., one in four Gen Zers feel their education hasn't adequately prepared them for the workforce (Wilkie 2019). Additionally, they believe they bear the responsibility to tackle big societal problems. They recognize they need critical thinking tools, leadership skills, and mentorship to confront future challenges. Therefore, they view their jobs as steppingstones toward broader ambitions, such as entrepreneurship, social advocacy, or zig-zagging up the corporate ladder. Thus, they seek employers willing to invest in their development.

To engage and motivate Gen Z, consider offering tailored development programs like leadership coaching, mentorship, and personal brand building.

New Leadership Paradigm in Action

In practice, mastery can take many forms. Access to tailored development and coaching empowers Gen Z to envision an attainable future, fostering hope, self-efficacy, and optimism. It also creates opportunities for "healthy friction" in the workplace, helping Gen Z develop essential soft skills for success and productivity.

Salesforce serves as a notable example of a company fostering mastery through its comprehensive personal and professional growth initiatives. Their Great Leader Pathways program "offers a personalized learning experience tailored to the skills, mindsets, and competencies required at each stage of leadership" (Sostrin 2022). What sets this initiative apart is its proactive approach to equip both current and aspiring managers with the tools to navigate the complexities and uncertainties inherent in leadership roles, by cultivating skillsets like resilience and mental toughness. Through personalization, tailored training, and synchronous and asynchronous modalities, Salesforce addresses the unique aspirations and growth trajectories of the next generation of leaders.

AceUp demonstrates mastery through its innovative approach to leadership development, particularly leveraging an AI-powered, human-centered team transformation approach to coaching. This tailored approach to leadership development enables larger enterprises to democratize the coaching experience and enhance leadership capabilities across the organization. An example of this is their collaboration with a leading Fortune 100 technology company. They aimed to foster a culture of "exploration and growth mindset" while addressing a pattern of reactiveness and fire drills, which served as significant roadblocks. The objective was to increase individual and team openness to change and uncertainty through improved communication, messaging, and accountability.

AceUp's offering of AI-powered team coaching is notable due to its ability to enable team transformation at scale, bridging the gap of connection and trust and equipping organizations to enhance performance amidst uncertainty. Through this process, outputs included increased trust and team cohesion, enhanced collaboration, and the cultivation of essential soft skills for early career employees. This experience also provided a "healthy friction" teaching opportunity for both teammates and people managers alike, which is essential as Gen Zers transition into leadership roles.

Another aspect of mastery is developing your employees' personal branding skills. Gen Z highly values employer support in cultivating their personal brands, seeing it as an asset for long-term success. Instead of traditional perks like game rooms, consider investing in facilities such as podcasts or production rooms. Aligning your developmental initiatives with their career aspirations and social media culture can provide a competitive advantage. Stephanie Nuesi, a rising Gen Z influencer and Google employee, shared how building her personal brand helped her land her dream job. Now, she leverages her platform of 400,000 followers to help fellow Gen Zers to find their voice. Consequently, companies that show they are invested in their employees will foster employee advocacy and generate invaluable brand awareness. According to a LinkedIn study (n.d.), "Candidates trust the company's employees 3× more than the company to provide credible information on what it's like to work there."

Purpose

The third motivator is purpose. Gen Z finds meaning through their contributions to the workplace and seeks fulfillment in pursuing goals aligned to their core values.

New Leadership Paradigm in Action

In practice, purpose may involve engagement through service and co-creation. Gen Z thrives when invited to design programs that represent their company values, fostering a form of "healthy friction" where they learn how to execute their purpose effectively. As Simon Sinek (2024) said, "When people are financially invested, they want a return. When people are emotionally invested, they want to contribute."

Deloitte research reveals that the majority of bosses (more than 7 in 10) are actually excited about Gen Z's influence on evolving the workplace, but alignment gaps must be addressed (Dunlop and Pankowski 2023). Managers and organizations can test and learn the following tactics:

Create seats at the table. Invite Gen Z into the conversation and move away from the traditional "command-and-control" leadership. Co-creating the future with Gen Z requires dialogue. Tactics like reverse-mentoring facilitate this dialogue at all levels of the organization. With AI poised to transform the way we work, live, and play, tapping into the most tech-savvy generation to shape a human-centered future of work makes sense.

Cultivate a connected culture. Building professional relationships is meaningful to Gen Z. In reality, Gen Z wants a hybrid culture where they can have flexibility and also the opportunity to foster these connections. Recognizing that success is a collaborative effort, Gen Z understands the value of enlisting supporters, mentors, and work allies to find meaning and drive their purpose forward. As Gen Z influencer Danielle Farage advises,

"Put yourself in as many rooms as possible and lead with your purpose." Thus, organizations that encourage Gen Z to align with their corporate values will succeed.

Connect with Gen Z for Success

Repositioning Gen Z for success requires our ability to engage and motivate this cohort to establish a human connection with work. Imagine the possibilities if we prioritize supporting Gen Z and rebuilding trust in our systems and institutions. To achieve this, we must address the root causes of their disengagement, most notably the decline of organizational trust. As author and speaker Dan Pink (2009) states, "There's a mismatch between what science knows and what business does." Companies that implement strategies rooted in the science of human motivation and human-centered leadership can bridge this gap.

Standing on the brink of the fourth industrial revolution, we are presented with an opportunity to redefine leadership paradigms and how we perceive and nurture talent. The responsibility rests with our business leaders to spearhead this transformation, embracing a more inclusive, empowering approach to leadership. My expert opinion is that businesses that view this as an opportunity will outperform those that see Gen Z as a liability. By focusing on autonomy, mastery, and purpose, we will reap the benefits of Gen Z finding meaning in work. Consequently, our businesses will experience a more engaged workforce, longer tenures, and dynamic cultures. And this generation might just change the world.

Biography

Adjunct professor of marketing at Columbia University, and New York University, Jenny Fernandez is a marketing executive, startup advisor, and leadership coach. She is director of leadership at Endeavor Venture Funds and Venture Studio. Previously, she was vice president of marketing at Loacker USA; vice president of sales and marketing at Merlin Entertainments; North America marketing director and head of commercialization at Mondelēz International; and global leader of the Oreo brand in Asia Pacific. Jenny also held roles at Kraft Foods, where she managed channel strategy and launched new platforms and brands, and at Accenture as a management consultant focused on the retail and manufacturing industries. She is a contributor at *Harvard Business Review* and *Fast Company*. Jenny holds an MBA from Northwestern University and a Certificate in Executive and Organizational Coaching from Columbia University. Jenny was named to the Thinkers50 Radar Class of 2024.

References

Ahir, H., Bloom, N., and Furceri, D. (2023). Global economic uncertainty remains elevated, weighing on growth [online]. *IMF Blog*. Available at: https://www.imf.org/en/Blogs/Articles/2023/01/26/global-economic-uncertainty-remains-elevated-weighing-on-growth

Coe, E., Doy, A., Enomoto, K., and Healy, C. (2023). *Gen Z mental health: The impact of tech and social media* [online]. McKinsey Health Institute. Available at: https://www.mckinsey.com/mhi/our-insights/gen-z-mental-health-the-impact-of-tech-and-social-media

Dunlop, A. and Pankowski, M. (2023). *Hey bosses: Here's what Gen Z actually wants at work* [online]. Deloitte Digital. Available at: https://www.deloittedigital.com/us/en/insights/perspective/gen-z-research-report.html#:~:text=More%20than%20other%20generations%2C%20Gen,a%20culture%20of%20reverse%2Dmentoring

Fernandez, J., Lee, J., and Landis, K. (2023). Helping Gen Z employees find their place at work. *Harvard Business Review*. https://hbr.org/2023/01/helping-gen-z-employees-find-their-place-at-work

Honestly Podcast. (n.d.). *Latest episodes* [online]. Available at: https://www.honestlypod.com/podcast/episode/1b1ee3ce/smartphones-rewired-childhood-heres-how-to-fix-it

Jabra. (2021). Hybrid Ways of Working 2021 Global Report. https://www
.jabra.com/thought-leadership/hybridwork-2021

LinkedIn. (n.d.). *The ultimate list of employer brand statistics.* https://business
.linkedin.com/content/dam/business/talent-solutions/global/en_us/c/
pdfs/ultimate-list-of-employer-brand-stats.pdf

Manyika, J., Lund, S., Chui, M., Bughin, J., Woetzel, J., Batra, P., Ko, R., and
Sanghvi, S. (2017). *Jobs lost, jobs gained: Workforce transitions in a time
of automation* [online]. McKinsey & Company. Available at: https://www
.mckinsey.com/~/media/BAB489A30B724BECB5DEDC41E9
BB9FAC.ashx

Masterson, V. (2023). *Future of jobs: These are the most in-demand skills in 2023—
and beyond* [online]. World Economic Forum. Available at: https://www
.weforum.org/agenda/2023/05/future-of-jobs-2023-skills/

Noenickx, C. (2023). The picky buying habits of Gen Z consumers. *BBC.*
https://www.bbc.com/worklife/article/20231218-the-picky-buying-
habits-of-gen-z-consumers

Pendell, R. and Vander Helm, S. (2022). *Generation disconnected: Data on
Gen Z in the workplace* [online]. Gallup.com. Available at: https://www
.gallup.com/workplace/404693/generation-disconnected-data-gen-
workplace.aspx

Pink, D. (2009). *The puzzle of motivation* [online]. TED. Available at: https://
www.ted.com/talks/dan_pink_the_puzzle_of_motivation/transcript?subt
itle=en&trigger=30s

Pollard, A. (2021). Gen Z has $360 billion to spend, trick is getting them to
buy. *Bloomberg.* https://www.bloomberg.com/news/articles/2021-11-17/
gen-z-has-360-billion-to-spend-trick-is-getting-them-to-buy

Sinek, S. [@simonsinek] (2024). *Post.* X.com. https://x.com/simonsinek/status
/205032187299508224?lang=en

Sostrin, J. (2022). Want to prepare your employees to lead from anywhere?
Salesforce reveals its playbook. *360 Blog.* https://www.salesforce.com/blog/
leadership-development/

Walensky, R., Bunnell, R., Layden, J., Kent, C., Gottardy, A., Leahy, M.,
Martinroe, J., Spriggs, S., Yang, T., Doan, Q., King, P., Starr, T., Yang, M.,
Jones, T., Boulton, M., Brooks, C., Ma, J., Butler, V., Caine, J. and Fielding,
D. (2022). *Morbidity and Mortality Weekly Report: Adolescent Behaviors and
Experiences Survey—United States, January–June 2021* [online]. Centers for
Disease Control and Prevention. Available at: https://www.cdc.gov/mmwr/
volumes/71/su/pdfs/su7103a1-a5-H.pdf

Wilkie, D. (2019). *Generation Z says they work the hardest, but only when they want
to* [online]. SHRM. Available at: https://www.shrm.org/topics-tools/news/
employee-relations/generation-z-says-work-hardest-want-to

28

How to Develop Strategic People

David Lancefield
Founder of Strategy Shift

Strategy Needs a Reboot

Strategy is one of the misunderstood and provocative words in business. How often do we add "strategic" to an initiative or a job title to signal its importance without being clear about what it means? Or we develop a plan for the business and confuse it with being a strategy? Or wonder why so many strategy launches are met with derision or apathy?

The causes are hardly surprising when you consider the lack of human connection in how strategy is often developed—behind closed doors on a need-to-know basis, before being broadcast to the organization in a series of announcements and events.

Too often, people lack:

- Knowledge of what a strategy is and what it isn't. In fact, it is a coherent set of choices that enable an organization (and team) to achieve an ambition. These choices center on where to focus (customers, products, geographies), how to stand out from the competition, and how to evolve the organizational capabilities, resources, systems, and culture to effect it.

- An understanding of why there needs to be a new strategy. "What's wrong with what we're doing now?" they wonder.

- A grasp of what the strategy is, and what it means for them. Hence, they do nothing, as they think it's for somebody else to do or they await instructions from their boss.

- A positive view of strategy because it's framed in terms of threats. The doomsday scenarios about the demise of the organization grab their attention. But instead of encouraging fresh thinking, they trigger anxiety and loss aversion, a concern to protect themselves from downsides. It's hardly the recipe for thinking about exciting new opportunities for growth.

- A sense of ownership because they're not involved in creating it.

It's even more remarkable when you realize that for strategies to work, they require the best of people: imagination to think of new possibilities, courage to make difficult choices, and honesty about what needs to change.

Open Approaches to Strategy Are an Improvement but Not Enough

Recent developments in the practice of strategy are encouraging. The C-suite, the group of the most senior leaders in an organization, is inviting more people to contribute their perspectives as they initiate, design, and implement strategy—this is called "Open Strategy." This includes the company's employees, ecosystem partners, customers, citizens, and investors. Organizations such as Adidas, Barclays, and IBM have used hackathons, crowdsourcing platforms, and competitions to do this.

Practiced well, these leaders frame the strategic topics to discuss, design the method of participation, and contribute their own thinking as they debate with the people invited. Importantly, they continue to make the decisions at the top level—open strategy shouldn't be confused with democracy—before cascading them in the organization.

But what happens when employees go back to their day job? This depends on their eagerness, courage, and capability. The best might develop a strategy for their team, coherent with the overall strategy, if they're empowered. But many will do nothing, whether due to fear of failure (having tried something outside their comfort zone) or their inability to work out what to do next.

The positive jolt fades away until the leadership team intervenes again, trying to convince people that the next effort will result in real change. It represents a missed opportunity to cascade strategy. It's no wonder that most strategies don't deliver the objectives they promise.

Imagine the Power of Strategic People

To change this—and propel this open strategy effort—executives need to develop strategic people systematically, not leave it to chance. These are individuals who make their own choices about where to focus, how to stand out, and how to develop their team to contribute to the overall strategy.

The most obvious candidates are business unit and divisional leaders, those with organizational power and, in companies, profit and loss responsibility. By why leave it there? Why shouldn't everyone become a strategic person?

Picture the benefits. The odds of implementing a strategy increase through greater coherence as it is cascaded throughout the organization. There's less wastage of time and effort on activities that don't contribute to the strategy. People feel more engaged as they feel more empowered to make decisions. Some also benefit from applying strategic thinking in other aspects of their life, such as relationships and their health and well-being.

Strategic People Require New Mindsets and Practices

Many people call themselves strategic as if it's a badge of honor. But they're far from it in practice. They're stuck in the present as they optimize and improve. They lack a clear ambition, afraid to make important choices and unable to improve the capabilities of their bureaucratic organization. Yet, they talk in theatrical terms about disruption and innovation without following through.

By contrast, strategic people do the following (see Table 28.1):

- Look to create a better future.
- Focus on addressing customer hopes, needs, and frustrations.
- Explore dynamics and dependencies as a system, recognizing the uncertainties involved.
- Don't hide from the truth about the challenges and limitations of the team and organization.
- Frame choices about where to focus, how to win, and what to change with clarity.
- Call out assumptions that underpin these choices with transparency.
- See the power of dialogue between people of different backgrounds, expertise, and styles to generate new possibilities and highlight challenges to overcome.
- Consider the organizational changes required to effect the strategy.
- Encourage people to be accountable.

Table 28.1 The mindsets, practices, and skills of strategic people.

Mindset	Practice	Skill
Future-orientated	Develop an ambition	Imagination, creativity
Customer-obsessed	Start with possibilities	Entrepreneurship, dialogue, observation, qualitative analysis
Systems	Look for signals, inter-relationships	Exploration, questioning, curiosity
Honest	Define challenges	Interrogation, investigation, forensic analysis
Clarity	Frame choices	Integrated thinking, trade-offs, precision
Transparent	Call out assumptions	Structured thinking, communication
Teamwork	Work with colleagues to stimulate ideas and surface challenges	Questioning, bridging, listening
Pragmatic	Consider organizational changes	Understanding of operational and cultural behavior, pragmatism
Integrity	Define accountability and reward mechanisms	Human motivation, financial

Developing Strategic People Requires a Deliberate Effort

If we know the mindsets, practices, and skills of strategic people, what does it take to develop them? The heart of this endeavor is a human connection—to your customers, to the strategy of the organization, to the people around you, and to your inner self.

Leaders

Establish an Emotional Connection to the Strategy

Rational, numbers-based arguments aren't enough to convince people to change. Would you be convinced to change your focus and activities if you were told that the organization should become three times bigger? You might buy the logic of the argument that supports it. But research shows that we need to feel a personal connection to what the strategy is looking to achieve, such as the impact it has on the lives of customers, citizens, or your colleagues. Use storytelling and visualization to help to create this connection—through encouraging curiosity, sparking creativity, and creating excitement in a better future, focusing attention on the opportunities and possibilities ahead.

Instill Belief

Similarly, convey your belief in the possibilities ahead, sharing what they mean to you—I call this skillful disclosure. Show your belief in the abilities and energies of others. Say it out loud: "I believe we are capable of delivering this strategy." Research in psychology shows that human beings tend to give more cognitive attention to negative rather than positive events or information across a range of contexts, so it's important to say it explicitly, especially during a time of change.

Cascade the Strategy Through Giving Responsibility

Describe your strategic decision clearly and how you've reached it. Invite your direct reports to make their own set of choices in their area of responsibility—some organizations, like Haier, have created self-managed enterprises to do this. You, as the corporate leader, might have decided to become the number-one provider of a specific service; the task of the person you are engaging with is figuring out how to win over customers to enable this. This might sound straightforward, but making strategic decisions may invoke a range of emotions from anxiety to excitement, especially if it's for the first time. Help them by giving them the full picture (of the strategy and context), be available for consultation, and be supportive, especially when they make mistakes.

Encourage Everyone to Focus on Customer Needs

Invite discussions about how well your team is serving current customers and what it will take to attract new customers. Seek to understand customers' underlying motivations (what jobs they want done) and imagine new ways of delighting them. Go to the extremes—focus on how much further you can satisfy already happy customers as well as minimize the frustrations of unhappy customers. This activity applies to everyone, including those in the back office. Everyone should be able to answer this question: "How does this activity deliver a better outcome or experience for our customer?"

Coach People to Focus and Make Choices

Few people are taught how to be strategic. We often associate strategy people as those with a business school education or the external consultants. It doesn't have to be this way. Start by embedding strategic practices into every aspect of the commercial, operations, and people agendas of the organization. Focus on the "imprintable moments"—the ones that have the biggest chance of being noticed and remembered. In practice, this might relate to the questions you use in recruitment interviews, the methods you teach in induction programs, and the way you make (and explain) important decisions. You act as a role model and teacher as you do this. As you do this, ask people to reflect on their decisions, especially when the outcomes were not as intended. Ask questions such as these: What didn't we consider? What factors did we underestimate? What perspective might have helped? Whom should we have involved? What would we do better next time?

Communicate Key Decisions Openly and Carefully

Strategic decisions—a new area of focus, a launch of an initiative, or an investment in new capabilities—are opportunities for people to learn about how judgments are made. In fact, the scrutiny that comes from this transparency might even improve the quality of decision-making too. Explain the thinking, logic, and evidence that supports the choices. For example, you might say, "This strategy is based on a number of important insights and assumptions."

Put in Place Resources and Incentives

Assess what the strategy requires of your people to cascade it effectively. Too often people are encouraged to pursue a new strategy yet assessed against old metrics and without sufficient resources.

Individuals

If you're somebody who wants to become more strategic in how you think and what you do, don't wait for your colleagues and bosses to lead the way. You have a choice—yes, strategy right there—about where you spend your time and what you do, even in the most tightly managed, bureaucratic organizations. Your aim is to make the best possible contribution to the strategy and to your performance and prospects.

Becoming more strategic involves the following:

- Anchoring your attention on your customers and their influences (signals about their willingness to spend, competitor activity, technology developments).
- Focusing on making strategic choices in your day-to-day life—e.g., the decisions you take, the meetings you hold with colleagues and external parties.
- Proactively suggesting initiatives that contribute to the strategy and that play to your strengths (experience, expertise, skills identified by others, and your own reflection).
- Encouraging collaboration (and dialogue) as you develop your strategy—invite your colleagues to contribute their ideas on how to delight customers and what this will entail in the capabilities, resources, systems, and culture of the organization.
- Figuring out what you need to change to deliver the strategy, starting with motivations, obstacles, and frictions.

What does it take for everyone to become a strategic person, making choices that help the organization and themselves? It's not the closed, technocratic exercise often associated with strategy. It is about instilling a sense of ambition, confidence, and capability—creating a powerful human connection.

Biography

David Lancefield is the founder of Strategy Shift. He has advised more than than 50 chief executive officers and hundreds of other C-suite executives to design bold strategies, supercharge their leadership, and transform their culture in 20 countries. David is a contributor to the *Harvard Business Review*, *MIT Sloan Review*, and a contributing editor of *Strategy + Business*, and a guest lecturer at the London Business School. He is a former senior partner in Strategy&, PwC.

References

Hamel, G. and Zanini, M. (2020). *Humanocracy*. Boston, MA: Harvard Business Review Press.

Lancefield, D. (2022, November). How to communicate your company's strategy effectively. *Harvard Business Review*. https://hbr.org/2022/11/how-to-communicate-your-companys-strategy-effectively

Markides, C. and Lancefield, D. (2020, July). Creating the right kind of urgency to bring about change. *Strategy+Business*. https://www.strategy-business.com/article/Creating-the-right-kind-of-urgency-to-bring-about-change

Martin, R. (2022, February). How to get buy in for your strategy. *Medium*. https://rogermartin.medium.com/how-to-get-buy-in-for-your-strategy-92a9b10af2e

Stadler, C., Hautz, J., Matzler, K., and von den Eichen, S.F. (2021). *Open strategy: Mastering disruption from outside the C-suite*. Cambridge, MA: MIT Press.

29

Your Imagination Is Your Currency

Natalie Nixon
Chief executive officer of Figure 8 Thinking, LLC

I'm always inspired by the breadth of imagination that other people exhibit. Here's an example.

For my last birthday, my husband gifted us tickets to attend a phenomenal work of art at Jazz at Lincoln Center. The jazz orchestral and spoken word composition, *Musings of Cosmic Stuff*, was a collaboration between Sherman Irby, a jazz wind instrumentalist and composer, and astrophysicist Neil de Grasse Tyson. The oeuvre intrigued and inspired me. While other physicists such as Stephon Alexander have connected the dots between jazz and physics (note Alexander's *The Jazz of Physics*), I had not up until then experienced a sensorial manifestation of the two realms.

Jazz + Physics? Now, that takes imagination.

William Blake's insight from the 1790s, "What is now prov'd was once only imagined," captures the timeless essence of innovation. Found in his poem "The Marriage of Heaven and Hell," these words underscore the critical role of imagination as the starting point for all enduring innovations. Our most logical and substantiated ideas often begin as mere figments of imagination—dreamy musings and speculative queries that pave the way for discovery and proof.

Our world, particularly the business sector, lauds objectivity, rationality, and logic. Yet, the genesis of the most groundbreaking products and solutions are rooted in the realm of the imagination. Take for example Marie Van Brittan Brown's invention of closed-circuit TV security systems. Brown was driven to find workarounds to provide a safe environment in the 1960s when her neighborhood in Queens, New York, was a high crime area. She used her imagination to develop a system that included peepholes, a camera (designed in an innovative way to look through multiple peepholes), monitors, and a two-way microphone. Her system ultimately laid the groundwork for modern security systems.

We now live in a time of incredible technologies—artificial intelligence (AI), automation, and robotics—that bring ease and speed to an average work day. Simultaneously, these innovations are accelerating at speeds that cause us to question our own relevance. In the face of such unprecedented ambiguity, business leaders have a critical decision to make: retreat in fear or embrace the unknown with open arms.

The most strategic tool at your disposal in such times is not quantitative data or historical precedents.

It is your innate imagination.

Your imagination is your currency.

And now, more than ever, we have the opportunity to leverage what makes us uniquely human.

I define *imagination* as the brain's capacity to integrate memory, awareness, analysis, and visual thinking. The Latin etymology of the verb *imaginari* means "to *picture* oneself." How appropriate, given that we are hardwired to be visual creatures. According to the *Interaction Design Foundation* (Few 2009), when we visualize data our brain leverages rapid processing. As a result, our cognitive load gets reduced and comprehension improves.

Imagination is the cornerstone for creativity which, in 2023, the World Economic Forum (2023) predicted would become the second most sought-after skill by 2027. Additionally, 2023 research from Thrive My Way (Todorov 2022) indicated that 60% of chief executive officers view creativity as a key leadership attribute, and 70% believe it's essential for economic growth. Despite this acknowledgment, 75% of individuals feel they aren't reaching their creative potential, and nearly half report rare opportunities for creative expression at work. This discrepancy highlights a significant gap: while the value of creativity is acknowledged, adequate opportunities and resources to cultivate it are lacking.

The brain and the mind are distinct. When the young Michelangelo (pre-*David*) was digging up corpses in peasant graveyards in fifteenth century Florence to study human anatomy, he was struck by how identical human brains are. At the same time, he marveled at how unique our individual personalities could be. That's because the brain is the medium. But the mind is a product of how that medium is used and adapts to our environment, life experiences, and unique DNA. It's the instrument for the imagination.

Building your imagination's capacity is essential for problem-solving and strategic planning. Albert Einstein was a devoted imagineer, often quoted for saying that "imagination is more important than knowledge" and that it fuels progress and innovation. Astronomer Carl Sagan's perspective aligned with Einstein's when he suggested that the imagination propels us toward uncharted territories and possibilities.

The imagination is the hearty companion to what makes us uncomfortable.

Disconcerting conditions—such as uncertainty, ambiguity, and boredom—are actually the perfect liminal spaces required to spark great ideas, unlikely collaborations, and magnificent experiments.

Liminal space is as relevant, necessary, and important as the concrete spaces in our lives. In fact, what is tangible cannot exist without ambiguity. For example, the wait at the traffic stoplight makes speeding down a country road sublime; the dormancy of winter makes spring magnificent; and the uncertainty of a work project's impasse can ultimately propel us forward into new directions that make the final outcome exceed our expectations.

The imagination is the premiere space for cultivating liminality. And liminal space is probably one of the most important realms for knowledge workers. Spending time to ponder and wrestle with ideas is critical prep time for when you actually do tackle the work at hand. These are the foundational spaces of innovation. And they bode well for both our productivity and our well-being. There's good reason for this. James Hewitt, a human performance scientist, pointed out to me that from an evolutionary perspective, pausing to ponder and make sense of ambiguity would have yielded the best results for problem-solving.

As humans, our imagination is one of the most fundamental assets we can use to venture forward. Your imagination is the catalyst for any journey, whether it's a literal journey equipped with maps and a compass, or a metaphorical journey like a career change or creating and launching a new marketing strategy.

Without the imagination we are frozen, stuck, disconnected from others, and disassociated from ourselves. The astrophysicist Neil de Grasse Tyson wrote in *Astrophysics for People in a Hurry*:

> To make this journey, we'll need imagination, but imagination alone is not enough because the reality of nature is far more wondrous than anything we can imagine. This adventure is made possible by generations of searchers strictly adhering to a simple set of rules. Test ideas by experiment and observation. Build on those ideas that pass the test, reject the ones that fail, follow the evidence wherever it leads, and question everything.

Tyson's process is one way to spark the imagination. I have an additional way, one that can be especially useful to help business leaders cultivate their imagination. It's called the LEAP Method™, a framework I developed to help individual managers and teams go from a fuzzy idea to a tangible and actionable early-stage product, service, or experience. Here are the four phases of the LEAP Method:

1. *Leverage*: Practice backcasting and identify and document all skills and experiences that have been acquired and developed. This might emerge in the form of a corporate "show and tell" or delving into the company's origin story and asking each colleague to reflect on their own origin story with the company.

2. *Envision*: Practice forecasting by scheduling time to audaciously dream about future scenarios of what you imagine could be possible. This could take the form of what I call "strategic daydreaming." Companies like 3M and Pixar have provided "thinking time" for employees, fostering an environment where daydreaming is recognized as a conduit for strategic breakthroughs and innovative solutions.

3. *Ask*: Learn to make inquiry and curiosity daily habits. Practice asking for advice about your audacious dream (see Phase 2: *Envision*) and ask for help from people within your sector as well as from unusual suspects *outside* of your industry. Encouraging team members to engage with diverse cultures and business practices through international assignments or partnerships broadens perspectives and sparks innovative thinking. Firms like IBM and Ernst & Young, which have robust global rotation programs, are setting themselves up to have cultures of curiosity.

4. *Prototype*: Oxygenate your ideas by building rough draft, conceptual versions of what you envision. Use the build-test-learn process in short, iterative phases so that your original

concept takes actual shape and form. Google's famed "20% time" policy encouraged employees to dedicate a portion of their workweek to creative projects. These innovative play initiatives normalized prototyping and birthed products like Gmail and AdSense, showcasing how play can fuel innovation.

In a recent engagement with a luxury hair care brand, I helped 40 leaders apply the LEAP method to envision "new ways of making." The process of backcasting, then forecasting; posing audacious questions, and then doodling very crude prototypes of their ideas made for an energizing day of applying the imagination for new ways to reframe their business. The LEAP method permits business teams to delve into the liminal spaces of reflection, dreaming, inquiry, and experimentation. In a counterintuitive way, the not-knowing sparks more interesting insights. In short, the process helps teams to "unstick their minds"—a phrase coined by Jane McGonigal in her book, *Imaginable*.

In conclusion, the era we're entering is not just about information processing but about leveraging imagination to drive business success. In the "Imagination Era," the businesses that thrive will be those that leverage their pasts; envision entirely new ways of solving old and new problems; ask different questions and foster curiosity; and prototype by encouraging experimentation. They will become adept at navigating the unknown by leaping into it.

Biography

Natalie Nixon is the creativity whisperer to the C-suite, helping companies connect the dots between creativity and business impact. At Figure 8 Thinking, she's a creativity strategist, global keynote speaker, and author of the award-winning *The Creativity Leap* (Berrett-Koehler, 2020). She was named to the 2024 Thinkers50 Radar cohort, and Real Leaders named Natalie one of the top 50 keynote speakers globally. She's been featured in *Forbes*, *INC*, and *Fast Company*.

Natalie received her BA from Vassar College and her PhD from the University of Westminster. She's a lifelong dancer, swimmer, and doodler. She lives in Philadelphia with her husband, John Nixon.

References

de Grasse Tyson, N. (2017). *Astrophysics for people in a hurry*. W.W. Norton & Company.

Few, S. (2009). *Data visualization for human perception* [online]. *The Interaction Design Foundation*. Available at: https://www.interaction-design.org/literature/book/the-encyclopedia-of-human-computer-interaction-2nd-ed/data-visualization-for-human-perception

Todorov, G. (2022). *16 top creativity stats to discover how common creativity is* [online]. *Thrive My Way*. Available at: https://thrivemyway.com/creativity-stats/

World Economic Forum. (2023). *The future of jobs report 2023* [online]. World Economic Forum. Available at: https://www.weforum.org/publications/the-future-of-jobs-report-2023/in-full/4-skills-outlook/

About the Editors

Des Dearlove is an internationally recognized expert on management thinking. Together with Stuart Crainer, he founded Thinkers50, which for more than two decades has championed the very best management ideas.

A former columnist for *The Times* (London) and contributing editor to *Strategy+Business*, Des is the co-editor of the *Financial Times Handbook of Management* and co-author of several best-selling books, including *Gravy Training: Inside the Business of Business Schools*, and *Generation Entrepreneur*, which was shortlisted for the WH Smith's Business Book of the Year Award. His books have been translated into more than 20 languages.

Des has taught at some of the world's business schools, including IE Business School and the Saïd Business School at Oxford University, where he is an associate fellow. Under the pen name of D.D. Everest, he is also author of the Archie Greene trilogy of children's books, which was shortlisted for the National Book Awards Children's Book of the Year.

Lisa Humphries is a freelance editor and writer. She has edited a number of business books including most recently *The Next Leadership Team* (shortlisted for the 2024 Business Book Awards); *Enterprise China; The Future of Global Retail;* and *Looking Ahead: The Sustainable Global Agenda*.

With a global portfolio of clients, Lisa has provided research and editorial consulting for several book and editorial projects, including *Government Reimagined: Leading Through New Realities*, and a series of articles for the Warwick Business School magazine

Core Insights. In 2020, she was responsible for curating a book on a private leadership program for a royal family in the Gulf region.

Lisa has worked as an editor for Thinkers50 since 2018, and teaches on the Full-time and Part-time MBA programs at Cranfield School of Management, Cranfield University. She has travelled extensively in Africa, Asia, and South America, and was previously the manager of an award-winning travel company in Australia.

Acknowledgments

We would like to thank all those who contributed to this book in one form or another.

We are especially indebted to all the members of the Thinkers50 Community who shared their insights: Matt Abrahams, Kai Anderson, Weslynne Ashton, Andrew Barnes, Jeanette Bronée, Michael Bungay Stanier, Malissa Clark, Kirstin Ferguson, Jenny Fernandez, Martin Gonzalez, Faisal Hoque, Neri Karra Sillaman, Susie Kennedy, David Lancefield, Pia Lauritzen, Stephanie LeBlanc-Godfrey, Poornima Luthra, Mita Mallick, Hamilton Mann, Amanda Nimon-Peters, Constance Noonan Hadley, Natalie Nixon, Kate O'Neill, Ludmila Praslova, Thomas Roulet and Soulaima Gourani, Ville Satopää, Giuseppe Stigliano, Daniel Trabucci and Tommaso Buganza, and Kandi Wiens.

We would also like to thank Rita McGrath for providing the Foreword and for her continuing, long-standing support of the Thinkers50 mission. Many thanks also to Shannon Vargo and everyone at Wiley: Jeanenne Ray, Michael Friedberg, Michelle Hacker, Sherri-Anne Forde, and Gabriela Mancuso for their enthusiasm for our partnership, and Sheryl Nelson for her exemplary copy editing.

Finally, our thanks also to the amazing team at Thinkers50: Monika Kosman, Adina Rizga, Mercy Tapscott, Elisabeth Sejbak, Aleksandra Walicka, Jakob Tonnesen, and cofounder, Stuart Crainer.

Index

Page numbers followed by *f* and *t* refer to figures and tables, respectively.

OTHER BOOKS FROM

Thinkers50

BECOMING THE BEST

FROM THE BESTSELLING AUTHOR OF *FROM VALUES TO ACTION*

BUILD A WORLD-CLASS ORGANIZATION THROUGH **VALUES-BASED LEADERSHIP**

HARRY M. JANS

"Values and culture are paramount to corporate leadership. This book provides leaders with the tools to develop their talent." —**JEFF IMMELT**, chairman and CEO, General Electric Company

FROM VALUES TO ACTION

THE FOUR **PRINCIPLES OF VALUES-BASED LEADERSHIP**

HARRY M. JANSEN KRAEMER JR.

Certain Uncertainty
ISBN: 9781394153459

"For anyone who seeks to lead a values-based life, *Your 168* is a personal and inspiring guide to making the most of what matters."
ALAN MULALLY,
Retired CEO of Ford Motor Company and Boeing Commercial Airplanes

MAKE **EVERY HOUR** OF YOUR WEEK COUNT

YOUR 168

FINDING PURPOSE AND SATISFACTION IN A **VALUES-BASED LIFE**

HARRY M. JANSEN KRAEMER, JR.

WILEY

Enterprise China
ISBN: 9781394153428

The Upside of Disruption
ISBN: 9781394192601

WILEY